Woodworking Plans and Projects

Guild of Master Craftsman Publications Ltd

First published 1983 by
Guild of Master Craftsman Publications Ltd,
Castle Place, 166 High Street, Lewes, East Sussex BN7 1XU

ISBN 0 946819 07 6

Reprinted 1984, 1986 (twice), 1987, 1989, 1992, 1994

© Guild of Master Craftsman Publications Ltd, 1983

Printed and bound in Great Britain by
Hillman Printers (Frome) Ltd

Metric Conversion Table
Inches to millimetres

Inches	0	1/8	1/4	3/8	1/2	5/8	3/4	7/8
0		3	6	10	13	16	19	22
1	25	29	32	35	38	41	44	48
2	51	54	57	60	64	67	70	73
3	76	79	83	86	89	92	95	98
4	102	105	108	111	114	117	121	124
5	127	130	133	137	140	143	146	149
6	152	156	159	162	165	168	171	175
7	178	181	184	187	190	194	197	200
8	203	206	210	213	216	219	222	225
9	229	232	235	238	241	244	248	251
10	254	257	260	264	267	270	273	276
11	279	283	286	289	292	295	298	302
12	305	308	311	314	318	321	324	327
13	330	333	337	340	343	346	349	352
14	356	359	362	365	368	371	375	378
15	381	384	387	391	394	397	400	403
16	406	410	413	416	419	422	425	429
17	432	435	438	441	444	448	451	454
18	457	460	464	467	470	473	476	479
19	483	486	489	492	495	498	502	505
20	508	511	514	518	521	524	527	530
21	533	537	540	543	546	549	552	556
22	559	562	565	568	572	575	578	581
23	584	587	591	594	597	600	603	606
24	610	613	616	619	622	625	629	632
25	635	638	641	645	648	651	654	657
26	660	664	667	670	673	676	679	683
27	686	689	692	695	698	702	705	708
28	711	714	718	721	724	727	730	733
29	737	740	743	746	749	752	756	759
30	762	765	768	772	775	778	781	784
31	787	791	794	797	800	803	806	810
32	813	816	819	822	826	829	832	835
33	838	841	845	848	851	854	857	860
34	864	867	870	873	876	879	883	886
35	889	892	895	899	902	905	908	911
36	914	918	921	924	927	930	933	937
37	940	943	946	949	952	956	959	962
38	965	968	972	975	978	981	984	987
39	991	994	997	1000	1003	1006	1010	1013
40	1016	1019	1022	1026	1029	1032	1035	1038

Woodworking Plans & Projects

Contents

Reproduction oak welsh dresser

Cutting List

All sizes are given in inches.

Oak

4 Corner Posts	$32\frac{1}{4} \times 2\frac{1}{4} \times 1\frac{1}{4}$	
2 Top Rails	$15\frac{1}{4} \times 6\frac{7}{8} \times {}^{13}/_{16}$	Inc. 1¼ Tenons
2 Bottom Rails	$15\frac{1}{4} \times 4 \times {}^{13}/_{16}$	Inc. 1¼ Tenons
2 Panels	$18\frac{1}{2} \times 13\frac{1}{2} \times \frac{5}{8}$	
1 Top	$60 \times 19 \times {}^{13}/_{16}$	
2 Drawer Rails	$58\frac{1}{2} \times 2\frac{1}{4} \times {}^{13}/_{16}$	Inc. 1¼ Tenons
2 Drawer Fronts	$27\frac{5}{8} \times 5 \times {}^{11}/_{16}$	
1 Base	$60 \times 5 \times {}^{13}/_{16}$	
2 Base Returns	$19 \times 5 \times {}^{13}/_{16}$	
6 Stiles	$20\frac{1}{4} \times 1\frac{3}{4} \times {}^{13}/_{16}$	
3 Top Rails	$17{}^{3}/_{16} \times 1\frac{3}{4} \times {}^{13}/_{16}$	Inc. 1¼ Tenons
3 Bottom Rails	$17{}^{3}/_{16} \times 2\frac{1}{2} \times {}^{13}/_{16}$	Inc. 1¼ Tenons
3 Panels	$16\frac{3}{4} \times 15{}^{7}/_{16} \times \frac{5}{8}$	
2 Ends	$47 \times 8 \times {}^{13}/_{16}$	Inc. 2 in. Tenons
2 Feet	$15 \times 2 \times 1\frac{1}{4}$	
3 Shelves	$57 \times 5 \times {}^{13}/_{16}$	Inc. ½ in. Housings
1 Top Rail (Shaped)	$57 \times 5\frac{1}{2} \times {}^{13}/_{16}$	Inc. ½ in. Housings
1 Top	$57 \times 4\frac{3}{4} \times {}^{13}/_{16}$	Inc. ½ in. Housings
1 Bottom Rail	$57 \times 2 \times {}^{13}/_{16}$	Inc. ½ in. Tenons
1 Cornice	$61 \times 2\frac{1}{4} \times 1\frac{3}{4}$	
2 Cornice Returns	$10 \times 2\frac{1}{4} \times 1\frac{3}{4}$	
4 Drawer Sides	$16 \times 5 \times \frac{3}{8}$	
2 Drawer Backs	$27\frac{5}{8} \times 4\frac{1}{4} \times \frac{3}{8}$	
Boarded Back	$\frac{3}{8}$ in. Thick – Enough to cover 57 ins. width × 45 ins. height.	

Plywood

1 Bottom	$58 \times 17\frac{1}{4} \times \frac{3}{4}$	Inc. 1 in. Lipping
1 Division	$21 \times 17\frac{1}{4} \times \frac{3}{4}$	Inc. 1 in. Lipping
1 Back Rail	$56 \times 6\frac{7}{8} \times \frac{3}{4}$	
1 Back	$57 \times 20\frac{3}{4} \times \frac{1}{4}$	
1 Shelf	$19 \times 16 \times \frac{3}{4}$	Inc. 1 in. Lipping
1 Shelf	$38 \times 16 \times \frac{3}{4}$	Inc. 1 in. Lipping
2 Drawer Bottoms	$27\frac{3}{8} \times 16 \times \frac{1}{4}$	

Various lippings $1 \times \frac{3}{4}$ for ply bottoms, divisions etc.

Hardware

Three pair brass H hinges or butts.
Two brass plate drawer handles.
Three brass tear drop door handles.
Three magnetic or ball catches.

All measurements given are finished sizes and include allowance for tenons, dovetails, etc. With the doors and drawers the sizes given are as a guide only. Accurate dimensions can be taken from the finished carcase.

Materials for such items as drawers, runners, kickers and guides, drawer divisions, pegs and the odd batten are not included in the above as these can usually be found in the scrap box.

Suppliers

Hardware – Caplins, London.
Wood (Oak) – North Heigham Saw Mills, Norwich.
Plywood – Cordys, Lingwood Norfolk.
Polishing Materials – Jenkins, London.
Hand Tools Used – Stanley, Record, Marples, Bosch.
Machines – Wadkin, Makita and Skill.

When back two or three centuries ago the country craftsmen were busy making, among other things, everyday pieces of household furniture in their small village workshops, they would have been very flattered to have known how much their work is appreciated and so sought after now. Good genuine antiques have become both expensive and very scarce, and this has led to the popularity enjoyed today by reproduction furniture. From the common joint stool, which was probably the first piece of constructed furniture and was a welcome seat to many a tired worker after a long hard day's toil, to the most elaborate cabinets seen in our big city museums, the best examples of the past are copied and adapted to suit the modern home.

The reproductionist is not just simply making a piece of furniture; he is also building history into it. I find it a great challenge and fun trying to copy the hundreds of years of everyday use, the wear, knocks and bumps, scratches, burns and other marks (Ah, if only that table could talk!).

Perhaps the reason why old furniture is so much desired today is that it is so "easy to live with". So much of the modern type of furniture although very nice and excellently made, can not be fully appreciated. We are, to put it bluntly, frightened to use it. A scratch or stain across say a lovely inlaid fiddle sycamore table top would be disastrous, but the same blemish would only add to and enrich the other qualities of the old or reproduction piece. A piece of reproduction furniture is like a good wine: it improves with time and this goes on long after it has left the safety of the workshop. In your home, the everyday wear and tear and abuse is added to the foundation of marks that has been built into the piece of furniture by its maker.

A hundred or more years ago an oak welsh dresser would have been the main feature of many country kitchens. As their name implies, welsh dressers originated from Wales, the ones with doors and drawers in the base from North Wales and the potboard dressers (the open bottom ones) came from Southern Wales. The dresser shown in this article is a splendid example and typical of many Northern pieces. Although not a project for an absolute beginner, with a little thought and determination most competent woodworkers can achieve first class results.

By looking at the plans and drawings you will get an idea of how the piece is put together. I would like to concentrate on the main points of construction and reproduction techniques, and therefore will leave the basic carcase construction to personal choice. To help you, I will just say that in the one made by myself – mortice and tenon joints were used for all framework and doors, housings for plywood bottoms to ends and for fixing shelves and dovetails in the drawer making.

A word about choosing wood. Try and pick out the nicely figured stuff for prominent features like door panels and tops. Good reproductions do not want to look too perfect, so also include some splits and knots (but not in such a way as to weaken the piece). Below is an outline of the main sequence of work.

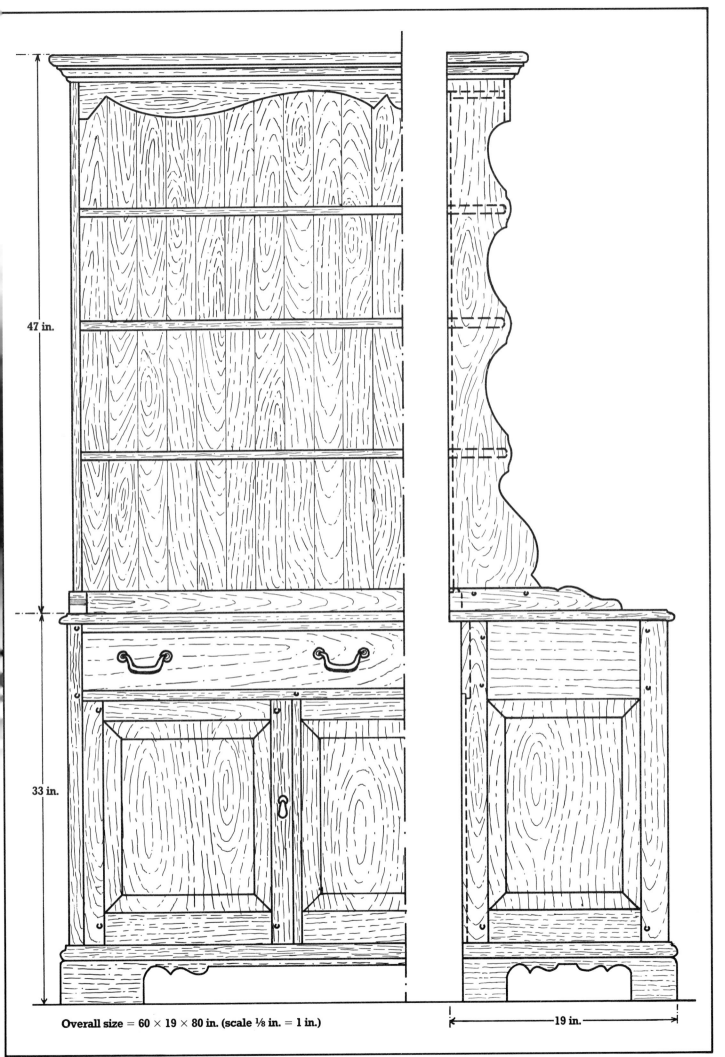

47 in.

33 in.

Overall size = 60 × 19 × 80 in. (scale ⅛ in. = 1 in.)

19 in.

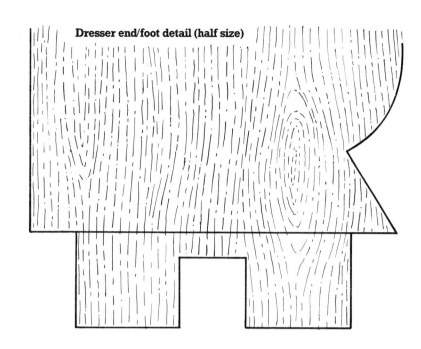

Dresser end/foot detail (half size)

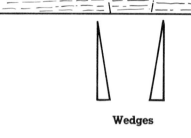

Wedges

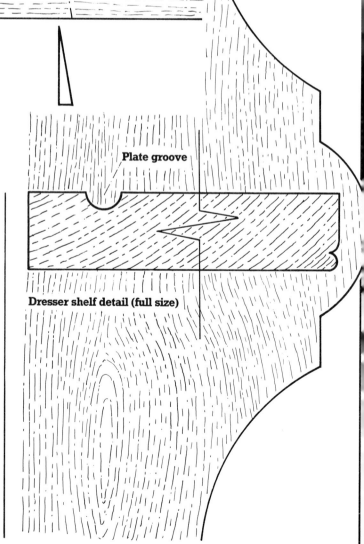

Plate groove

Dresser shelf detail (full size)

Base Cupboard

1. The two end frames are jointed, glued together and cleaned up.
2. Join the two end frames to make up the main carcase; clean up the front.
3. Cut out, shape base and fix round the bottom front and sides of the carcase.
4. Screw and glue in drawer bits, runners, kickers and guides.
5. Mould, clean up and fix top.
6. Joint, assemble and hang doors.
7. Make up and fit drawers.

Dresser Section

1. Shape the two end uprights; joint and fit feet.
2. Make up shelves, top and bottom rails, work plate grooves and mouldings and shape top rail; join together to make main structure.
3. Make up and fit cornice moulding.
4. Make up and fit tongue groove and vee jointed back boards.

In the following paragraphs I have highlighted the main details and points of the piece and given you some idea as to how these are achieved.

Fielded Panels

The panels in the end and door frames are all fielded. These can be cut on a spindle moulder (if you are lucky enough to own one) or worked by hand with a bench rebate plane against a fence, which takes a little longer but gives better results as you get an irregularity and unevenness associated with old furniture and is, after all, what we are trying to achieve when making reproductions.

When cleaning up the face of the panel, "sluff off" the edges of the raised centre panels Fig. 1. When doing this, as when creating any other type of wear, it must be remembered that what we are doing with the spokeshave in minutes would have taken hundreds of years on an antique. Therefore a little thought as to the most likely spots where the bangs and rubs would have occurred will help you to get that old look.

The panel sits in a $5/16 \times 3/8$ in. deep groove worked round the inside of the frame (Fig. 2) and a small bead moulding is worked round with a scratch stock with a chamfer on the bottom rail. The scratch stock gives good results on small mouldings (with a little tidying up afterwards using sandpaper). If you have not used one before it is best to practice on a piece of scrap wood to get the hang of how they go and also get the right size of moulding you want to finish with. (Fig. 3.)

Joint Pegs

When the oldtime craftsmen made their furniture in their little workshops they did not have the luxuries of modern glue. Mortice and tenon joints had a peg through them to pull and hold them together. These would have finished flush originally but with the movement of wood around them they may now stand slightly proud. On our reproduction these pegs can be passed right through to give extra strength or just in $3/8$ in. or so into the surface as a cosmetic gesture only. The pegs are made of $5/16$ in. square section with the corners planed off to make an octagonal. These fit nicely into the $5/16$ in. hole drilled through the joint. *(Drawer Pins might have been useful here. – Ed.)*

Top Moulding

The detail round the three edges of the top is the traditional thumbnail moulding, Fig. 4. This can again be made with a bench rebate plane worked against a fence and rounded with a spoke shave.

When cleaning off and 'wearing' the top, bear in mind where the dresser top is going to stand and wear around it rather than underneath it. Remember that the furniture we are reproducing was made in a time when only "crude" tools (compared with today's metal planes etc.) were available. Wooden planes and spokeshaves gave a very uneven surface and this has been accentuated by time. They were really more concerned with the functional aspect, and finish was not too important. You can copy these effects by planing hollows into the surfaces with your smoothing plane. *(The use of a 'scrub' plane blade in the smoothing plane might also be considered. – Ed.)* Use of a spokeshave on flat surfaces, allowing it to "chatter", will create tool marks and a good sanding will blend these into the finish. The top is fixed down by screwing through the kickers and top rails. Allow for shrinkage by enlarging the top side of the screw holes.

Doors/Drawers

The doors and drawers are best left until the carcase has been assembled and an accurate measurement can be taken.

The doors are a framed and panelled construction in much the same way as the end frames. When cramping doors up it is advisable to keep them flat during the glue drying time so you will avoid a top or bottom corner of the door that kicks out when it has been hung.

Behind the doors are a double and single cupboard with an adjustable shelf in each. A false upright is fixed to the leading edge of one of the double pair of doors to match the fixed division.

Drawers are dovetailed in the usual way; they have a $1/4$ in. ply bottom grooved into the sides and front. Runners, kickers, and guides are screwed into the carcase after assembling, Fig. 5. A central runner and kicker and dividing guide is tenoned between the drawer rails and the back rail.

When choosing wood for the drawer fronts try and find a nicely figured piece that you can get the two fronts out of in one length. Keep them in this order so that when in position the grain follows through the length. (This shows some thought has been taken.) The same can be done to the base and cornice so that the grain follows around the corner, but this is not so important.

Originally drawer bottoms were made of solid wood. On very early pieces the grain ran from back to front. This was all right until the bottom either shrunk or expanded, resulting in a sloppy or jammed drawer. They learnt from this and always had the grain running from side to side. On our drawers we do not have to worry about shrinkage using ply, but it is a good thing to get into the habit of doing, if only to have all drawer bottoms with the same direction of grain.

Base and Cornice

A bracket foot type base with moulded top edge, Fig. 6, is fixed round the bottom of the cabinet, mitred at the corners and screwed and glued into place. A cornice moulding, Fig. 7, is fixed in much the same way round the top edge of the dresser.

Boarded Back

Dressers are made with either boarded or open backs. If a boarded back is required a rebate must be worked round the back of the main structure to accommodate this. The back is made up of $3/8$ in. thick tongued groove and veed boards of equal or random widths. It is fixed from behind by nailing but this is usually best done after staining and polishing.

Ageing Brassware

Although you can buy "antiqued" brass fittings most come highly polished and protected with a coat of lacquer. What we need to do is get rid of this so that we can get down to the bare metal. You will find that this coating is often very stubborn to remove and the only way to shift it is to soak for a few hours in cellulose thinners. Some .88 ammonia can be bought from the chemist. This is used to "corrode" the brass. Pour a little into an old container (not too big, four or five inches diameter) so that it covers the bottom to about the depth of $1/2$ in. Suspend the fittings over this and leave to fume until the brass discolours and stains. When they have reached the desired effects (an overall greenish colour) the scum can be removed with fine wire wool and a dull shine achieved. A word of warning when using ammonia. You will almost certainly find out that it is not a very pleasant substance to breathe, but other than giving you a bit of a shock and watery eyes I don't think it is too harmful if used correctly. Just avoid standing directly over an open container of it.

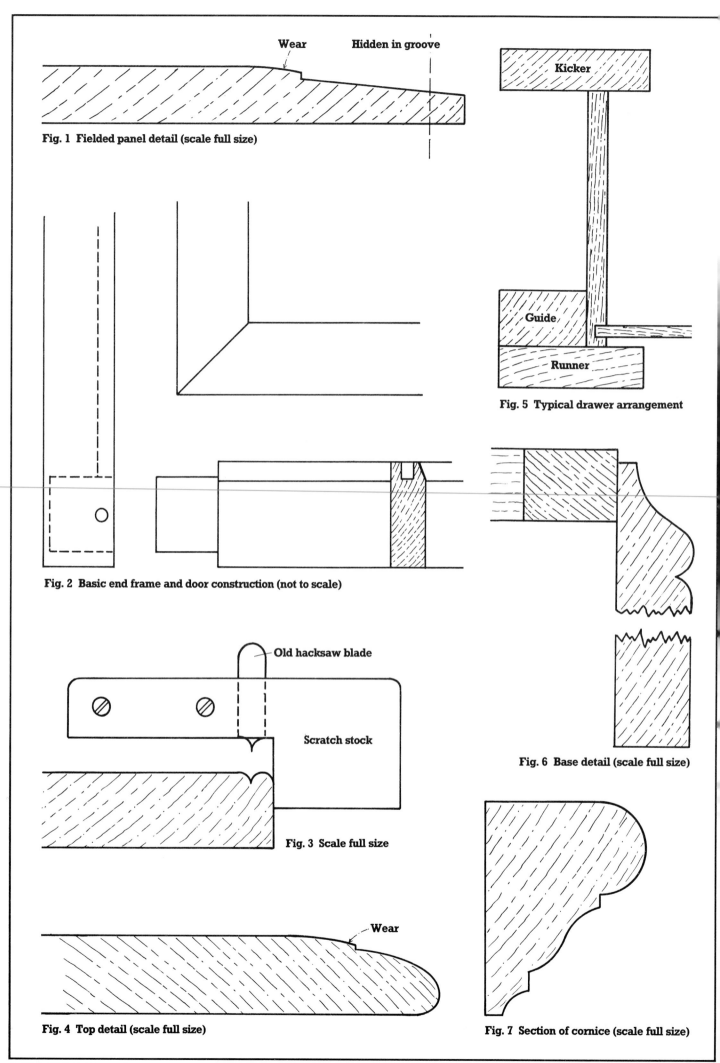

Wear   Hidden in groove

Fig. 1 Fielded panel detail (scale full size)

Kicker

Guide

Runner

Fig. 5 Typical drawer arrangement

Fig. 2 Basic end frame and door construction (not to scale)

Old hacksaw blade

Scratch stock

Fig. 3 Scale full size

Fig. 6 Base detail (scale full size)

Wear

Fig. 4 Top detail (scale full size)

Fig. 7 Section of cornice (scale full size)

Distressing

(Putting in all the little marks, bruises and scratches.)
Before you set out on this next stage it would be an
advantage to go and look closely at some old furniture.
Local museums usually have good examples. Note the
colour and overall feel and shape of the piece. The
thing to try and do when distressing is get the balance
right. You may be surprised how much banging and
scratching you have to do to get the right result, but
even so many fakers overdo this not really thinking
about "how" and "why" the marks got there. Distressing
and ageing is much like polishing: you can either
improve a beautifully made piece of furniture or
completely spoil it. Again, what we are trying to do
when we age our pieces of furniture has taken
hundreds of years to create on an original. Think which
places would be badly marked and which would have
remained nearly unscathed. There would be severe
damage around the base where generations have
kicked their feet. It may have also stood in a damp
kitchen; puddles on the floor would have blackened the
lower parts. On the other hand, the cornice being high
up and out of reach would have very little wear or
damage. Any part which protrudes or shelves out would
suffer badly; mouldings would be damaged and have
bits missing. Around door and drawer handles constant
opening would have left its mark.

Fakers have differing opinions on how these marks
can best be achieved. Irregularly shaped rocks and
wire brushes are but a few of the tools. I find an old file
handle, which has various sizes of chains, bolts and
washers attached, works well. This can be banged
about in a random fashion and gives very good results.
The thing to do is to try and achieve a varied selection
of marks. Nothing looks worse than the same pattern
duplicated say along the front edge of a top. Small
scratches can be put in with the corner of a sharp
chisel.

Finishing

When all the construction has been completed you
should now have a piece of furniture that is just about
finished. The finish you see on antiques has been
achieved by many years of use and waxing. We have to
produce an old looking finish in a much shorter time, so
we speed the process up quite a bit in the form of
staining and polishing. As we are using water stain the
grain must be raised. This is done by wetting over the
complete piece with warm water. It is left overnight to
dry and cut down with 150 grade paper. Pigments are
obtained in a powder form (walnut or vandyke for a
medium dark brown) and mixed with cold water. Add
some ammonia to give it a little extra bite. Brush the
stain on fairly evenly to cover the complete piece and,
as it starts to dry off, use a damp sponge to even out the
stain and create the highlights and shadings. Common
sense will tell you which bits remain dark and which
bits can be lighter (internal corners, deep mouldings
and out of reach places can remain dark, edges and
external corners light etc.). After leaving to dry
overnight, cut down with 000 wire wool then seal with
one coat of button polish brushed on. This dries very
quickly and you will find by the time you have worked
through the piece you can start at the beginning again
cutting down with 220 paper, taking care on edges not
to go through the stain and polish. Next fad on three to
four coats of button until the grain is chocked up and a
reasonable depth has been achieved. With old oak a
dull shine is required, so do not build up too much of a
lustre with a fad. Leave again to dry overnight, then dull

down with 0000 wire wool. Apply a good quality
furniture wax to finish.

Summary

As mentioned before a welsh dresser is not the easiest
of pieces to begin with, but if desired the above
techniques can be used to practise on smaller items.
This design is only one of many variations of welsh
dresser and I see no reason why you could not tailor it
to suit your individual requirements by adding such
refinements as spice drawers, different hardware or
different knobs, cup hooks to the underside of shelves,
lining drawers for cutlery or altering the overall size.
You can also change or design new shapes for the
mouldings to suit the cutters or moulding planes that
you own.

You will notice that plywood has been incorporated
in the structure for bottoms, backs and other interior
panels. If you wanted to keep your piece authentic you
could certainly use solid; the old craftsmen would have
used soft woods for such items. I have used plywood
because I believe it is a better material and is usually
suited for such situations as it remains stable and is of a
regular thickness, but also to conserve solid material.

A great deal can be learnt, from making
reproductions, about the people who made the furniture
many years ago and the conditions they worked in. I
find reproduction furnituremaking very absorbing; you
are always looking for new ideas and ways to make the
finish older looking. This keeps your interest alive, and
it's very rewarding when a visitor to your house remarks
on the beauty of your "old" welsh dresser.

Making a dining table

The under frame of this dining table follows a breakaway from normal practice regarding the jointing of legs and rails. It will be seen that the legs have an open right angle section instead of a solid square section. The processes involved are simple in appearance when compared with the traditional M and T joined legs and rails. However, it cannot be emphasised too much that the craftsmanship required to successfully use this construction must be of the highest order. Where care and precision are present in the making there need be no fear of an early breakdown in use. The original table, made in mahogany, has been in constant family service, without need for repair of any kind, throughout 20 years.

The height of the table is 1½" lower than is often casually quoted when dining surface heights are under consideration. (Research concerning domestic dining tables favours the height shown here.) Ellipses can be blunt or pointed and one's choice can be exercised in scribing the final shape of the table top. The ellipse used to make the drawing was struck by the four arcs method but the trammel method is very near to this one in shape.

To begin the practical work prepare four lengths of wood to size say, 2' 4½" by 3" and four lengths of wood

to 2'4½" by (3" less ⅞") plus ¼" for groove depth = 2⅜" for the legs. In the 3" wide pieces plough a ⁵/₁₆" groove ¼" deep and ⁹/₁₆ths from the edge. On the 2⅜" width pieces, either with a rebate plane or a plough plane fitted with a narrow cutter, cut to shape the tongues. Try to have the tongue thickness slightly oversize to be trimmed later most carefully with a rebate or shoulder plane and working for a press-in-tight fit. Check each rebate adjoining the tongue for accurate squareness. When all is ready arrange sufficient G cramps, or sash cramps, and protection slips for each cramp position. After making a dry trial, glue up and tighten cramps to leave the inside surfaces on an exact right angle.

Next, follow No. 2 of the drawing notes. Use either a plough plane or a scratch stock fitted with a ⅛" home-made profile blade to make the groove to receive a ⅛" square rosewood string; or a lighter coloured string if preferred.

The rectangular frame is made from wood 3" by ⅞" finished. Common dovetails as shown are used for the corners. After a dry assembly of the four sides, mark out and cut the stopped mortises to take the wooden buttons.

Follow notes 3, 4 and 5 (4 screws to each corner) and make corner blocks as noted in No. 6. A dry try out is recommended and, after adjusting any irregularities, mark each leg to match its allotted corner of the frame. Proceed to apply the glue and cramp up. Leave to dry hard after checking. Follow note No. 7 now.

Depending on the size of boards obtainable from the timber merchant the number of boards required has to be worked out. Pair off the boards to show the most attractive grain figure when assembled. The most common way to strengthen the edge joints is to use ½" dowels. Rectangular blocks, made with the grain running at right angles to the edge joints, and fitted firmly into mortises where dowel holes would be, make a strong job. Stopped tongue and groove joints are another method some seasoned craftsmen might use.

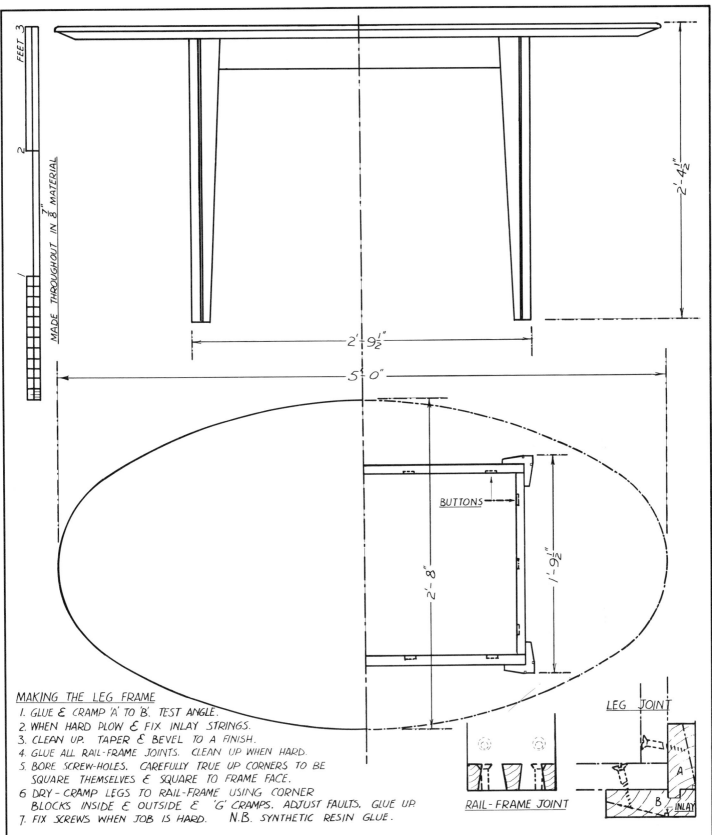

FEET 3

2

1

MADE THROUGHOUT IN $\frac{7}{8}$" MATERIAL

2'-4$\frac{1}{2}$"

2'-9$\frac{1}{2}$"

5'-0"

BUTTONS

2'-8"

1'-9$\frac{1}{2}$"

MAKING THE LEG FRAME
1. GLUE & CRAMP 'A' TO 'B'. TEST ANGLE.
2. WHEN HARD PLOW & FIX INLAY STRINGS.
3. CLEAN UP. TAPER & BEVEL TO A FINISH.
4. GLUE ALL RAIL-FRAME JOINTS. CLEAN UP WHEN HARD.
5. BORE SCREW-HOLES. CAREFULLY TRUE UP CORNERS TO BE SQUARE THEMSELVES & SQUARE TO FRAME FACE.
6. DRY-CRAMP LEGS TO RAIL-FRAME USING CORNER BLOCKS INSIDE & OUTSIDE & 'G' CRAMPS. ADJUST FAULTS. GLUE UP.
7. FIX SCREWS WHEN JOB IS HARD.   N.B. SYNTHETIC RESIN GLUE.

LEG JOINT

A

B

INLAY

RAIL-FRAME JOINT

Smoothing up the main surface, with a wooden or metal smoothing plane, should be carried out while the table top is still rectangular. When the ellipse is marked out protect the surfaces while cutting away the waste wood with a hand saw and, where necessary, a bow-saw; spoke-shave to a finish. Use a cabinet scraper before glasspapering ready for the polishing process.

There are french polishes with a plastic base available for those familiar with this craft. Spraying or brush applications of polyurethane varnishes may be used. The point at issue, however, is that normal french polish is too likely to be damaged on a table required for everyday use; one of the more modern damage resistant finishes seems to be a likely choice. (Rustins

Plastic Coating is recommended for a heat and moisture proof finish. Danish Oil is excellent for gloss or matt finish. – Ed.)

When one takes up the challenge of designing and making some of the things we have to live with, the urge to diversify is always strong in mind. On one of these occasions I started on researching a non-solid leg mostly for use on tables. I applied this idea to many different designs and the results have been most satisfactory. The advantages over the solid leg, in practical terms only, are many. Aesthetically, the light play and shadow add much to the appearance.

The tripod tapered dovetail joint

In high class work this joint is used to secure three legs to a central column and is found in tip top tables, wine tables, lamp standards and old fashioned music stools with revolving tops. It is a very strong joint and even if the glue eventually fails the taper of the dovetails will hold it secure. A view of the joint from underneath is shown in Fig. 1.

Because the legs are dovetailed to a turned pillar several complications arise. The first difficulty of fitting the legs to a curved surface can be overcome by cutting flats on the pillar where the legs meet. There are however no straight surfaces from which to mark the joint. The dovetail on the leg is cut to a taper, being narrower at the top than the bottom and this adds considerably to the firmness of the completed joint. The socket has to be cut to the same taper and because it is "stopped" at its upper end requires accurate marking out as well as careful work with both dovetail saw and bevel edged chisel.

It is advisable when making these joints to draw a full-size plan and elevation (Figs. 2 & 3). Not only will this reduce the possibility of making mistakes but will also ensure that the dovetails are reasonably proportioned. If the tails are too wide the wood of the pillar between them could be so weakened that it could split.

Guide
The centre of the pillar is marked by the tailstock of the lathe and from this centre at 120° are drawn three equally spaced radii. These lines not only indicate where the tapered sockets for the dovetailed legs are to be cut but also act as a guide to ensure that the legs are correctly aligned. On either side of these three radii are marked the thickness of the three legs (Fig. 4). Flats are cut between these two lines to enable the square shoulders of the legs to abut snugly against them. An ordinary square cannot be used to draw the upright lines along the turned column which are needed to mark out the flats. This little difficulty is overcome by cutting a piece of cardboard with parallel sides of a width equal to the depth of the turned column. One end of the card is cut perfectly square and the card is then wrapped around the column with its top side snug against the turned member. A sharp pencil drawn along the square edge of the card will produce the required upright lines (Fig. 5).

The column between these lines is carefully pared away with a wide chisel (Fig. 6) to form surfaces which are flat along and across the grain and also out of winding. A sharp finely set bullnose plane can be a great help in trueing the three flats.

Tapering
In order to give an appearance of lightness it is customary to taper the legs so that they are thicker at the dovetail than at the foot. Such tapering is best left until after the dovetails have been marked and cut. Using a shooting board the ends of the legs are trimmed absolutely square. A marking gauge is used to mark the depth of the dovetail all round the top of the leg. The shape of the dovetail is marked on the lower end of the leg where the dovetail will be at its widest. Parallel guide lines are drawn to assist in drawing the taper correctly (Fig. 7).

A fine dovetail saw is used to cut the tails. These dovetails are now used to mark the sockets on the pillar flats. The same setting of the marking gauge which marked the depth of the dovetails marks the depth of the sockets on the pillar base.

A leg is turned upside down, placed on the pillar and the socket is marked (Fig. 8). The other end of our piece of parallel card is now cut to the same taper as the dovetail and is used to mark the slope of the sockets on the flats.

The sides of the sockets are sawn as far as they can be with a dovetail saw after which a narrow bevel edged chisel cuts down the end and sides at the top of the socket. Waste wood is pared away with the chisel taking care to cut just within the lines. This will allow a little bit for trimming when fitting the leg. The dovetail should fit into its socket throughout its length and it should be possible to push it to within ⅛" (3 mm) of the end of the socket. A light tap from the mallet will then drive the joint home.

Steel Strap
When the legs fit properly it is advised that identifying marks are put on both dovetails and sockets to ensure that the legs are glued into their rightful positions. Before glueing takes place the joints are tapped apart and the legs tapered to make the feet narrower than the dovetailed ends. Sharp edges are rounded to produce a pleasing contour. A suggested shape for a leg is shown in Fig. 9 and a cardboard pattern should be cut to assist in marking out the legs uniformly. If the legs have to bear a fair amount of weight as in the case of a music stool or tip top table they will need to be of a stouter section than those of a wine table. To prevent the leverage of the legs from splitting out the sockets of the pillar it is advisable to cut out a mild steel strap as shown in Fig. 10. A central screw secures the strap to the base of the pillar while the remaining screws are run into the underside of the legs.

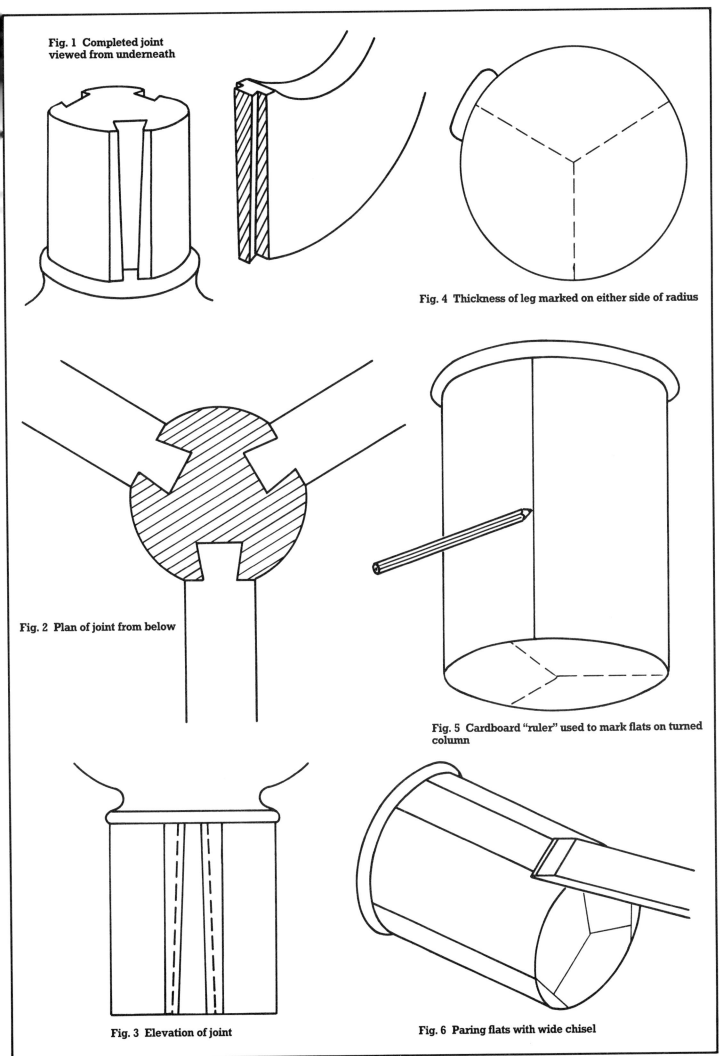

Fig. 1 Completed joint
viewed from underneath

Fig. 4 Thickness of leg marked on either side of radius

Fig. 2 Plan of joint from below

Fig. 5 Cardboard "ruler" used to mark flats on turned column

Fig. 3 Elevation of joint

Fig. 6 Paring flats with wide chisel

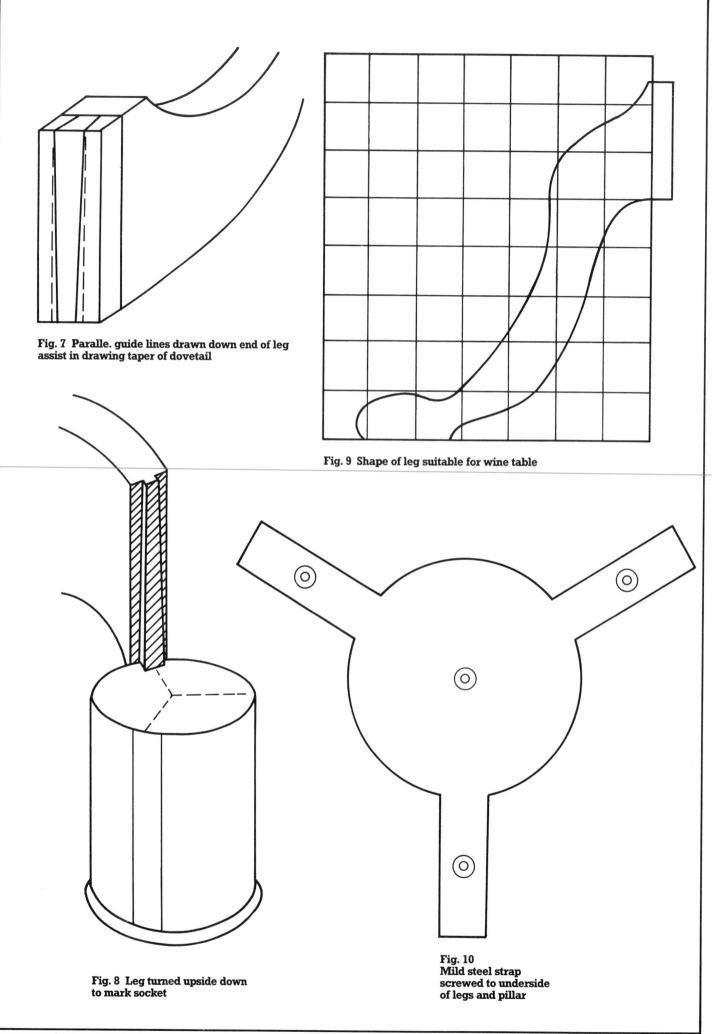

Fig. 7 Paralle. guide lines drawn down end of leg assist in drawing taper of dovetail

Fig. 9 Shape of leg suitable for wine table

Fig. 8 Leg turned upside down to mark socket

Fig. 10
Mild steel strap
screwed to underside
of legs and pillar

Wood carving and wood sculpture bench

This Sculpture Bench is ideal for carving generally and can be adapted for most woodworking. Easily folded and carried, it will meet the needs of persons with limited accommodation or storage. The sizes are flexible and materials can be chosen as available, although ideally the top would be constructed of solid beech.

The design, which is from the Bahco Record Tools Education Department, has a dog vice which provides the usual vice features. The dog also works in conjunction with single or double dogs which can be located in any position along the length of the bench to hold flat material of any contour. A collar insert allows the use of a Bench Holdfast which acts as a top vice for holding work securely on the top of the bench. A woodcarver's screw can also be located in one of these holes. Thus, the majority of work holding problems can be met.

The bench is solidly built, the dowelling jig being used for joint work and the craftsman will find it possible to sit on it for ease of working with some jobs whilst the seat, not only gives stability at the vice end of the bench, but also offers seating particularly useful when carving in low relief on the top of the bench.

For ease of reading, sizes have been omitted from the general assembly drawing. Reference to the Cutting List will give the overall finished size of each piece of material. Where actual settings of the M148 Marples Dowelling Jig are not given, the procedure may be found in the Dowelling Jig instruction leaflet.

Cutting List

All dimensions are *finished* sizes. No allowances has been made for waste or cutting. Sizes are given in millimetres except where otherwise stated.

Description	No. Reqd.	Dimensions L	× W	× Th.	Material
LEG FRAMES:					
Legs (a, b, e & f)	4	780	70	45	Good quality softwood
Top rails (c & g)	2	300	70	45	Good quality softwood
Bottom rails (d & h)	2	140	57	22	Good quality softwood
Bench top supports (i)	2	140	45	45	Good quality softwood
CENTRE FRAME:					
Stiles (l & m)	2	600	57	22	Good quality softwood
Rails (j & k)	2	675	57	22	Good quality softwood
STOOL FRAME:					
Stile (n)	1	450	57	22	Good quality softwood
Stile (o)	1	500	57	22	Good quality softwood
Rails (p & q)	2	400	57	22	Good quality softwood
Seat supports (r)	2	57	57	22	Good quality softwood
Feet (s)	2	150	57	45	Good quality softwood
Seat (t)	1	250	250	18	Hardwood or blockboard
Bolt Block (u)	1	100	100	18	Hardwood or blockboard
BENCH TOP:					
Top (v)	1	625	275	18	Blockboard
Cross battens (w)	2	275	57	22	Good quality softwood
End battens (x)	2	300	70	40	Suitable hardwood
Edge strips (y)	2	625	40	12	Suitable hardwood
Vice cheeks (for 52D)	1	300	80	22	Suitable hardwood
or (for 57)	(1	300	80	22)	Suitable hardwood
	(1	300	25	22)	Suitable hardwood
Vice mounting block (z)		200	100	25	Suitable hardwood

Sundries
1 length of ⅜ in. (9 mm.) dia. dowel
1 length of ¾ in. (18 mm.) dia. dowel
3 prs. 2 in. (50 mm.) steel back flap hinges
1 – 3 × ½ in. (75 × 13 mm.) dia. bolt
4 – 2 in. (50 mm.) coach screws

Countersunk steel screws
1½ doz. ¾ in. (18 mm.) – No. 10 gauge
1½ doz. 1¼ in. (38 mm.) – No. 10 gauge
4 – 1 in. (25 mm.) – No. 8 gauge

Bench fittings
No. 52D Record 'Dog' Vice or
No V175 RECORD Woodcraft Vice
No M146 MARPLES Bench Holdfast

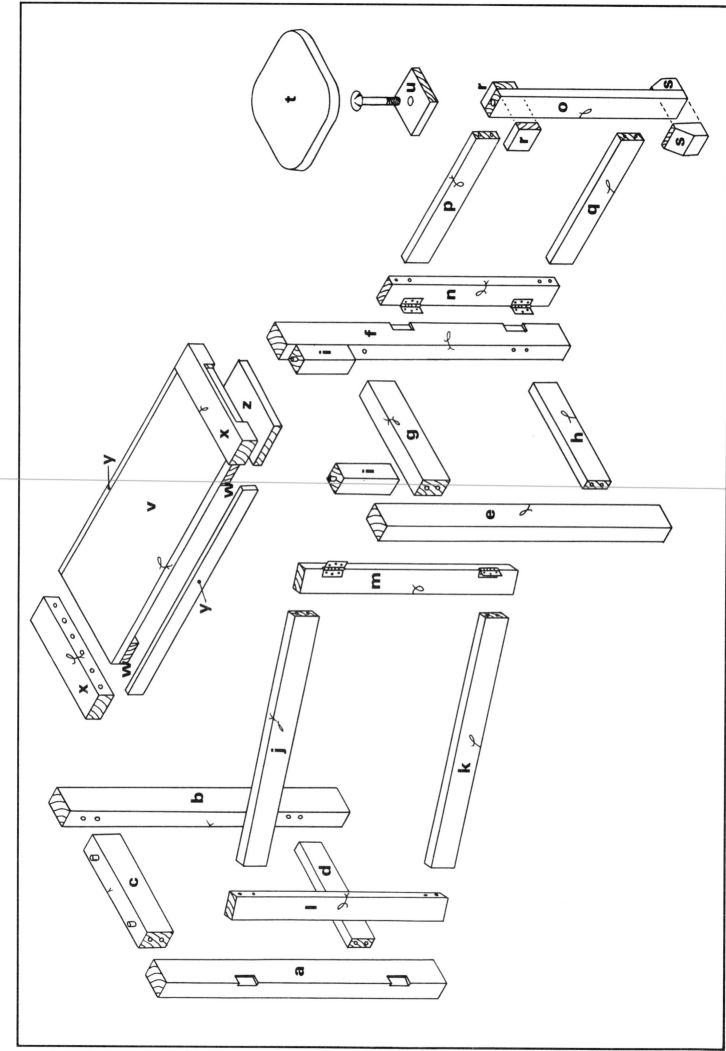

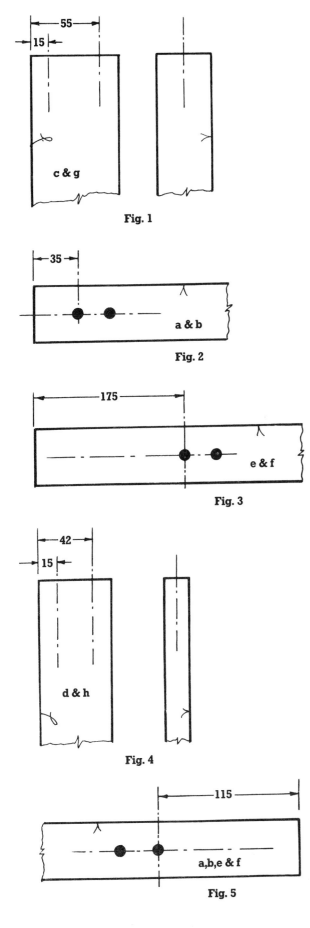

Fig. 1

Fig. 2

Fig. 3

Fig. 4

Fig. 5

Making the Leg Frames

Cut and prepare pieces (a), (b), (c), (d), (e), (f), (g), and (h). If planed timber is used, then the only preparation necessary will be to cut *all* the above pieces to the lengths shown in the Cutting List. Care should be taken to ensure that all ends are sawn squarely if they are not to be finally planed. Mark a face side and face edge on each piece.

Set the Marples M148 Dowelling Jig bush carriers and fences to the sizes in (fig. 1).

Assemble Jig on the end of piece (c) and drill (through the ⅜ in. (9mm) bushes) to a suitable depth – i.e. 30 mm. Repeat this process on the other end of the piece. Repeat for piece (g).

Mark a line across the face edge of pieces (a and b) as shown in (fig. 2). This is the centre line of the first dowel hole. Remove the reference head and adjustable head from the Jig and assemble it on the face edge (a) with the aid of the clamp provided. Ensure that the fences rest against the *face side*. Drill both holes.

Repeat on the face edge of piece (b). Mark lines across the face edge of pieces (e and f) as (fig. 3). Follow procedure for pieces (a and b).

Replace both reference and adjustable heads. Set bush carrier datum lines and fences to sizes as (fig. 4). Assemble Jig on the end of piece (d). Drill both holes. Repeat on other end and both ends of piece (h). Remove reference and adjustable heads from Jig. Assemble Jig, with clamp, to face edge of (a) – (fig. 5). N.B. Fences must rest against *face side* when drilling pieces (a), (b), (e) & (f).

Drilling for dowels is now complete.

Cut 16 pieces of ⅜ in. (9 mm) dia. dowel to 55 mm in length. Both leg frames may now be glued, cramped and checked. Glue and cramp both pieces (i) to inside of legs (e) and (f) and to the top edge of rail (g).

Making Centre Frame

Cut and prepare pieces (j), (k), (l) and (m). Replace reference and adjustable heads. Check settings of bush carrier datum lines and fences. N.B. the settings are the same as (fig. 4).

Assemble Jig on the end of piece (j). Reference head *must* be against the *face edge, fences* against the *face side*. Drill both holes 30 mm. deep. Repeat on other end. Repeat procedure on both ends of piece (k). Remove adjustable head (*not* reference head) and assemble Jig, with clamp, to the face edge of piece (l). Reference head should rest against the end of piece (l) with fences against the face side. Repeat on face edge at other end. Repeat procedure on face edge of piece (k). All drilling is now complete. Cut 8 pieces of ⅜ in. (9 mm.) dowel to 55 mm. in length. Glue up framework.

Making Stool Framework

Cut and prepare pieces (n), (o), (p) and (q). Replace adjustable head. Jig settings are the same as for Centre Frame. Jig can be assembled on the end of pieces (p) and (q) with no further resetting of bush carriers or fences, and all four ends drilled – again to 30 mm. depth.

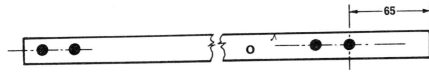

Fig. 6

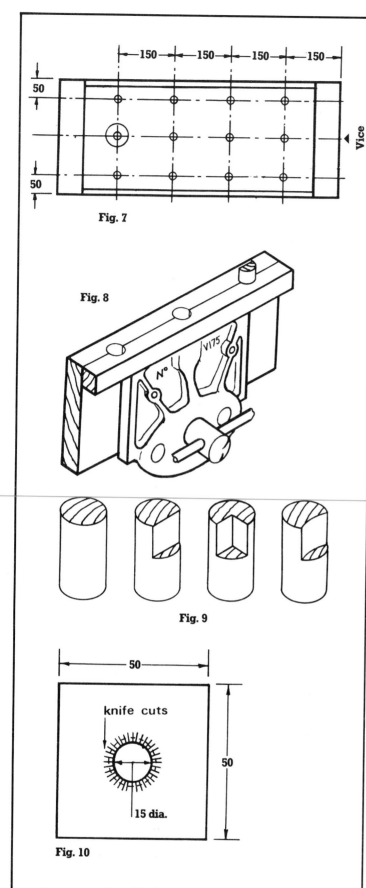

Fig. 7

Fig. 8

Fig. 9

Fig. 10

Remove adjustable head and assemble Jig on face edge of piece (n) – same procedure as for rails (j) and (k). Assemble Jig similarly on the face edge of stile (o) with reference head against top end. Drill both holes. By removing reference head the Jig can now be inverted and removed along the face edge of stile (o) to the position indicated in (fig. 6). Drill both holes.

Cut 8 pieces of dowel, as before, and glue up the framework.

All the jointing of the underframing is now complete. If instructions regarding correct assembly of the Jig

against face sides and edges have been followed, all face sides should be perfectly flush. Final cleaning up, therefore, should be limited to glasspapering.

Making the Bench Top

Prepare pieces (v), (w), (x) and (y). Glue both pieces (w) to underside of blockboard top – edges flush with the ends of piece (v). Glue pieces (y) to each edge of (v). Final trimming of both ends of bench top may be necessary before attaching pieces (x).

It is suggested that six dowels be used on each joint to ensure maximum strength. Although it is possible to obtain additional bush carriers and longer capacity rods to complete this joint in one simple operation, it is appreciated that the reader may only have the facilities of the standard Dowelling Jig. In this case, set the bush carrier datum lines at 25 mm. and 75 mm. from the reference head. Fences shold be set at 20 mm. from centre datum lines. With adjustable head removed, hold Jig (by hand) firmly against the face side and at the end of piece (x). Drill both holes. Repeat on second piece (x). Hold Jig similarly on the end of bench top, fences firmly against face side and drill corresponding holes.

Remove reference head, place a piece of dowel, say 50 mm. long, in second hole to locate first bush carrier, drill through other bush to produce the third hole. This method can be repeated to provide the remaining three holes. Each dowel hole will be centred 50 mm. apart. Repeat procedure on other three edges. Further information of this method can be found in the 148 Instruction Leaflet under 'edge to edge' jointing.

Cut 12 pieces of dowel, 55 mm. long and glue and cramp end battens to bench top.

Mark out complete top as (fig. 7) and drill through each centre ⊕ with a suitable ¾ in. (18 mm.) centre bit for the 'dogs'.

Details of fixing the collar of the Marples M 146 Bench Holdfast may be found in the Instruction Leaflet supplied with the tool. It is recommended that the collar be placed in the position indicated in (fig. 7). Additional collars are available should the user wish to fit alternative holding positions.

Assembly of Framework

Both leg frames are hinged to the centre frame with suitable 2 in. (50 mm.) steel back flap hinges. The bottom edge of the centre frame should be raised off the floor by 40 mm. Care should be taken to ensure that the centre frame be positioned exactly the same distance from the bottom of the two legs. To enable the framework to fold correctly, the centre frame must be hinged diagonally to the inside faces of the two diametrically opposite legs (a & f). Location and securement of the hinges will be improved if a recess is cut to receive each flap, rather than simply screwing each flap to its respective frame. Use ¾ in. (18 mm.) screws for fixing to centre frame, 1¼ in. (35 mm.) for fixing to legs. Similarly, hinge the stool frame to the outside of leg (f) taking care to position the bottom of stile (o) level with legs (e & f). Glue two pieces (r) to the top of stile (o). This will provide extra thickness to accept seat bolt. Similarly shape pieces (s) and glue to bottom of stile (o). This will ensure vertical stability of seat frame.

Making the Seat

Most carving and sculpture work can be carried out in a comfortable sitting position, and whilst the seating unit gives this facility, it also adds to the stability of the bench.

The seat can be made from any suitable material (preferably hardwood) and may be shaped to individual requirements. It is advantageous for the seat to swivel and also to be removed for storage. This can be achieved simply by recessing a 3 in. (75 mm.) × ½ in. (13 mm.) bolt in a piece of wood (u) and finally gluing and screwing (u) to (t) with four 1 in. (25 mm.) screws. A hole bored down the end of stile (o) to a depth of 60 mm. will permit the seat bolt to be simply dropped in. When stored away, the seat can be attached to the top through one of the 'dog' holes.

Fixing the Top to the Frame

The easiest method of locating the *four* positions for placing *metal* dowels is achieved by driving a 25 mm. panel pin into the centres of the blocks (i) to approx. half their length. Similarly, two panel pins placed in the top edge of rail (c) will locate the other two dowels. Cut the heads off each panel pin, place the bench top in position and press down. Remove the bench top, pull out the panel pins and drill ⅜ in. (9 mm.) holes at each of the eight centres to a depth of 25 mm. Cut four pieces of ⅜ in. (9 mm.) mild steel rod (or shanks from bolts) at 40 mm. Glue into holes in framework with epoxy resin (Araldite).

Fitting the Record 52D Vice

We recommend the fitting of a Record 52D ('dog') Vice. In addition to the usual facilities, the 52 D has an adjustable 'dog' to assist the holding of work on the bench top. Prepare a suitable piece of wood, 25 mm. thick (z) and glue it to the underside of the bench top – set back 15 mm. from the front edge. N.B. the top rail (g) has been lowered to avoid fouling the vice. Offer the vice to the front edge and mark around the body jaw. Cut a recess within this area to a depth of 15 mm. to allow the face of the body jaw to fit flush with the bench front. Attach the vice with FOUR 2 in. (50 mm.) coach screws. A suitable piece of hardwood can be screwed to the sliding jaw and finally planed level with the bench top.

If funds are limited, then a cheaper version – the Record V175 Woodcraft Vice can be substituted. However, this has a smaller opening capacity and does not have the advantage afforded by the 'dog'. Some modification of the wooden vice cheek will be necessary to make provision for the addition of 'dogs' – similar to those envisaged for the bench top. (fig. 8).

'Dogs'

These can be made from ¾ in. (18 mm) dowel. (Fig. 9) gives an indication of various adaptations to overcome the many problems of holding awkwardly shaped items on the bench top. Each one should be approx. 35 mm. long, overall, but must be shorter for fitting in modified vice cheeks.

If the dowel 'dogs' are a loose fit in the holes, prepare *eleven* pieces of polythene (from empty bottles) as (fig. 10). Glue these, with contact adhesive (bostik) to underside of bench top, using a 'dog' to locate them centrally at each hole. The flexibility of the polythene will allow the 'dogs' to be raised or lowered with ease without dropping through the hole.

All surfaces should be given a couple of coats of polyurethane varnish to protect and enhance the finished bench.

This basic design is capable of size modification, particularly if heavier work is envisaged. Whilst the model in the photograph is constructed largely in softwood, the user may introduce any timber which is

available, but care should be taken in its selection to avoid cracks and loose knots.

For advice on any aspect of tool usage, it is suggested that the reader write to the Bahco Record Tools Education Service at Parkway Works, Sheffield, S9 3BL.

Details of the Dowelling Jig – Marples No. M148, the Bench Holdfast – Marples M146, the Record 52D and V175 Vices and the Marples M277 Carver's Screw, can be obtained from Bahco Record Tools Ltd., Parkway Works, Sheffield, S9 3BL.

Garden seat

Tools used
Steel Measuring tape
Steel Foot rule
Tri-square
Straight edge
Bench hook
Cross-cut saw
Tenon saw
Bow saw
Metal plane No. 5
Metal plane No. 4
Chisels, firmer
Chisels sash mortise
Mallet
Brace
Centre bits
Shooting board
Marking knife
Spokeshave
Hand drill
Twist drills
Screwdriver
Sash cramp
Sliding bevel

The garden seats used in municipal parks, promenades and public walks are made to withstand not only careful use but the ill-use of a mindless minority who seem to delight in punishing artefacts provided to make life more pleasant. Tough materials and rugged construction are called for in the latter case.

For private gardens lighter constructions and a wider choice of timbers may be considered. A seat which will remain exposed to all seasons must, of necessity, be built in weather-resisting timbers, e.g. teak, oak or a carefully chosen timber from the many 'dominion' woods available. It goes without saying, perhaps, that waterproof glue should be used during construction. Preservation much depends, when facing the all-weathers situation on the regular use of teak oil, raw linseed oil or one of the polyurethane varnishes. The 'summer-use' only type of seat, built maybe in pine, could be either varnished or finished in gloss paint.

With one's mind made up on the kind of seat needed to satisfy all requirements, the first step could be to visit a timber yard where the varieties, rough sawn or machine planed, are discussed. Unless one has the skill and the time to prepare the pieces from rough sawn timber, wielding a wooden jack plane or a Record or Stanley No 5 metal plane, it is well worth while ordering the pieces P.A.R. (planed all round). But, first of all a "cutting list" must be made. Briefly, the various pieces are grouped so that all those parts with the same width and thickness appear on your list as one item. (Varying lengths of the same width and thickness could be added end to end if some of the pieces are unduly short. It is a simple matter to cut them down to length

when required). Allow ½ in. more on the length of *each* piece when ordering serveral short pieces in one length as this much will be needed when jointing and squaring off ends. As an example, the 14 slats fitted into the seat back frame, each at 15 inches long. Rather than ordering 2 pieces seven times longer than 15½ in. = 108½ in. or 9 ft-½in., which could be unwieldy, the writer would ask for two lengths 5 times 15½ in. or say, 6 ft. 6 in., and one piece four times 15½ in. or 5 ft. 3 in. which would be strictly economical but adequate.

Now study the drawings which should clearly explain the shapes and sizes of the joints (Note carefully any off-centre placing), mark out and cut the joints at the top of the front leg and the arm of the seat. Next, mark out and cut the joint between the end rail and the front leg. Assemble these pieces dry and lay flat on the bench. Place the back leg member across the frame and, having set a sliding bevel, with the aid of a protractor on the drawing, and the angle transferred to a spare piece of wood, mark the shoulder line at the top of the leg. By the same procedure, proceed to mark the shoulder line at the back end of the end rail. Cut and fit these joints.

Tenons
The long front and back rails should be next on the list. Having located the end rails in earlier work there should be no difficulty in carrying round the necessary limit lines for these long rails. N.B. As the tenons are rather wide it might help someone to know of the following method: After marking the shoulder lines with a marking knife and trysquare, use the mortise gauge (if available) or take extra care making two settings and two markings to scribe the tenon thickness with marking gauge. Saw the shoulders, on the waste wood side of the shoulder line, to their proper depth. Make one or two extra parallel saw cuts on the waste wood side of the shoulder line and, *lightly* with a chisel bevel side downwards, chip away down the grain most of the waste wood. Clean up across the grain with a wide chisel bevel side up. Finally, with a marking gauge mark the tenon widths, and the haunches where shown. Use a tenon saw and, where required, a bowsaw, to complete the shapes.

(Normally, the standard method of sawing tenons would be used, making all saw cuts down the grain first, then the shoulder cuts to remove the wastewood cheeks in one piece. – Ed.)

The seat stiffening bearer rails with their dovetail housings could be marked out next and cut to a fit. Close up and clamp together the front and back rails to locate the stiffeners exactly. When the joints are cut and fitted the hollow curve which provides the 'spring' in the seat should be marked out and cut with a bowsaw before using a spokeshave to a finish.

At this point, when the mortises which are to receive the thin tenons have been opened out (i.e. tapered) at the wedge-fitting side, the wedges made, surfaces skimmed up with a wooden smoothing plane, or a No 4 Record or Stanley metal plane, any necessary rounding of the front rail done on its top edge, all sharp corners lightly eased, the main seat frame may be glued, cramped together, wedges fitted, ¼ in. holes bored at

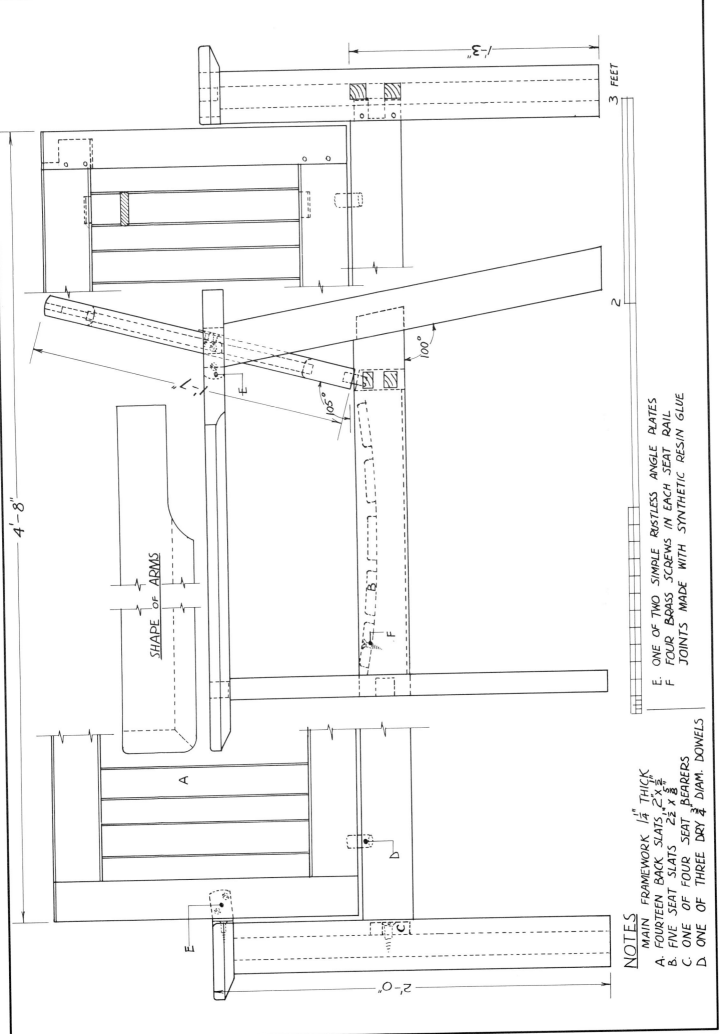

4'-8"

SHAPE of ARMS

1'-7"

100°

105°

1'-3"

B

A

C

D

E

F

2'-0"

2

3 FEET

NOTES

MAIN FRAMEWORK $1\frac{1}{4}$" THICK

A. FOURTEEN BACK SLATS, 2" x $\frac{1}{2}$"
B. FIVE SEAT SLATS $2\frac{1}{2}$ x $\frac{5}{8}$"
C. ONE OF FOUR SEAT BEARERS
D. ONE OF THREE DRY $\frac{3}{4}$ DIAM. DOWELS

E. ONE OF TWO SIMPLE RUSTLESS ANGLE PLATES
F. FOUR BRASS SCREWS IN EACH SEAT RAIL
   JOINTS MADE WITH SYNTHETIC RESIN GLUE

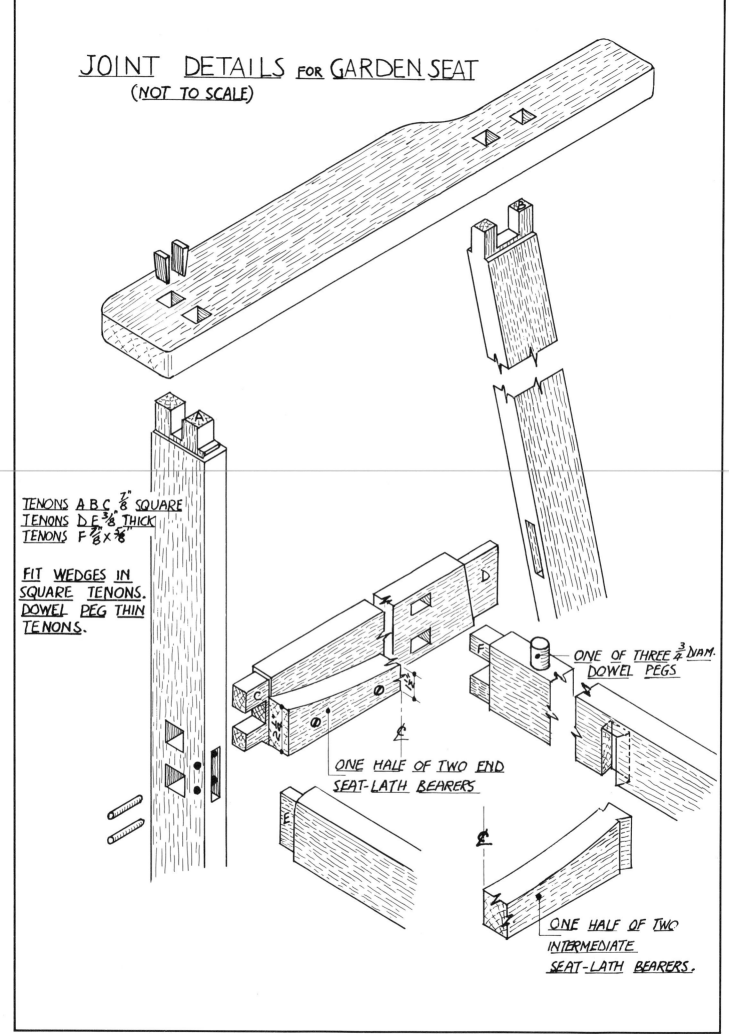

JOINT DETAILS FOR GARDEN SEAT
(NOT TO SCALE)

TENONS A B C $\frac{7}{8}$" SQUARE
TENONS D E $\frac{3}{8}$" THICK
TENONS F $\frac{7}{8}$" × $\frac{5}{8}$"

FIT WEDGES IN SQUARE TENONS. DOWEL PEG THIN TENONS.

ONE OF THREE $\frac{3}{4}$" DIAM. DOWEL PEGS

ONE HALF OF TWO END SEAT-LATH BEARERS

ONE HALF OF TWO INTERMEDIATE SEAT-LATH BEARERS.

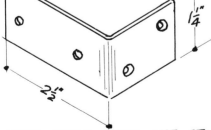

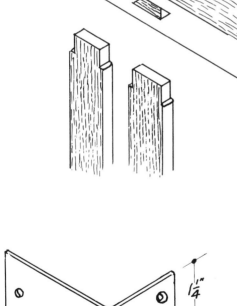

METAL ANGLE PIECE. USE STOUT
STAINLESS STEEL, IF POSSIBLE.

'BEND ANGLE' DETERMINED BY
FIRST MAKING CARDBOARD PATTERN.

no more than ¼ in., from the shoulder line through the
thin tenons, and dowels glued and fitted. Later, when
the glue is set hard, proceed with gluing and cramping
the stiffener rails in place.

The end bearers of the seat slats may now be cut,
shaped as were the stiffener top edges, holes bored for
screws and finally fixed in place.

The back support frame should present rather less
difficulties than those encountered in the larger seat
frame. Carefully mark face edges on the four inner
faces of the oblong frame. Bring each pair together and
hold firmly while locating the positions where one end
of each long rail enters the edge of its companion short
rail. Gauge tenons and mortises. If required use the
wide tenon method, described earlier, to shape tenons
and haunches.

Mortises

The corner mortises and the slat mortises present quite
a session of chopping away waste with either mortise
chisel, sash mortise chisel or a registered chisel of the
right sizes. It is possible to remove most of the waste
wood by using a wood bit of diam. one sixteenth less
than the tenon thickness fixed in the brace and on a
centre line drawn (or marked with a marking gauge)
bore a string of stopped-depth holes and chisel the final
mortise shape with paring chisel.

Next, close up the two face edges of the longer rails
and hold firm while locating the 14 slat positions. Notch
the ends of each slat to form a simple tenon and transfer
the tenon widths on to the mortise positions.

Assemble the seat back now and check for twist and
squareness dry in the cramps. When satisfactory,
dismantle and round the frame's top edge. Clean up and
soften off sharp corners. Glue, cramp up and check
again for 'wind' and squareness.

The three ¾ in. dowels fitted into the long back rail of
the seat frame should be carefully located and bored
not quite vertical but parallel to the back-slanting line of
the back frame. It the dowel holes are absolutely of
equal centres it will be possible to fix the back frame in
either way round: a useful ploy if any movement is
detected as the seat is used.

The angle plates used to secure the back frame are
mentioned on the drawings. Use brass or chrome plated
raised head screws.

Constructing a tambour

Tools used

3' Boxwood folding rule
6" Trysquare
Marking gauge
Tenon saw
Jackplane
Smoothing plane
Bead plane
Round plane
Ripsaw
Firmer chisels and gouges for cutting grooves

Although tambours are most frequently found on Roll Top desks they also make effective doors on cabinets where hinged or sliding doors may not be suitable. Visiting the Ideal Home exhibition some years ago I saw a tambour incorporated into a draw leaf table. When I commented on the tambour the salesman remarked that I was the first person who had not called it a roll top table!

The tambour comprises carefully shaped strips of wood glued to a canvas backing. The ends of the strips are shaped to allow them to run freely in grooves. The grooves are either straight or gently convex. They cannot be concave because the canvas backing prevents the strips from hingeing in that direction.

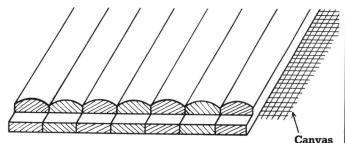

Fig. 1 Simple form of tambour

The simplest form of tambour consisting of slightly rounded strips is shown in Fig. 1 and is adequate for flat or slightly convex surfaces. If a sharp curve were on view the canvas backing would be revealed as the strips opened up when negotiating the curve. The situation would increasingly worsen as the canvas stretched with use.

Fig. 2 Improved form of strip

To prevent the canvas from being seen when the tambour passes round a curve a bead shaped as in Fig. 2 is used. A small projection on the edge of one strip fits under a hollow worked on the edge of the adjoining piece. This projection hides the canvas even when the strips open up on the curves.

Probably the most straightforward way of preparing moulded strips is to plane a thoroughly seasoned straight grained board to a thickness a trifle greater than the width of the finished strips. Then by altering the shape of the cutter of a bead plane the thicker edge of the lath can be planed to the desired shape (Fig. 3). The face of the strip is shaped with a round plane to which a suitably shaped fence has been fitted (Fig. 4). Finally a small bead plane shapes the thin edge of the strip (Fig. 5). The quirk of the bead is used as a guide when sawing off the strip from the board in readiness for shooting the edge prior to moulding the next strip.

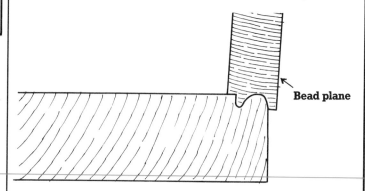

Fig. 3 Bead plane moulding thick edge of strip

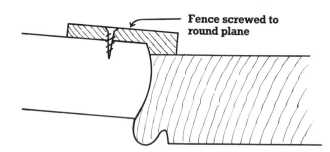

Fig. 4 face of strip shaped with round plane

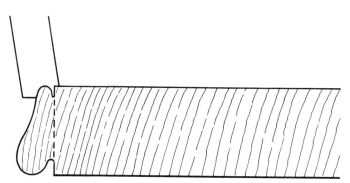

Fig. 5 Thin edge of strip worked with small bead plane

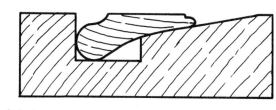

Fig. 6 Strip supported in planing cradle

Cradle

The backs of the strips have to be planed and to ensure that they are all planed to exactly the same thickness a planing cradle (Fig. 6) is prepared. A board is ploughed and splayed to enable the strips to be accommodated in it to the required depth. The upper faces of the cradle act as a guide to the plane so that a uniform thickness is achieved throughout.

Fig. 7 Angled rebate in leading edge of strip permits tambour to negotiate slight concave curve

With some roll top desks the tambour has to negotiate a slight concave curve, generally when it is about half open. To enable this to take place a small amount of clearance in the leading edge of one bead allows the adjacent bead to slide under and permit the tambour to bend back on itself (Fig. 7).

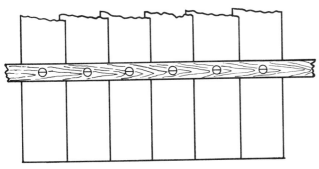

Fig. 8 Steel strip screwed to back of tambour

In the case of a large tambour it is a wise precaution to add a little reinforcement rather than rely solely on the ability of the canvas backing to keep the strips together. The simpler method is to obtain two or three steel strips about ½″ (12mm) wide and 1/16″ (1.5mm) thick. Holes are drilled and countersunk the same distance apart as the width of the backs of the laths. The strips are then screwed to the backs of the laths as in Fig. 8. The second method is to bore two or three holes through each lath and pass cords through. To achieve smooth operation of the tambour all the holes must be at the same distance in all the strips. To ensure this necessary accuracy the planing cradle is adopted. Using a fine bit, holes are bored, correctly spaced and at the same distance from the top. A piece of wood cramped over the top of the board as in Fig. 9 secures each lath in turn while the holes are bored through.

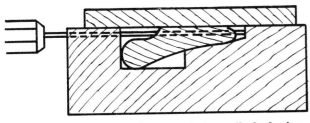

Fig. 9 Top board holds strips securely in cradle for boring

Glue

It is essential when gluing the canvas to the backs of the strips to ensure that the glue does not run between the joints of the strips. One way of safeguarding this is to brush thin glue on one side of a sheet of drawing paper.

After the glue has dried the paper is cut into ¼″ (6mm) wide strips. Having laid out the tambour on a flat surface and damped the glued side of the paper the strips are stuck over the joints on the back face and allowed to dry. After about two hours the canvas backing is glued on, taking care not to disturb the paper strips.

The ends of the tambour are cut to size with a fine-toothed saw and if necessary rebated as in Fig. 1. It is usual to insert the tambour after the carcase of the desk or cabinet has been assembled and to enable this to be done the grooves are run out at the back of the cabinet (Fig. 10). If a tambour has to be repaired and the grooves are not run out the probability is that grooved inner ends were screwed in after the carcase was assembled. If this is so then unscrewing the ends will enable the complete roll to be removed.

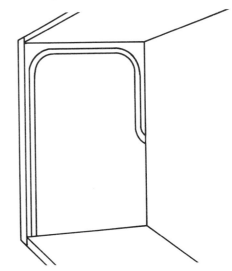

Fig. 10 Groove run out at back enables tambour to be fed in

When designing a tambour there are several important features to bear in mind. Firstly there must be sufficient room in the piece to allow the entire length to fold away when the tambour is opened. Secondly the length of the roll (measured across the strips) must be as long as possible in proportion to its width (the length of the strips). Failure to ensure this may cause the tambour to skew and jam in its grooves instead of sliding smoothly. Thirdly keep the width of the strips as small as practicable and thereby avoid having to enlarge the width of the grooves at the curves. Finally because the end strip has to stand up to a great deal of pushing and pulling it should be stouter in section than the other strips. To enable it to negotiate the curved grooves the rebated ends of this strip are reduced to the same dimensions as the others (Fig. 11).

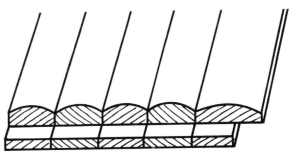

Fig. 11 End strip of tambour being of stouter section has its rebated ends reduced in width for easy running

The strips of the tambour are individually polished before assembling and gluing otherwise it is extremely difficult to achieve a first class finish.

More than just a stool

Ever hear of a *stoolman*? How about *stooling* a committee? Of course not . . . because the *chair* (not the stool) is represented in history as a seat of authority; a place of power, such as the chair or throne of the king. The austair bench (which is just a long stool) was part of Puritan, Quaker, Shaker and other religious expressions where one sat in common for worship.

At first, the chair was somewhat uncomfortable and awkward like the stool, but it soon gained acceptance by all, and the common person's seat (the stool) was diminished in size. Perhaps this was an expression of distaste for its symbol of lowliness. Then, in what seems to be a final act, it was made a place for the feet!

Although the footstool became very practical for keeping the feet off draughty, wooden floors, the trend of discontinuing the stool for seating begs the question as to why it was virtually eliminated. The footstool as a companion for the wingchair certainly speaks of emerging affluence, but desire for comfort alone may only be part of the story. Over the years, the seating stool has never really quite survived its symbolic ancestry to find a permanent place of general acceptance in the home. The single exception to this appears to be found in its admittance into the bedroom as a familiar part of the dressing table. So the chair is functional today, but the stool really is not. And although the stool is not considered a status symbol, yet it has somehow managed to survive in its limited way. Maybe there *is* something about it that makes it more than just a stool.

And so when I set out to find an alternate seat to complement our limited writing desk line, I returned again and again to the design illustrated in this article. Not wanting our customers to be placed in too lowly a position upon the stool, I figured that the least I could do would be to provide one as beautiful as possible. Perhaps you'll agree with me that the beauty of this piece that I show being built makes it more than just a stool in that sense as well.

Some Background

The basic proportions in this project are from an original piece at the Victoria & Albert Museum, South Kensington, London. My particular thanks is given to Mr. John Hardy, Assistant Keeper, Department of Furniture, for supplying me with a large reproduction of the original stool and historical data about it.

The museum stool is Irish; early 18th century, purchased by the museum in 1910 from W.D. Hodges & Company. The name of the craftsman is not known. I wish I knew who he was, as a person's name adds that human involvement with the wood that is so important in beautiful handcrafted furniture. I look at the stool, and I think about the person who crafted it – how he put his hands to it – how he planned it. There is a person inseparably linked to that antique – an expression of himself.

In this sense, wood lives as does the art form it is moulded into. Here this Irish fellow put his hands to the wood to bring about a beautiful sitting stool in the midst of a shop and tools common to that period. Over 250 years later, an American across the Atlantic closely approximates another stool from his very design. And then writes an article about it from the heart of surburbia. Does wood live? I heartily agree with Laurence Schmeckebier (Dean Emeritus, School of Art, Syracuse University, New York) that museums have become the conservators of our artistic and cultural heritage as well as active educational and cultural centres.

The original stool is rare for several reasons. In my opinion, the principal reason is its Queen Anne/Chippendale design influence at a period of time when Queen Anne/Chippendale chairs – not stools – were the focus of the craftsman/designer.

Layout, Cutting and Finishing the Legs

In my own build, I have taken the liberty of slightly modifying the trifid foot and working it closer to my own design. In addition, I have incorporated different shell carvings – ones from 18th century Newport (south of Boston) – similar to a Christopher Townsend design. Lastly, a somewhat different fabric was chosen. One which would enhance the elegance of design and would be not unlike the New England types rather than the geometrical wool-work as on the original.

Photo. 1 To reproduce a museum piece exactly, or to pick off the essential measurements for an innovative build, I need only a view of the front and side together with a single dimension (height, depth and width); a top view may also be required if there are compound curves involved. From this, a scale is developed that enables me to find any other dimension on the piece. In the case of a picture in perspective (where the three dimensions appear as the eye sees them), a special scale is made, because the length of the lines decrease as they extend out into the distance.

I maintain an active file of 18th century design sketches. Over the years, my trips to the library with sketch pad in hand has provided me with a good source of traditional designs. On the sketch containing this stool I find the note, "Victoria & Albert Museum, South Kensington, England. Charles H. Hayward's book." The note is dated in October 1969. I encourage others to keep a file of designs pertinent to their area of interest. You never know when you'll use one of them.

I start the build with the legs.

Photo. 2 All cabriole legs with deep ankle swings and extended knees are started by cutting a template from a grid pattern. The template can be any hard, stable material up to about 6mm/¼" thick. The four leg blanks are cut from *solid* stock (60mm/2½" square). I'll explain my emphasis on the word "solid" when I get to carving the trifid foot. The four blanks have been stickered (use of 19mm/³⁄₄" spacers between the blanks) for about a week after ripping and planing to allow the wood to stablize prior to cutting.

Photo. 3 The outline has been drawn on each leg blank on two adjacent sides – Knee to knee and toe to toe.

Photo. 4 Before bandsawing the leg to rough shape, we drill the mortises into the leg stiles. Here, the mortise is about 9.5mm or ³⁄₈" wide by 44mm or 1³⁄₄" long. A mortising attachment can be used which will produce square holes, but I prefer using a bradpoint drill bit and overlapping the holes during drilling.

The brad point drill bit the author has in mind is similar to the English Lip and Spur bit specifically designed for boring in wood. (Manufactured in U.K. by Bahco Record.) – Ed.

Photo. 5 The mortise is being finished to size with the use of a mortising chisel. The mallet is not necessary for this operation if the chisel is *sharp.* This requirment for sharpness applies to the paring chisel as well as any other. All of us have long since learned that a new chisel usually comes to us with the edge ground to the proper angle, but for it to be usable, we need to hone and strop it.

The novice usually encounters a problem with the first through-cut on the bandsaw, because the pencil line from the adjacent side disappears when the final cut severs the wood. To meet this problem, some craftspeople tack the severed piece back with brads while others wrap tape around it. As far as I'm concerned, the easiest answer is to proceed as follows:

1. Turn the face of one side upward and bandsaw to about midpoint along one of the lines;
2. Now back the piece out along this path of the sawline just cut.
3. From the other direction, saw along the same line, but stop just short of meeting the first cut. This allows the waste piece to be held intact by the short, uncut piece;
4. Again, back out the piece along the path of the sawline just completed.
5. Cut each line on this side in the same manner, each time leaving a short, uncut piece to hold the waste (three are indicated by arrows in Picture 7).

When all the lines of this one side have been cut, we will have a leg blank which is still square and intact for sawing the adjacent side. But we will also have managed to preserve the leg lines on the adjacent side as well. Now we can turn the blank over so that the adjacent side is up, and bandsaw along these lines. The difference here on this side is that we will saw away the waste wood completely. A moment's reflection will tell us that the outline of the leg on the other side now no longer needs to be preserved , because the line has already been cut.

even though the waste of the second cut be removed entirely, there is a permanent line retained which was produced by the first cut.

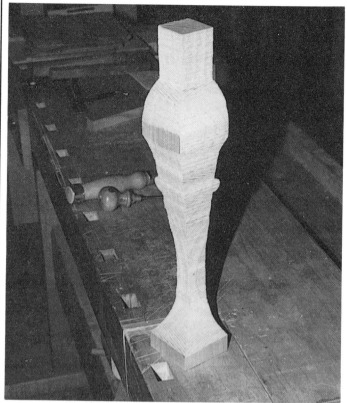

Photo. 8 After the short, uncut portions are severed, all waste is cut away. This picture shows the rough cut leg ready for rough shaping.

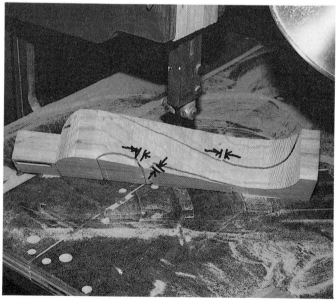

Photo. 6 and 7 Picture 6 shows the second through-cut leaving the waste severed, while number 7 shows that

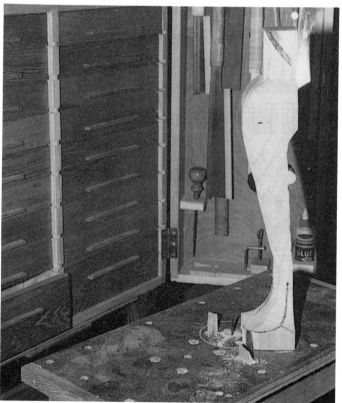

Photo. 9 There is a jig saw bolted to the bottom of this shop-made stand which is about 99cm/39″ high. The blade is shown protruding above the table between the foot and the waste (shown with blade guard removed). After cutting, the foot is bevelled slightly around the circumference.

The note in the background, *Wait for the Dust to Settle,* unexpectedly found its way into this shot. It refers to a couple of very poor financial decisions I made some months ago as regards the shop. If I had just waited and given it more time, waited for more information to come about, the decisions would have been quite different. And so I tacked up the note on the tool cabinet door and set revised goals for the shop, steering my small business around a hole in the road. It's been a constant reminder to me. Incidentally, I made the tool cabinet from wood common to my state of California: Western Pine cabinet and Redwood drawer fronts and stand. Redwood is a most untraditional wood and both woods are *very* impractical, because they're so soft. But I did it anyway!

Photo. 11 Four tools are essential to my shaping the leg: one is a coarse, double-cut bastard file with one side half-round and the other side flat. Another file (also the half-round and flat-sided combination) is a medium double-cut bastard. The double cuts quickly remove wood with minimum effort. The remaining two tools are spokeshaves. I prefer the Kuntz 51 and 83 as shown. One of the spokeshaves has a flat surface and the other is rounded.

During initial shaping, there is a tendency for the leg to continuously twist between the pressure of the bench stops (and occasionally slip out altogether) as the files aggressively bite into the wood. Some time ago I built a bench jig as a holding fixture rather than constantly stopping to readjust that leg position. It fits into the bench's square dog holes. On the back side of the jig, I have an indexing pin which allows me to position the leg on its side or at 45° angles. This jig is better seen in the next picture.

I should say at this point that just as I have a peculiar way of building our letter compartments separately from the desk, so I depart from the norm in the shaping of the leg. I prefer to complete the legs separately prior to glue-up. It is common practice, however, to glue-up to the rails first, and then finish the legs as a complete unit.

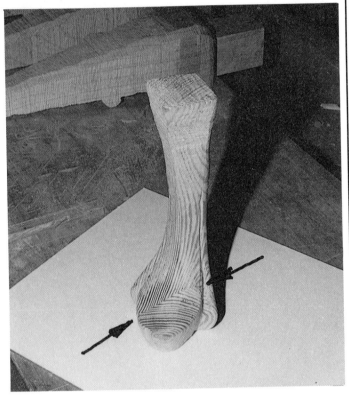

Photo. 10 I include this picture for two reasons. First, when I work out a different foot design, I usually try several designs first. This foot is about the fifth trial, and it finally "felt right". These trial pieces are out of a soft, inexpensive wood (usually Fir) that I glue-up to the proper square size prior to carving. And that brings me to the second reason for this picture. I always carve cabriole legs from *solid* stock. The arrows in the picture show the glue joint seam that will be apparent whenever (for reasons of economy) pieces are glued-up. Production furniture people try to "grain match" to hide this seam prior to inserting them into the automatic carving machines. Dark stain many times aids them in this attempt. But a fine piece of furniture (referred to as "high upper-end" here in America) will always be executed from a solid blank – never from glue-ups.

The trifid foot ("trifid" meaning split into three parts) can be interesting to the carver. It takes patience with the various contour levels that may not be apparent until executed. It may also require a carving tool or two that has not previously been used that often. Where the bird's claw-and-ball foot is exacting and demanding in its shaping, I can visualize it easier than working the trifid. Over the years, I have better understood why the trifid foot in all its variations was said to be the preferred alternate by Philadelphia chair makers to the claw-and-ball foot.

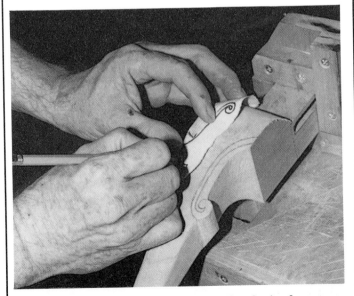

Photo. 12 Once the leg is shaped to the desired contour, the carving outlines are drawn onto the leg from our sketches.

Photos. 14 and 15 These two pictures show the wood being removed which surround the outlines of the C-scroll, shell and head of wheat. A number 8 bent gouge is being used (14mm).

Photo. 13 A V-parting tool is being used to cut the outlines previously drawn in. Here, a continuous, unbroken sweep is necessary to provide a clean line. To go into more detail would be unnecessary in light of the outstanding articles on carving by Guild Member Ron Butterfield (see *Teach Yourself Woodcarving*, volumes 4, 5 and 6).

Traditionally there are two distinct carving tools used for marking and texturing.

The Vee Parting Tool – vee shaped in section giving a vee cut of varying depth depending on the size of the tool – still available ⅛" to 1".

The Veiner is generally only available in the smaller sizes ¹/₃₂, ¹/₁₆, ⅛, is gouge shape but deep and can only be used for shallow cutting. – Ed.

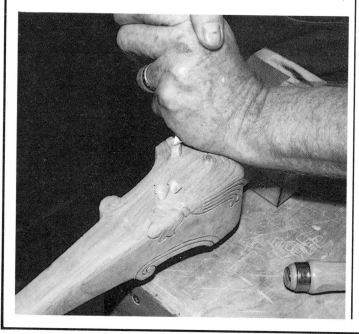

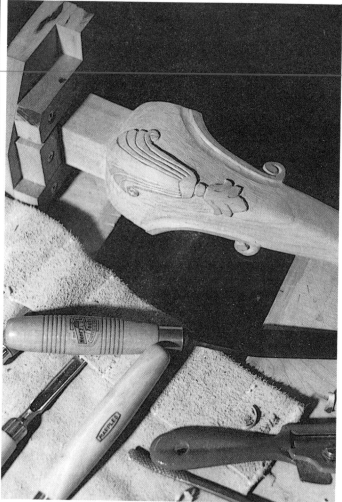

Photo. 16 The carvings are now "sitting proud" – elevated. An Italian rifler file was used to level all the valleys left by the gouge. Next, the lines inside the carvings will be contoured and progressively deepened. The edges of the rays of the shell (both leg and centre rail shells) will be rounded and smoothed. The file marks left by the rifler outside the carvings will be smoothed with 1/0 (80 grit) sandpaper and then with 4/0 (150 grit).

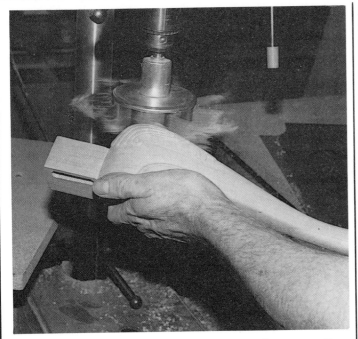

Photo. 17 The entire leg is being flap sanded with a fine sandpaper using an attachment on the drill press.

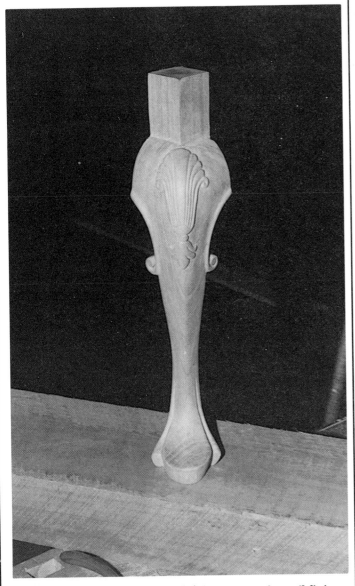

Photo. 18 The finished leg is shown ready for rail fitting. Incidentally, the leg stile above the knee does not need finishing, because a final fit to the rail may require paring to bring the two surfaces flush to one another.

Cutting the Rails and Cross-Grain Skirt

Photo. 19 This tenon and dowel combination make a strong joint. The tenon, when glued-up, is pinned for strength and stability; the dowel, in addition to adding some strength, is used primarily for stability below the joining of rail and stile. The entire end of the rail could be cut for a tenon, or a variation of tenons – we could get so sophisticated and scientific that we lose sight of what we are doing and never get to building it at all – just sit and stare at the joint and worry whether its best or not. When I want to get back to the basics of joinery (and woe to the overly experienced ones who never do that sort of thing), I invariably reach for two reference books: One is C.H. Hayward's entitled, simply, *Woodwork Joints.* It is authoritative, inexpensive and excellent reference material which allows for innovative combinations. The other book is Tage Frid's, *Tage Frid Teaches Woodworking; Joinery.* Frid's book is a little expensive by comparison, but he's definitely one of the best authorities in the field of woodworking and the book is outstandingly well illustrated. While I'm on the subject of books, there is another one that is really a tool catalogue, but it's as thick as some books, and they have spared no cost to get the best pictures; it's a New York firm by the name of Garrett Wade. And the prices are very competitive for the finest tools from around the world. (Honest, I don't own stock in the company.)

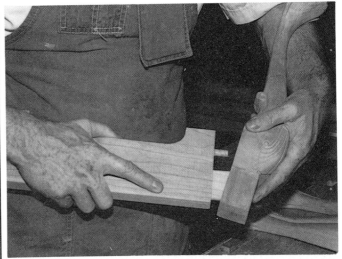

Photo. 20 This is a dry fit stage to ensure that the side of the stile protrudes slightly above the face of the rail.

This allows me to pare the stile and rail flush to each other with a shoulder and block plane. The joints will then be locked in place by pinning the mortise and tenon through.

Over the years, I have seen very few cabriole legs without ears (those little wing blocks on each side of the bend in the knee). These ears, other than adding strength to support the rail under the weight of a person, give the eye a directive line to move from leg to rail. Without the ear, the leg appears incomplete and the eye is stopped and somewhat confused as to where next to move. The method that was used for the ears of the cabriole leg on the original stool was most unusual and very pleasing to the eye, although I have seen adaptations of it applied to low tables and a couple of chairs. If you look at the completed stool, you'll see a continous, unbroken line that was formed starting from the vein in the ankle of the foot up to the C-scroll at the back of the knee (part of which intentionally extends into the rail), where the skirt (or long "ear") picks up the eye and leads it along the rail (by means of the bead) to the centre carving. Then, the cross-grain of the skirt moves the eye upward to the rail where the fabric of the seat now complements nicely with the rest of the design. Even the seat fabric contains a bead that is set into the rabbet of the rail. In this way, the craftsman created a frame that continuously leads the eye to the centre and upward. I've never seen another stool anything like it!

Photo. 22 The grain must go from front to back *as well as* up and down. The top piece shows proper direction on the front, but the rays of the grain start at the front only to bend around, never quite reachig the back, then wind up again in front. That's not the grain to use. The bottom piece is the correct one. The grain may not always be uniformly straight, but it starts at the front, and it ends at the back; we call it *quarter-sawed* or *edge-grained*. I prefer to cut this quarter-sawed lumber from *plain-sawed* or *flat-grained* lumber, which I use for the legs.

Photo. 21 Cross-grain can fool you. Early in my apprentice training, I learned that straight grain on the face of the wood may not always retain its straight characteristics when cut on a contour. The 76mm/3″ × 165mm/6½″ cherry plank shown in this picture had to be visualized prior to cutting, or a lot of scrap would have been generated. These pieces will be glued together and contoured for the cross-grain of the skirt.

Photo. 23 Here, pieces of the 165mm long cross-grain are being glued-up. There is no need for a lot of glue or for a great deal of pressure on the clamps – only a light to moderate pressure is necessary.

Photo. 24 Once the cross-grain is dry, I cut the lengths so that the ends (towards the centre) exactly meet at both sides of the centre block where the carving will appear. The top line is sighted and checked to make sure it is level and that all heights now correspond.

I want to draw attention to the marking line for the trim along the edge of the skirt. The quality of the build requires that the edge trim be of the same wood so that the grain will run in the same direction. A trim added after contouring would certainly make the job a lot faster, but it would also introduce a grain going in the wrong direction; the discerning eye would unconsciously pick it up immediately. Patience is tested as the gouge is moved along near the edge, removing the necessary wood to the proper depth. The wood grain running at right angles to the gouge along the edge wants to lift and splinter out. A previously sawn kerf line helps retain the proper bead (trim width).

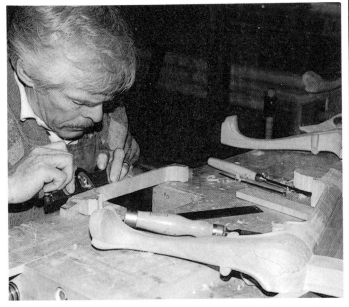

Photo. 25 I pencil-in the contour lines of the leg and centre carving on the ends of each length of cross-grain. This picture shows shaping a cross-grain skirt to nearly the exact contour with my Stanley 93 shoulder plane. The low angle of the shoulder plane allows me to achieve a smooth end grain cut with no tear-out. After repeated fittings, holes are drilled through the rail, and the cross-grain skirt is secured from the back in position with screws. Because the cross-grain expands and contracts at a rate greater than the plain-sawed rail it is secured to, no glue is applied. The cross-grain is simply fitted dry and finished. The results have been excellent.

Ideally, I need to build a low angle plane for cutting future cross-grain. Shaping it a segment at a time is effective, but the most desirable of all is to construct a moulding plane to the proper profile. This produces a clean, highly uniform result – a method that would have been common in the 18th century. I would not want to use a special shaper cutter ground to my specifications because of the tendency to tear-out even with carbide faces. The hand plane is superior in all respects for this operation . . . perhaps I might add, "in my opinion." Once the cross-grain skirts are all roughed out and attached, the edge trim bead is checked for relative straightness. Adjustments are made at this point with a pencil.

Photo. 26 The centre shell lines that were drawn in and started with a V-parting tool are now deepened. The edges of each shell segment will be rounded over and sanded.

Final Steps
Photo. 27 The time for glue-up has arrived. Just prior to taking this picture, a mahogany-cherry stain had been

applied and allowed to dry overnight. After the clamps had been secured, I measured the perpendicular distance between two legs. Then I took another perpendicular measurement between the other two legs. Any difference between the distances means the piece is out of square. If that occurs, I must adjust the clamps until the stresses give me identical measurements. To illustrate this, distance *a* must be equal to distance *b*.

The last step in joining will be to remove the clamps and bore a hole into the leg stile through the mortise and tenon. Glue will be added to a precut dowel pin which will be driven through the hole and set flush with the surface.

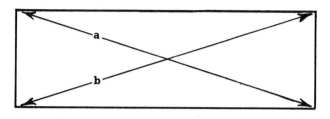

Photo. 28 A rabbet is being cut which measures the width of the blade which is about 3mm (⅛″) × 19mm (¾″) high. This rabbet is cut for the fabric to slip over and be secured in place.

A 19mm (¾″) thick seat board has been cut and secured to oak stringers, which were glued and screwed to the inside rails. The seat board is fastened with screws only – not glued. At this point, I'm surprised at how heavy the stool is as I turn it back on its feet to apply a couple of coats of sanding sealer.

Upholstery

I want to achieve a favourable combination of wood grain, design and fabric; the fabric will be chosen to enhance the wood's character, but also to set off the design of the piece itself – not the other way around. The print of the fabric and the print of the wood's growth seen in its fibre and texture should be used to complement each other. Fabric selected without regard to the wood (or to the design) will usually wind up as a mismatch. The marriage of man-made synthetic fibres and God's imprint as an expression of natural wood growth can be a combination of beauty.

Although I'm not an upholsterer, there are a few things I can do to bring this part of the project to a close. For example, I bought the fabric. I removed the seat board, drilled air holes and tacked black cambric to the bottom. Then I replaced the seat board and secured it once again with screws. A professional upholsterer then cemented a 50mm/2″ thick piece of foam rubber to the seat board, and stretched unbleached muslin over the foam rubber and tacked it to each of the four sides just above the shoulder of the rabbet. Then a fabric beading was tacked all around the stool at the shoulder of the rabbet. After sewing and fitting the fabric, its was stretched over the foam rubber and blind stitched to the previously attached fabric bead.

Completion
Photo. 29 The completed project.

Photo. 30 The stool was placed in front of one of our desks, and that upstart, the chair, was overthrown!

P.S. The registered trade mark of my work is a "cross" at the base of a "7" flanked on each side by my initials. The year of build completion is at the bottom. This is barely seen on the back of the rail in Photo. 28 and on the foot in Photo. 26.

Building a 1:12 Scale Georgian dolls' house

See Plans enclosed.

Dolls' Houses of various types and qualities can be found in most of the larger toy shops, most of them in the £20 to £50 price range, all of them to contemporary designs with plastic fittings and furniture and often inconsistent as far as scale is concerned.

I have seen an instance where quite a reasonable effort was spoiled by the use of "brick" elevation paper of the wrong scale so that a front entrance door appeared to be only about six courses high. At full size, this would make a brick about one foot thick!

However, such dolls' houses cannot be dismissed on the grounds of scale and finish, for they are not expensive and they do serve a useful purpose for the small number of years they are needed.

At the other end of the range, beautiful period dolls' houses are obtainable from specialists at prices which at one time would have bought a full size house. These are not only toys but also collectors' items and can be furnished with perfect reproductions of period furniture.

The design of this dolls' house is an attempt to produce something which is not too difficult for the amateur to build using the simplest of hand tools and easily obtained materials, but will also result in a toy which can give joy to many generations of children and can be furnished with many items of 1:12 scale furniture and fittings available.

Construction

In practice, I have always found it easier to make all the fittings such as doors, surrounds, steps, windows, staircases etc. first and then make the building to fit them. This applies specially to the staircases which sometimes have a tendency to "grow" during construction. We will therefore begin with the staircase.

Staircase

This is of the open well, baluster type consisting of a long flight of 13 risers and a short flight of 4 risers joined at right angles to each other by a square quarter landing.

On drawing No. 2 are shown the profiles of the inner and outer strings of both stair flights. These can be traced off the drawing (after checking to make sure that the print has not shrunk or stretched) and transferred on to 0·8mm plywood. Note that the strings for the long lower flight include supports for the quarter landing. Form the carriage as shown with ¼ in. (6mm) plywood, glue the strings on each side of the carriage and fill in with balsa wood to the underside of each tread. Cut out and fix the treads next in ¹/₁₆ in. Obechi and note that these project beyond the outer string.

The bottom step is bullnosed, formed in balsa wood, the riser being formed in thin plywood or veneer curved round. The rest of the risers can now be fixed (refer to notes on drawing) and the upper flight glued to the quarter landing.

At this stage you should have something that looks like the assembly sketch. Check dimensions for "growth", any discrepancy can be adjusted in the width of the upper landing which could be made next.

The Upper Landing

This needs little further explanation except that its veneer or thin plywood facing also forms the top stair riser and also covers the edge of the ceiling which is of 4 sheet mounting card. Mark in fine pencil line the floor board joints on the 1/16th in. Obechi floor. Also the position of balusters and newel posts (these and the upper flight balusters and handrails are fixed after the staircase and landing are in position).

The balustrading etc. can be fixed to the lower flight now, as once the staircase is in the house it will not be so easy. The balusters are equally spaced, two on every tread, the upper and lower newels and handrail are fixed first so that there is something for the balusters to stick to. Time should be taken to cut the upper newel around strings and tread nosings (cut away nosings slightly to make the job easier).

Entrance Surround (Drawing No. 3)

This consists of Roman Tuscan half columns. (Like Roman Doric but with a moulded base and, thank heaven, no flutes!) The columns support a simple moulded pediment whose details I have simplified so that simple carving and sandpapering of the various laminations produce a convincing result. The very thin laminations (1/32 in.) could well be made from plasticard if desired though wood has been specified on the drawing. The capitals and base should present no problems being carved from Jelotung which is easily worked.

The half columns can be carved or turned in wood or, as on the original, heat moulded in 30-40 thou. Plasticard.

Heat forming in Plasticard is very easy once the basic shapes have been carefully made. First carve a half column without base and capital. This can be of medium (not soft) balsa wood and when doing this, note that the column has a curved taper known in Classic Architecture as the entasis. It is important that the entasis forms a regular curve from top to bottom, so avoid a straight taper with all the curve near the top or bottom as this spoils the appearance.

When this is made, now draw the outline of the column on ¼ in. medium balsa wood and cut out the middle leaving a hole which must allow the column to pass through and as the plasticard will be 40 thou. thick, enlarge the hole so that the column when pushed through the hole will not produce paper thin edges to the final unit. Leave about 1½ in. all around the hole and glue a balsa wood edging about 1 in. deep round on the underside to give strength.

Now cut a piece of white 40 thou. thick plasticard the same size as the ¼ in. balsa wood sheet and fix it around the outside edges with large paper clamps or Sellotape. Hold this unit up to the light and trace the position of the hole on the plasticard.

Then place the unit under the cooker grill and heat until the plasticard is softened (about half a minute) and starts to sag in the hole. Remove from the grill and immediately push the wood column, flat side upwards, into the hole so that the flat side is just below the rim of the hole.

After half a minute remove the wood column and take off the plasticard which is now hardened and has in it a hollow depression, an exact replica of the wood column which can now be trimmed. Repeat for the second half column. Both half columns can be formed in little more than the time it has taken to describe the operation.

The sketches should explain the process clearly. A balsa wood backing can now be glued into the open side of the hollow half columns to provide glueing surface for fixing to walls. Fix the capitals and bases to columns.

The entrance surround is now complete and the pediment and columns can be set aside for fixing at a later stage in the work.

Doors

These are fully detailed and explained on the drawing and the only other instruction required is that at every stage they should be kept completely flat during construction while glue is setting and that any glue that squeezes out should be wiped off straight away.

Windows

Made entirely in white and clear plasticard, these can be built up over the drawing (or a tracing would be better). The glue used is polystyrene cement (not the liquid type) lightly applied.

Polystyrene cement is the natural solvent of plasticard and makes a welded rather than glued joint. For this reason be careful to prevent it squeezing from under glazing bars on to the "glass" areas as it cannot be removed. As for the doors, keep the windows flat during construction.

Door Frames

The construction of the door frames is fully detailed but the semi-circular fanlight over the Entrance door requries further clarification. It is laminated in very thin ply (0·4mm) forming two semi-circles with the plasticard "glass" sandwiched in between them.

Before fixing the frames to the "glass", the pattern of glazing bars must be painted on with white enamel, the "glass" being placed over the drawing as a guide. When complete the whole of the exposed face of the frame can be covered with thin plasticard to mask construction joints.

Fireplaces

There are four fireplaces, the two smaller ones are in the bedrooms. Their construction is rather similar to that for the entrance pediment except that they are simpler. Each fireplace, surround and "brick" chimney breast can be made up as a unit extending from floor to ceiling, to be added at a convenient stage in the erection of the walls. When making these items do not forget that the drawings are half full size. Quite a good representation of a glowing fire can be made using bright red tinsel packed up so that it is easily visible above the fire bars.

The House

At this stage it is now time to begin making the house. On drawing no. 4 is a complete set of dimensioned patterns for every floor, landing, wall and roof with the position of all frame members where they occur. All these shapes can be set out on 5/32 in. plywood with a fine pencil line and as cutting will be done with a no. 11 craft blade no allowance need be made for trimming provided that setting out is accurate and all cutting exactly on the lines; therefore no space need be left between each item.

Cutting against a steel straight edge must be done with a sharp new blade and all edges should be clean and square (keep a dozen new no. 11 blades handy!)

First make all those items that have internal framing or framing on one side or the other such as the front wall ground floor, first floor, landing and upper ceiling/roof support.

Take plenty of time over the front wall to ensure that it goes on and off easily and fits properly. Remember that the back wall fits between the end walls and the removable front wall overlaps them.

When fixing the mounting card linings to walls and ceilings (the front wall lining is continuous) make sure that floors can fit in between areas of wall lining giving good glue joints between wood parts as the whole construction is based on plywood glued edge to side and any joint made between wood and mounting card is a weak joint.

When all units are complete, set the base down on a flat surface and glue the two end walls to it pressing a fairly heavy weight against the ends to hold the joints tight, and propping the end walls with paint tins, using a set square to get them vertical.

If possible one could glue the back wall in at the same time though this might result in a frantic rush to find enough implements to hold the vertical joints and the long bottom joint before the glue sets (I find that tons of Sellotape is very good for this purpose!).

With the two end walls and back wall fixed, the two ground floor fireplaces could be put in at this stage, the chimney breasts being trimmed to fit under the ceiling.

Cross Walls

Before fixing the cross walls, the doors, frames and architraves should be fitted. Very light nylon of a type used for covering certain model aircraft makes very good hinges as it shows very little under paint, is very strong and allows the door free movement. A painted bead about 3/16 in. diameter also makes a very fine door knob. Glue the cross walls in position and when set, the two bedroom floors can be fixed. If the setting out and cutting have been accurate the floors should slide in between the end and cross walls. It may be necessary to trim a small strip off the ceiling lining to allow the floor to slide in for a good glue joint, which may also apply at the back wall (1/32 in. or less).

Skirting and Cornices
These are detailed and could be made and fitted in the two ground floor rooms at this stage and should be painted before fixing.

Staircase and Landing
The staircase goes in first, glued to the lining of the back wall and left hand side wall, but note that if a skirting is required on the staircase it should be glued to the staircase first and arranged to join with the ground floor skirting which incidentally should have gone in first anyway! The landing is L shaped and that part running from front to back must have its width adjusted to fit in with the staircase, (this is a "floating" dimension to give a perfect fit). Skirting can now be fixed around all the walls and landing on the first floor (bedroom floor).

At this stage, the bedroom fireplaces can be added as for the ground floor.

Balustrade to Landing
This must be fixed now, for if not it will be difficult, if not impossible, to fix later. It also includes the balustrading to the upper stair flight similar to that on the lower flight described earlier. The main newel posts and the half newel are fixed first, then the handrails and when all glue is set, the balusters. Take time over this, fix the balusters at equal spacing, get them straight and vertical and do not use too much glue.

Upper Ceiling and Roof Support
This member should slide in the same way as the bedroom floors except that it is glued at both end walls and the back wall and the mounting card ceiling is glued to the tops of the cross walls.

Roof
Patterns for the two roof panels are not shown on the drawings and in order to get a good fit, they must be measured on the job before being set out. They are splayed at the ridge and eaves, glued to the end walls and to the thick battens which run along front and back of the building. Veneer or thin plywood strips can now be glued along the roof to represent tiles as shown on full size section.

A ridge can be made of thicker material such as 0·8mm plywood.

Front Wall Support Batten
After roof has been fixed an L shaped or rebated batten is glued along the front of the 1 in. × 9/16 in. member shown in the full size section of the front wall. In positioning this L shaped batten reference must be made to the front wall, a space being allowed so that the front wall can be raised for easy removal. NOTE: A splayed batten glued to the base supports the foot of the wall and this should be glued on before any attempt is made to glue on the L shaped batten at the top.

This method eliminates the need for any other means of retaining the removable front wall.

It should now be possible to get the exact positions of and to fix skirtings to the front wall. Remember! Do not fix the ceiling cornices to this wall otherwise you will never move the wall, so glue them to the ceilings only.

Chimney Stacks
These can be made up in 5/32 in. plywood, or cut from solid soft wood such as deal. One wall of each stack is already included in the end walls and will provide a template for the opposite wall. Capping is of hardwood (ramin) and the chimney pots (two per stack) can be made from hardwood dowel about ⅜ in. diameter.

Copings
These are out of ⅜ in. × ¼ in. ramin as indicated and run the full length of front and back walls, up gable ends to finish at the stack.

Painting
This must be done before windows and front door etc. are fixed and can be of matt emulsion paint, pale colours to represent rendering or a matt brick colour (Humbrol Matt 70). If desired this can be laboriously lined in cream/grey to represent bricks in Flemish bond as shown on drawing no. 2. This is rather a mammoth task and might be eliminated by covering the whole exterior with "brick" paper at the correct scale which in this case will be four courses to one inch vertical.

There should be no trouble in cutting as the dimensions were designed to give whole course depths, but remember that over each window will be a flat gauged arch which will have to be drawn on paper and glued on first. It must match as nearly as possible the type of "brick" paper used. After covering, the joints of the removable front wall can be cut and edges sealed.

Paint roof tiles dark red, chimney flashings grey for lead, consult an old Building Construction book preferably Mitchell, to get this right, or better still look at a Georgian house for guidance.

Paint coping and steps stone colour, top of entrance surround grey, columns and all cornices mouldings and door frames white. Windows already of white plasticard need no paint.

Paint skirtings, cornices, internal door frames, fire surrounds and architraves white. Internal doors, light pastel colours, (all these should be painted before fixing). Staircase and balustrade can be painted white or varnished before fixing and touched up afterwards.

The landing can be varnished. If the floors are not to be carpeted these should be varnished.

Internal wall faces are of mounting card and if possible should be of very light colours and will save a lot of extra work, but you must keep the visible surfaces free from glue smears and generally clean.

The external entrances door can be a soft pastel colour (apple green was a Georgian favourite).

Windows, Cills, Entrance Door, Columns etc.
All these items can now be fixed with the minimum of glue, internal cills or window boards are 1/16 in. obechi painted white, projecting external cills are shaped as shown and glued in position after being painted stone colour.

Front Steps
These are made of hardwood painted stone colour.

The house is now complete except for a little black soot at the top of the chimney pots. Carpeting and furnishing can now be done using the various types of very fine 1:12 scale furniture available.

Build sense into your fence

Photo. 1 Plastic ranch fencing by Marley.

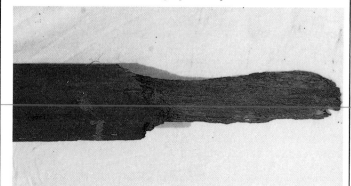

Photo. 2 Beyond repair! A well-rotted stump of a fence post.

Photo. A Past redemption!

Before starting to enclose a garden or repair a boundary fence make sure it is your responsibility and not that of your neighbour's.

The deeds of your house will tell you this and also give permitted maximum heights. If you build a high wall at the intersection of two roads you will naturally be interfering with the vision of road traffic users.

The prevalent idea that it is your fence if arris rails (longitudinal timbers) are on your side of a wooden fence is erroneous. It is generally erected that way as a compliment to your neighbour, affording him the plain, unobstructed surface.

Brick Wall

Whole brick construction – about 220 mm (8½ in.) – will last much longer than a lifetime. Half brick – 110 mm or 4¼ in. – will cost very much less but could be knocked down by a reversing lorry, even when reinforced with supporting piers at intervals of 4.5 m (5 yards) – particularly if a damp-proof course is included which will prove a weak point (Fig. 1).

You may have noticed how brick walls built on a frontage to a curved road tend to bulge outwards in time. This is due to frost expanding the mortar joins. The walls cannot tilt inwards because the curve acts as an archway laid horizontally, the inner edges of the bricks pushing one against another.

The way to counteract this bulge is to build the wall so that it leans ever so slightly towards the inner part of the curve – just sufficient to throw the bubble of your vertical spirit level a degree off its precise mark and no more. This won't be noticeable and frost damage will correct a possible bulge.

When erecting brick gate posts, drive a length of scaffold pole down the centre as a reinforcement so that the cars of friends who have partaken too liberally of your hospitality will be damaged and leave the post intact.

Other types of fence

Interwoven reed fences don't last very long. Palisade fences consisting of spaced uprights and those of split larch bound together with wire don't afford privacy. The galvanized coating of wire netting will eventually wear and lead to rusting unless further preservation is afforded by a coat of calcium plumbate primer followed by two finishing coats of an alkyd resin paint such as Dulux.

The quickest way to paint netting is to lay it on the ground and roller on the paint. Then turn it over and, without applying more paint, roller out the other side, using the exudations from the first side.

Some modern wire fencing is protected with plastic which lasts very much longer. In any case, these types are really only suitable for the tops of more permanent structures – for securing rambler roses and climbing plants.

Ranch fences (Photo. 1) though only suitable for front gardens, are simple to make and erect. You can use old floorboards, imperfections stopped with hard stopping, nailed onto oak posts; or use plastic lateral members which are much longer lasting. The traditional colour for

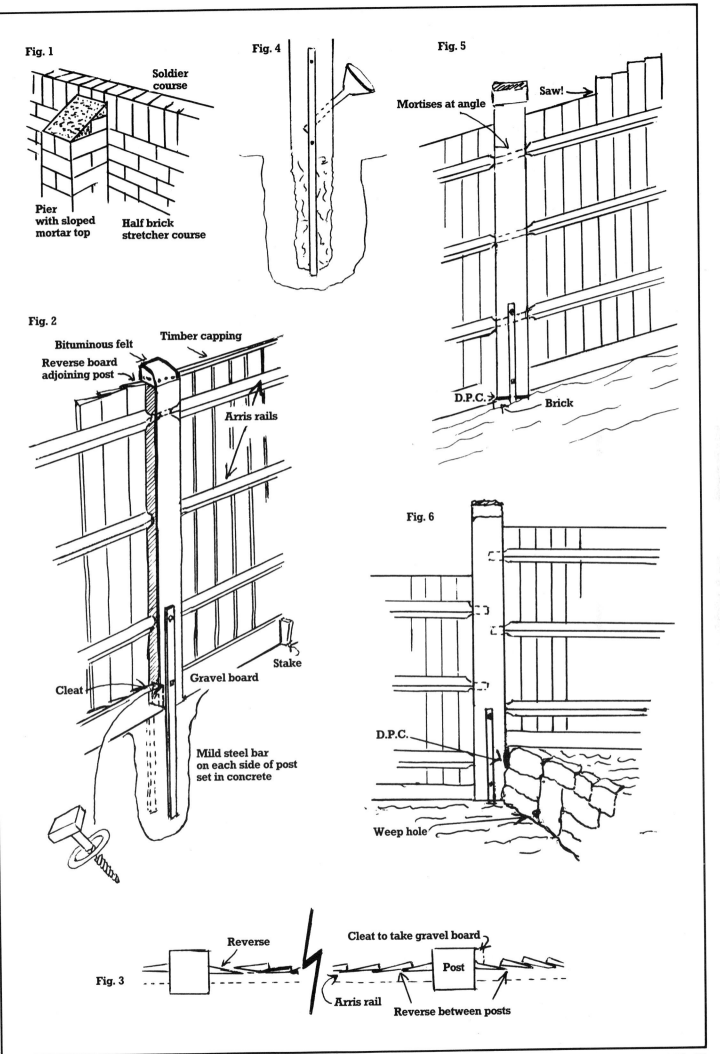

Fig. 1

Soldier course

Pier with sloped mortar top

Half brick stretcher course

Fig. 4

Fig. 5

Mortises at angle

Saw!

D.P.C.

Brick

Fig. 2

Bituminous felt

Timber capping

Reverse board adjoining post

Arris rails

Cleat

Gravel board

Stake

Mild steel bar on each side of post set in concrete

Fig. 6

D.P.C.

Weep hole

Reverse

Cleat to take gravel board

Fig. 3

Post

Arris rail

Reverse between posts

Photo. B New fence.

Photo. C Ground floor!

Photo. D Reinforced gate pillar – GOING UP?

ranch fencing is white.

Old-fashioned front-garden iron railings are quickest painted with painter's "mitts"; or use old gloves dipped into the paint and wiped on. Make sure as much rust as possible is removed first by scraping and wirebrushing.

Close-boarded fences

Apart from brick, close-boarded fences are longest lasting, preserving privacy, and are superior to the prefabricated type – and also the most expensive. Their weakness lies in rotting of the submerged stump (Photo. 2) and in the end grain of the tops of posts and feather-edged planks being exposed to rain; and so their life is only some 16 years unless you follow one of these methods of erection which will last 30 years or longer:

Concrete posts are one way of combating rot underground, but they look ugly. Concrete spurs also are obtrusive. If the posts are sunk in concrete, the concrete on setting will shrink and leave a gap all round for rain to enter.

Use oak posts that aren't themselves sunk into the soil but kept erect by mild steel bars, one at each side of the post, let into concrete as is shown in Fig. 2. These can be cut at a foundry and holes bored in the tops 50 mm (2 in.) from one end and 255 mm (10 in.) apart. Size: a metre (3 ft) long 40 mm (1½ in.) wide and 7 mm (¼ in.) thick will do for a chin-height fence. Anything much higher will require longer and stouter bars.

Attach half their lengths to the bottoms of the posts, one on each side, with galvanized coach screws which can be tightened with a spanner. Prebore the holes and grease the screw threads for easing entry into such a tough timber. Touch over screw heads with bituminous paint.

Insert the "prongs" of the first post in a hole in the ground and shovel round pieces of broken brick. Tip in a mix of concrete sufficiently sloppy to permeate the bricks, and allow to set before tackling the second post which should be at a distance of about 2¾ m (9 ft). Ensure the posts are upright with a vertical spirit level or plumb bob.

After erecting the first post insert the tenons of arris rails. Insert the tenons at the other end in the second post before sinking its prongs into broken bricks and concrete. Lay a spirit level on top of an arris rail to make sure it's horizontal. The remainder of the levels can be tested by standing back, facing the edge of the fence and "sighting".

To prevent concrete "spreading" too far over a flower bed arrange a shuttering of stout cardboard tied round at about 100 mm (4 in.) from the post you're working on. It will soon rot so leave it where it is and tamp in surrounding soil firmly. Trowel the top of the concrete with a slight slope outwards and leave a small gap between it and the foot of the post; or you can squeeze in a small piece of bituminous felt or damp-proof coursing.

Pointed metal end pieces can be bought and screwed into the bottoms of the posts for insertion into concrete. But as they're attached to end grain and have only one point of contact with the concrete and not two, they aren't so strong.

Nail feather edged upright boards onto the arris rails, overlapping one another, thick edge over thin, by 12 mm to 25 mm (½ to 1 in.) – one galvanized nail to each board and arris rail.

On nearing the second post measure the distance so that remaining overlaps can be equalized without leaving an awkward gap. The last board should be reversed as is seen in Fig. 3.

In the case of a long fence, total over-lapping may be reversed to catch differences of light and shade and avoid monotony. This is shown in Photo. B of the completed fence and also in Fig. 3.

Feather edging easily splits, so either prebore holes to receive the nails or blunt the nail tips with a blow of a hammer or pass a file over them. Sharp points cause splitting because they divide wood grain. A blunt point will merely break it.

Last, attach a gravel board to the posts by wooden cleats nailed to the bottoms of the posts.

The feather edging is supposed to rest on the top of the gravel board. But as the latter often warps leaving the feather edging swinging loose and adding an unfair strain on the arrises, drive creosoted wooden stakes into the ground each side and half-way between each post.

Creosote each piece of timber before erection and give a second application after the fence is built. It should then require recreosoting about every third year after wirebrushing off deposited muck and brushing with a soft banister brush. This can be done quickly with a 2-gallon garden sprayer, one whose pressure is kept up periodically with a hand pump. The first application should, however, be done with a 4 in. brush – to force the preservative well in.

The tops of the posts should be slanted to shed rain and further protected with small pieces of bituminous roofing felt secured with large-headed clout nails. Add capping over the exposed tops of the featheredging; or leave some bituminous paint exposed to the air for a couple of days to start evaporating and knife this over the top.

The gravel board is the only part needing renewal from time to time – and this is easily done. An alternative to a gravel board is to stand the feather-edging on lengths of plastic guttering laid on the ground upside-down between the posts.

Repairing an old fence

Broken arris rails can sometimes be replaced by "springing" new ones into the mortises of the posts. Or you can buy brackets made to screw into both arris rails and post.

Stumps that have started to rot but are not too bad can be strengthened by removing surrounding soil and scraping off the spongy parts, followed by an application of creosote; also pour a little creosote into the hole to kill deposited fungi. Replace soil and tamp firmly.

Then, about 100 mm (4 in.) above groundlevel bore a 12 mm hole (½ in.) downwards at an angle of 45°, to reach some two-thirds the thickness of the post. With a funnel, fill with creosote. Leave to soak in and refill. Then close the mouth of the hole with hard stopping. The creosote will work up and down with the grain of the wood and prevent further rotting (Fig. 4).

Fences on sloping ground

Where a garden is on a slope, either of the methods shown in the illustrations may be employed.

Fig. 5 shows mortises of posts cut at the required slope, and also the tops and bottoms of the feather-edging. Fig. 6 indicates stepping of the garden by means of retaining walls with weep holes strategically left at the bottom to prevent too much saturation in wet weather.

Don't forget bituminous damp-proof course along the vertical edges of the posts where they adjoin soil. Stick it on with mastic compound.

Photo. E Top floor!

Photo. F This post has been repaired with mild steel bars in concrete. The bar is off centre here to avoid the shake in the timber.

Photo. G Old age has caught up with this arris rail. Needs renewal!

Making a lady's make-up box

This project was made in contrasting woods. The box part in mahogany and the underframe in ash. An attractive-grained piece of sapele mahogany was chosen for the panel the underside of which carries the mirror. The grain for this panel runs at right angles to the length of the box.

Instead of being solid the legs of the underframe are built up of two lengths of material as shown in the 'Leg Joint' sketch. In appearance the tongue and groove joints look simple enough but the quality of craftsmanship must be of the highest order to guarantee a permanent lasting union.

Commence practical work by preparing for the legs four pieces 22½" long, 2" wide and ⅝" thick finished, and four pieces 22½" long, (2" minus ⅝") + ¼" leaving 1⅝" wide thick finished.

On the 2" wide pieces, with a ¼" blade, plough a groove ⅜" away from one edge ¼" deep. On one edge of the remaining pieces fashion a tongue using either a rebate plane, or a plough plane fitted with a narrow blade. Try to leave the tongue thickness a little oversize and, later, trim back with a rebate or shoulder plane; working for a press-in-tight fit. When ready, arrange sufficient cramps, and protection slips, for each cramp position. After a try up, dry, and a check for an exact inner right angle, proceed with the gluing and check the inner right angle again before finally leaving to dry hard. Clean up and plane the taper as per drawing.

The rectangular underframe is jointed together with common dovetail joints. Make this frame, glue up and, when the glue is set hard, trim up. Bore three screw holes in the corners; see drawing. Make corner blocks to fit inside and outside the corners. Try each leg up dry and, when any corrections have been made, mark each leg to its allotted corner. Apply glue to both surfaces, cramp up till hard dry, then fit the screws.

For the box part of this project prepare two ends and the front and back members of the box. Cut the stopped tenon joints and their mortises. Prepare the divisions and cut the stopped housing joints to receive them. Make a rebate all round the bottom edges to receive a piece of colour-matching plywood about ⁵/₁₆ths thick. Bring the various division pieces to size. Locate and bore screw holes through the bottom; enough to secure the carcase top to the table underframe.

Before gluing together, cut and finish to size the hinge-plate which runs along the top back edge of the box. Make provision for an ⅛" deep housing to receive the ends of this hinge-plate piece; shouldered for the sake of neatness.

Finish all parts and glue up the whole assembly. A generous string of glue-blocks under the hinge-plate (see drawing) are fixed while the hinge-plate is held firmly down.

The availability and size of the mirror are needed before the frame enclosing the top panel can be planned. The mirror used in the prototype job is 22" by 10" and it came from a second-hand frame. Using the drawing as a guide no great difficulties need be encountered before the right frame is produced. The piano hinge shown is not essential, of course, but it adds an elegant appearance.

Some details are given for the necessary metal stays. Failing the means to fabricate these in a home workshop a visit to a commercial supplier is indicated.

Each compartment is fitted with a neatly measured piece of formica, completely protecting the wood bottom from spoiling agents. A small piece of tape glued to each loose panel facilitates its removal.

Fine grain cabinet woods respond well to a french polish finish, but the special purpose of this piece almost chooses for itself a hard resistant acid catalyst finish.

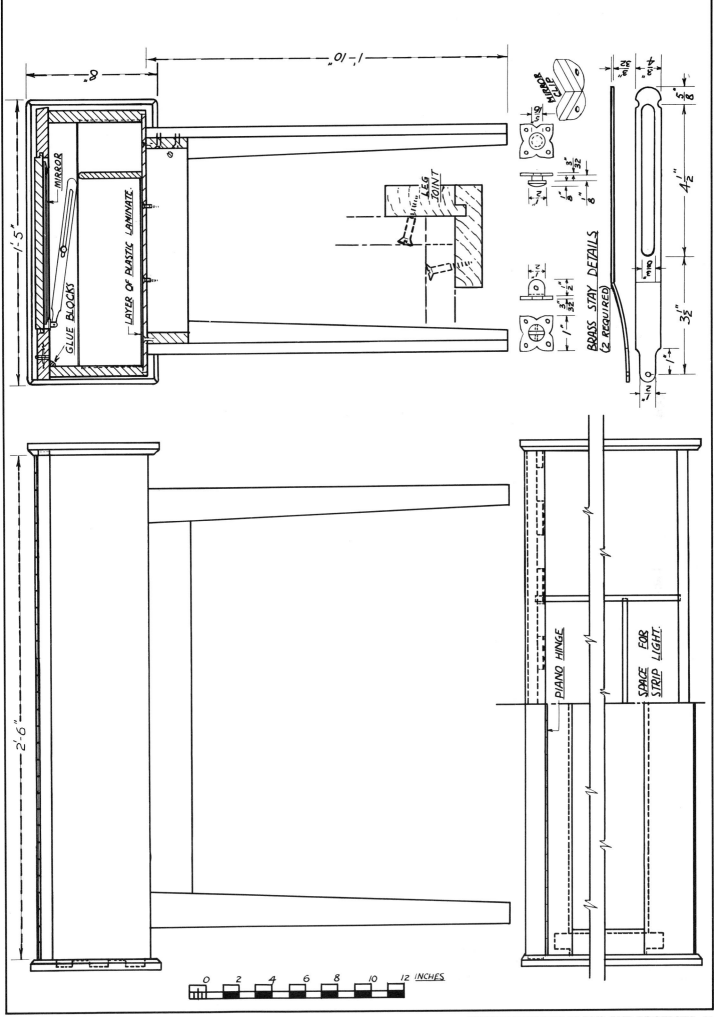

MIRROR

LAYER OF PLASTIC LAMINATE.

GLUE BLOCKS

1'-5"

8"

1'-10"

MIRROR CLIP

5/16"

3/32"

1/8" 2"

3/32" 1/2"

1"

2"

LEG JOINT

BRASS STAY DETAILS
(2 REQUIRED)

3/32"

1/8" 1/4"

5/8"

Ø10"

4 1/2"

3 1/2"

1"

1/2"

2'-6"

PIANO HINGE

SPACE FOR STRIP LIGHT.

0   2   4   6   8   10   12 INCHES

Making a gate-leg table

The table shown in the photograph is straightforward to make and will give many years of useful service. It has been constructed of oak, the top measures 1½m × 914mm (5ft × 3ft) with the leaves open and 457mm × 914mm (1ft 6in. × 3ft) when closed. It does not therefore take up much space in the latter position but can accommodate six people when opened.

Unless it is intended to turn one's own legs it is advisable to obtain these before starting the construction. For a table of this size legs should be 57mm (2¼in.) square although gate-legs can be 51mm (2 in.) square if desired. The side top rails and the end top rails measure 107mm × 22m (4 in. × ⅞in.). The lower side and end rails are of 57mm × 22mm (2¼in. × ⅞in.) The two lower end rails are on their edges whereas the side rails have their faces uppermost. This gives a better bearing for the gates to pivot on.

To keep the construction simple the framework was dowelled together. As a rough guide the size of the dowel to be used is usually one half of the thickness of the wood being joined. In this case where the framwork is 22mm (⅞in.) thick 10mm (⅜in.) dowels were used.

Dowels

Both marking out and boring for dowels must be accurate. The marking gauge is set to half the thickness of the rails and working from the face side the ends of the rails are gauged. Measure at equally spaced intervals the positions for the dowels (three in the top

rails and two in the lower) and square these lines across the ends (Fig. 1).

As the upper end rails are set back 3mm (⅛in.) from the faces of the legs the pin of the marking gauge is set 3mm (⅛in.) further from the stock and gauge marks are made at the tops of the legs and on the inner faces of the legs at their lower ends. As the lower side rails are "on the flat" their two dowel holes will be level and not vertical (Fig. 2). When marking the legs for dowelling remember to mark them out as two pairs to avoid mistakes.

Auger bits are preferable to centre bits because they drill true holes and do not wander. Make sure the bit is sharp and if necessary touch it up with a triangular file. It is essential to keep the bit at 90° to the surface to ensure a good joint and it helps to check the directions or angle of the bit with a trysquare. The holes should all be drilled to the same depth, namely just over half the length of the dowel. If this precaution is not observed the dowels may "bottom" and keep the joint apart. It is worth making a wooden depth gauge as shown in Fig. 3. This consists of two pieces of wood screwed together, one on either side of the bit. The lower edge is positioned the desired distance from the cutting edges.

To facilitate entry the ends of the dowels should be slightly pointed. A saw kerf is cut along the length of the dowel to allow surplus glue to escape and the tops of the holes slightly countersunk. This helps the joint to come together and also forms a reservoir for surplus glue (Fig. 4.)

Gates

The gates are jointed and assembled in a similar fashion. Both the upper and lower rails are "on the flat". The hinging legs are shortened so that they fit easily between the upper and lower rails of the table. A 13mm (½in.) dowel is glued into the top of the leg and protrudes so as to fit into a hole bored into the centre of the upper rail. A stout screw is run through the lower side rail directly below the dowel and up into the bottom of the leg to form the lower pivot. The outer legs are notched to fit against the upper side rails and into notches cut half-way through the lower side rails. The halvings are made an easy fit so that the gates may open and close freely without jambing. To prevent the gate from binding on the lower side rail a steel washer is slipped on the pivoting screw between the top of the rail and the bottom of the hinging leg.

The Top

The top is 22mm (⅞in.) thick and comprises three parts, the centre section and the two leaves. All three pieces will require to be jointed up from several widths of wood. The joints are shot true with the trying plane and the pieces are dowelled together taking care that the dowels are not too close to the ends of the finished leaf. Failure to watch this point could result in the dowels being exposed when the leaves are trimmed to shape. When fitting the pieces it is advisable to arrange them so that alternate pieces have the heartside uppermost (Fig. 5). Any drying out of the wood and subsequent "cupping" will then be less noticeable.

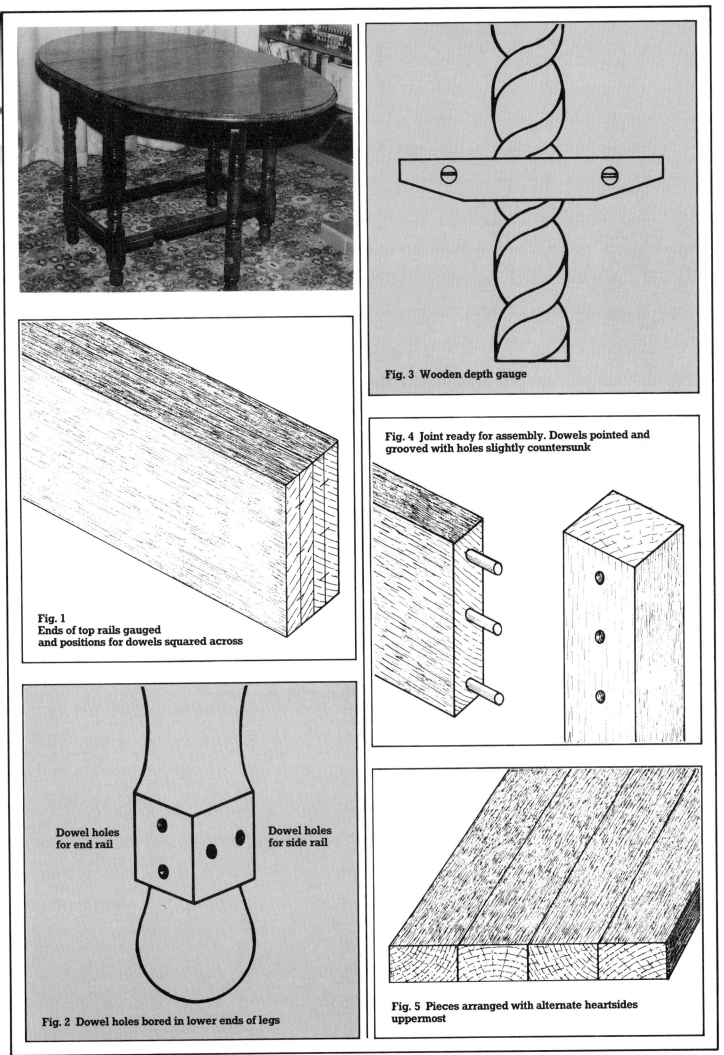

Fig. 3 Wooden depth gauge

Fig. 1
Ends of top rails gauged
and positions for dowels squared across

Fig. 4 Joint ready for assembly. Dowels pointed and
grooved with holes slightly countersunk

Dowel holes
for end rail

Dowel holes
for side rail

Fig. 2 Dowel holes bored in lower ends of legs

Fig. 5 Pieces arranged with alternate heartsides
uppermost

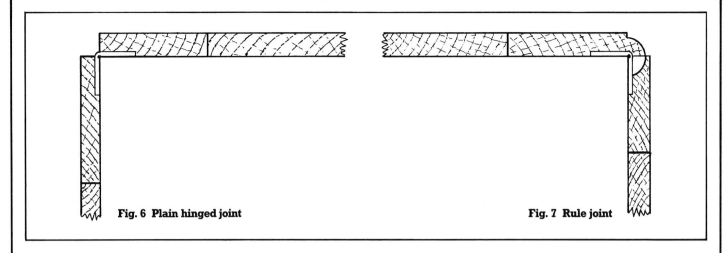

Fig. 6 Plain hinged joint

Fig. 7 Rule joint

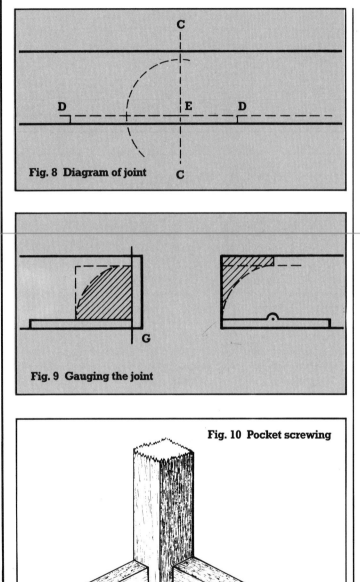

Fig. 8 Diagram of joint

Fig. 9 Gauging the joint

Fig. 10 Pocket screwing

The eliptical shape is best drawn full size on sheets of paper gummed together. A horizontal line AB is drawn 1¼m (5ft) long and is bisected by a vertical line XY 914mm (3ft) long. With a radius equal to the length AO an arc is drawn with Y as centre. Where it cuts the horizontal line at E and F two nails are driven through the paper and into the board underneath. A third nail is driven in at Y.

A loop of string extending round points E,F and Y is slipped over the nails. The nail Y is withdrawn and with a pencil held upright and pressed firmly against the inside of the loop an elipse is drawn.

Having cut the top to shape, the hinging of the leaves must be considered. In common work a plain hinged joint (Fig. 6) will suffice but the rule joint (Fig. 7) is much superior. Not only is the appearance better but the weight of the leaf when open is taken by the moulding and not by the hinges. If a rule joint is to be worked, special back flap hinges with one leaf longer than the other must be obtained. Smooth operation depends on the position of the pivot and it is from this point that the arcs are struck. A section of the joint is shown in Fig. 8. The dotted lines CC and DD indicate at intersection E the centre of the hinge pin from which the quarter circles are struck. CC is the joint line which determines the edge of the rebate and DD is the depth to which the hinge is let in.

Gauging the Joint

The method of gauging the joint is shown in Fig. 9. The first step is to work the rebate, after which the mouldings are formed with a pair of rounds and hollows or a universal plane. The arcs are first marked on the edges with compasses. Marking the table top or fixed part is straightforward and marking the leaves is simplified if they are left a trifle full at G. The joint is marked out before the edges of the leaves are planed true.

Set out the fixed part by squaring lines across the top, underside and both ends. Mark the thickness line of the hinge on the edges and this will give the centre of the arc. The radius can be the thickness of the table top minus two and a half to three times the thickness of the hinge flange. The line on the underside will give the centre of the recess for the knuckles of the hinges. A chisel and a small gouge are used to cut the recesses. Short stout screws are used to secure the hinges and care must be taken to keep the hinge pins dead in line.

The centre of the top is secured to the framework by pocket screwing through the inner faces of the top rails (Fig. 10). A slanting hole for the screw shank is drilled through the centre of the top edge of the rail and comes

Gate-leg table

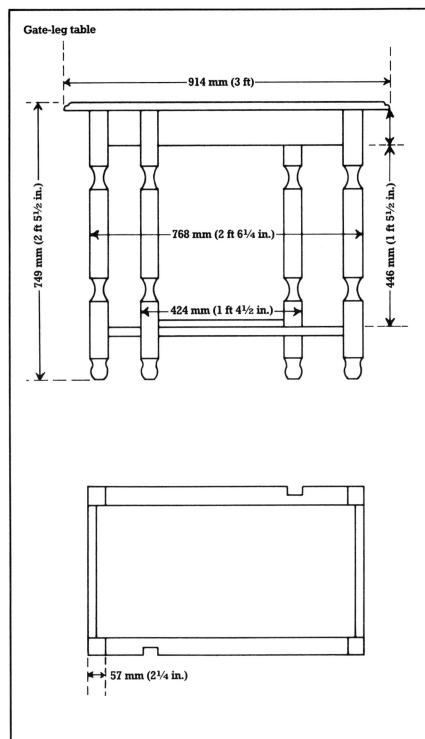

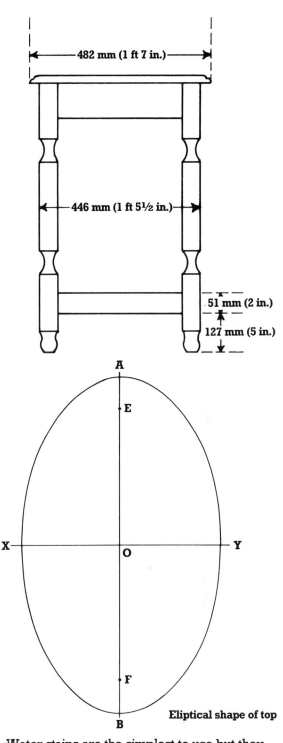

Eliptical shape of top

through its inner face. A channel to accommodate the head of the screw is then gouged out.

Having fitted the two leaves to the top a plain thumb moulding is worked round the edge. Two small stops are fixed to the underside of the leaves to keep the gates in their proper positions when opened.

Finishing

The table is now ready for finishing and no matter what finish is used the procedure is the same. All plane marks are removed by the careful use of a steel cabinet scraper after which smoothing is accomplised by using garnet paper. Grade 2/0 followed by 5/0 should prove satisfactory. Garnet paper is used in preference to glasspaper because although a little dearer it is longer lasting and is obtainable in finer grades.

Staining is necessary to enrich the grain, to give uniformity of colour and to match up with existing furniture. Water stains are the simplest to use but they raise the grain. Spirit stains do not have this disadvantage but they dry rapidly and speed of application is essential. Oil stains available from polish houses have much to recommend them for they do not raise the grain, are slower drying than spirit and allow the grain to be clearly seen.

Allow the stain to dry overnight before polishing begins. This table, being oak, was wax polished. To seal the pores of the grain two coats of white french polish are brushed on. This will assist the more rapid build up of a good wax film. When the french polish has hardened it is smoothed with worn fine garnet paper and thoroughly dusted off. A good wax polish, obtained from a supply house, is well rubbed in with a clean cloth and allowed to stand for about ten minutes. It is then rubbed vigorously with a clean duster. The process is repeated several times until a deep mellow shine is obtained.

Entrance gates

Tools and Materials used

Jack and smoothing planes
Brace
Screwdriver
Spokeshave
Bow saw
Mortice and marking gauges
Firmer chisels
Mortice chisel
Tenon saw
Try square
Mallet
Sash cramps
Cascamite (one-shot) Adhesive
(Ures formaldehyde synthetic resin glue)
Paint

The overall dimensions obviously depend on individual requirements but the constructional details shown would apply to larger or smaller gates. Those illustrated were made of redwood finished with four coats of paint. The 'segmental arch' shaped braces could be replaced by a straight length of wood in each gate if simplicity of construction is required but the shaped braces give added attractiveness to the design. My gates are hung on wooden posts fixed to concrete walls but they could be hung to concrete or brick piers.

Marking Out

A full size drawing on a sheet of plywood of one gate should be made, Fig. 1. To find the centre for the curved brace join points A and B and bisect at right angles by line CD. Continue the inner line of the closing stile down from A to meet bisector CD at O which is the centre from which the curves are struck. A thin lath with a nail driven through it to enter the plywood at O and with its other end at A can be used, by holding a pencil against the end of the lath at A (and then lower down), to draw in the brace. A stile and rail are marked out by placing each on the drawing and ticking off the lengths and positions of the joints on the face edges of the wood. These lines are then squared across the face edge of stile and rail. This stile is then placed alongside the other three stiles and the lines are transferred to them. The rails are treated similarly. Mortices and tenons are all gauged keeping head of mortice gauge against the face side of all pieces of wood.

Identification

Before beginning the marking out, the wood will, of course, have been trued up accurately to width and thickness. The timber for each gate should then be arranged (face side up) on the bench as it will appear in the finished gates with all face edges inwards. Indentification letters or figures should be placed on rails and stiles approximately where each joint is to be. It is also useful to write the word 'top' near the top ends of the stiles and also 'left-hand gate closing stile', 'l.h. gate hanging stile', 'left-hand gate top rail', etc on the various pieces of wood and similarly for the right-hand gate. All the other pieces of wood should be clearly identified for each gate. This notation may help to avoid errors later.

Tenons

The top and bottom rails are through-tenoned to the stiles and wedged. Thickness of tenon should be about one-third the thickness of the wood. The uprights are bareface tenoned to top and bottom rail and the mortices need not be more than 20mm deep. Tenons in this case can be about 10mm thick. The horizontal slats are bareface tenoned to the stiles (like the uprights to the rails) but double shoulder tenoned to the uprights. Each joint should be fitted individually and then each gate is assembled to see that all joints fit collectively. Sash cramps can be used to pull the shoulders of tenons up tightly.

Braces

Each brace is made by half-lap jointing two pieces together. The full size drawing will show what lengths and width of timber is required. About 100mm should be added past the centre line of the curve to give the length of the pieces. A sliding bevel is set to the angles on the full size drawing and the two pieces of wood are marked out and their ends cut to these angles. The bottom end of the lower part of the brace will be to fit notch in bottom rail. See Fig. 2.

A template of cardboard or thin plywood of both halves of the curve is now required. This can be got by fixing a sheet of greaseproof paper (or tracing paper) over the full-size drawing of the braces and tracing it out on this (including the centre line and the lines on either side) marking the length of each template. The templates are then used to mark out the wood. After bowsawing and spokeshaving the wood to shape the half lap (halving) joint is sawn and both pieces of each brace are glued together and cramped until the glue (synthetic resin – Cascamite – which is waterproof) has hardened. The braces are then fitted in place – tongued to the closing stile and notched to the bottom rail.

Final Assembly

The gates are taken apart and all inner surfaces cleaned up ready for final assembly. All joints are glued and the sash cramps are used to pull the stiles tightly in to the rails. The wedges are glued and driven into place. Surfaces of uprights and horizontal slats, where they come in contact with the brace, must also be glued. (An alternative to glue is lead paint in all joints and between braces and other timbers.) Finally screws are used through the braces to keep them up tight to the uprights and slats. The gates are cleaned up ready for painting and all sharp arrises should be removed with glasspaper. Screw heads should be covered with a suitable exterior grade filler.

The hinges are fixed to the gates and tried in place, after which the hinges are removed so that the gates can be painted. A good quality primer (perhaps with a lead base) followed by two undercoats and a finishing coat are recommended. (The hinges would have been fixed in place before the finishing coat, having been

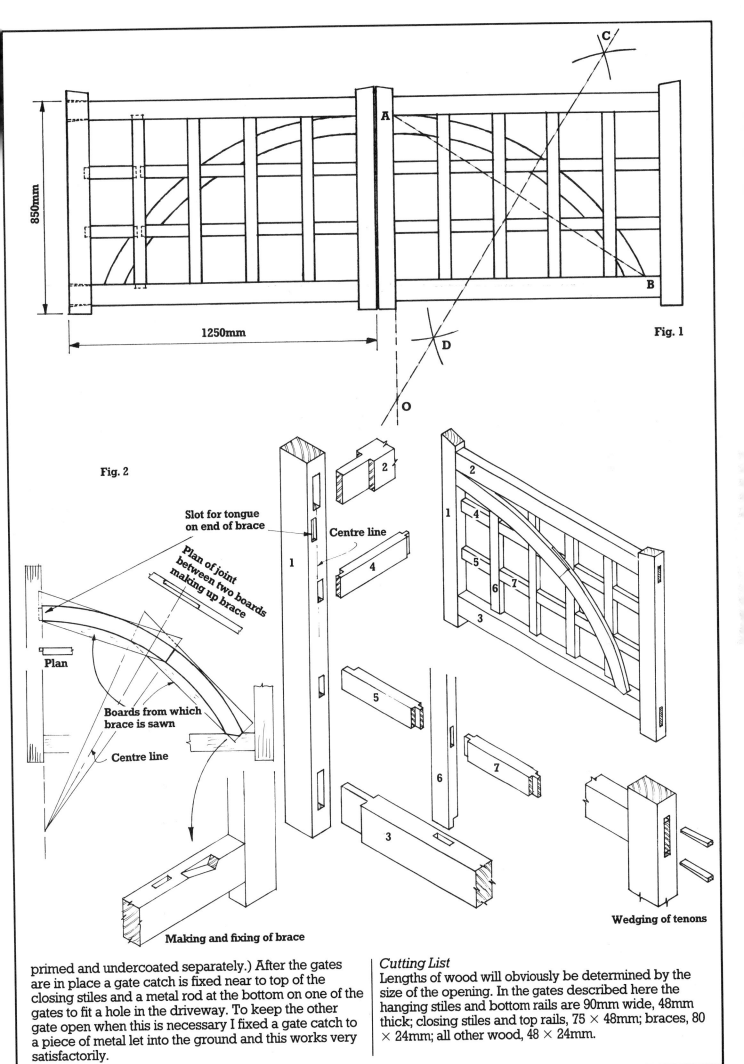

Fig. 1

850mm

1250mm

Fig. 2

Slot for tongue
on end of brace

Centre line

Plan of joint
between two boards
making up brace

Plan

Boards from which
brace is sawn

Centre line

Making and fixing of brace

Wedging of tenons

primed and undercoated separately.) After the gates
are in place a gate catch is fixed near to top of the
closing stiles and a metal rod at the bottom on one of the
gates to fit a hole in the driveway. To keep the other
gate open when this is necessary I fixed a gate catch to
a piece of metal let into the ground and this works very
satisfactorily.

Cutting List
Lengths of wood will obviously be determined by the
size of the opening. In the gates described here the
hanging stiles and bottom rails are 90mm wide, 48mm
thick; closing stiles and top rails, 75 × 48mm; braces, 80
× 24mm; all other wood, 48 × 24mm.

Refectory table

Tools Used
Carpenters Adze
Carving tools
Turning tools
Planes
Mallets
Market gauge
Boxwood Rule
Lathes
Hand saw
Panel saw
Tenon saw
Glue Pot
Glue Pearls
Oilstone
Screwdrivers
Glue kettle (electric)
Glue and brushes
Clamps
Beeswax
All polishes
Planes
Chisels

One of the most interesting ventures which has a universal appeal is a good table, preferably something solid which I am working at and writing about now.

It is thirty years since I made it with a view to its being the centre-piece of my home. It will seat four people very comfortably, even six at a pinch. Should a larger table be required it can be scaled up. Just a word of warning here, however: the larger the table, the more amount of overhang can be allowed to enable a chair to be pushed right under. Mine, being only 4 ft. long × 2 ft. 11 in., will not allow this. As I could not do with a bigger table, this suits me.

Should you make a larger one, it is as well to draw it to scale to enable you to get the balance right. The average chair height is eighteen inches, so I made my table top height twenty eight inches. My forearms rest comfortably on the table top when sitting.

All furniture sizes have been arrived at by trial and error over many years, so a general standard has evolved to accommodate the average person. However, it is you who is making the table so it is you who adds on or knocks of an inch or so to suit the height you want. Give it a lot of thinking about and try other people's furniture. At the same time, carry a rule around with you and jot down the sizes.

Wood to use
The choice of wood to use is a personal preference coupled with suitability. Mine was English oak. I suspect most people will choose a hardwood; walnut, teak or mahogany are excellent. In New Zealand I saw some tables made of Kauri which is a very hard timber. However, what your timber merchant stocks may have to be your choice. The main thing is having well seasoned stuff. Bring it in to somewhere with the same atmosphere in which it will be used when you have cut it up prior to machining. This gives it time to adjust and stabilise. Central heating plays havoc with green timber or timber which is not dried out and thoroughly seasoned.

I was, early in my career, weaned on air drying, but necessity needs quick results so kilning is often the order of the day. Somehow, though, kiln dried wood does not appear to have the same working qualities. Is it the nature of the wood or *human* nature?

Construction Joints and Matching Up
Joints in the table are all of the mortice and tenon variety. These can be cut and bored by hand though machinery does speed up the process. One thing to have in mind is that hand tools are slower but mistakes can be seen often before it is too late, whereas machines tend to carry on in a fast momentum and sometimes take too much off unless carefully set.

When sorting out your planks for the table top to mark the mortices (my table is in two planks joined with false tenons, loose tongue and draw-bored) juggle them about to get the very best match up of the grain. If oak, the flower or figure may be more prominent on one side – or any other visual characteristics of the wood may be matched to better advantage. Straight grained stuff will make it hard to spot a good joint when finished. People often ask me what the pins are for in my table, not realising their purpose.

I say, take a closer look; then I point out the joint at a place where the grain is slightly out of line. If you can arrange the medullary rays and the grain going the same way over most of the top, it makes it easier to clean up with little or no tearing out of the grain.

A very sharp plane finely set can leave a finish which makes rubbing down with glasspaper and scraping an infringement on the beauty of wood. This is not to say glasspaper is unnecessary but too often it is used before it is necessary, and to excess.

In other words, use your tools effectively at each stage and get the ultimate finish from them.

False Tenons
The false tenons should be straight grained and free from knots as they have to be a good push fit into the mortices which are in the middle edges of the table top. The false tenons are 8″ × 4″ × ½″.

Wedges
A good wedge needs to be a little longer than the tenon to enable the end to be trimmed off when cleaning up. It should tighten the joint slightly more at the shoulder than at the extreme edge.

8° or 10° of taper is all that is required. No wedges are used in the table top.

Mortices
There are three in each side of the top so that when the planks are together the mortices receive the three false tenons. The outside mortices are two inches in from the ends and the other one in the middle.

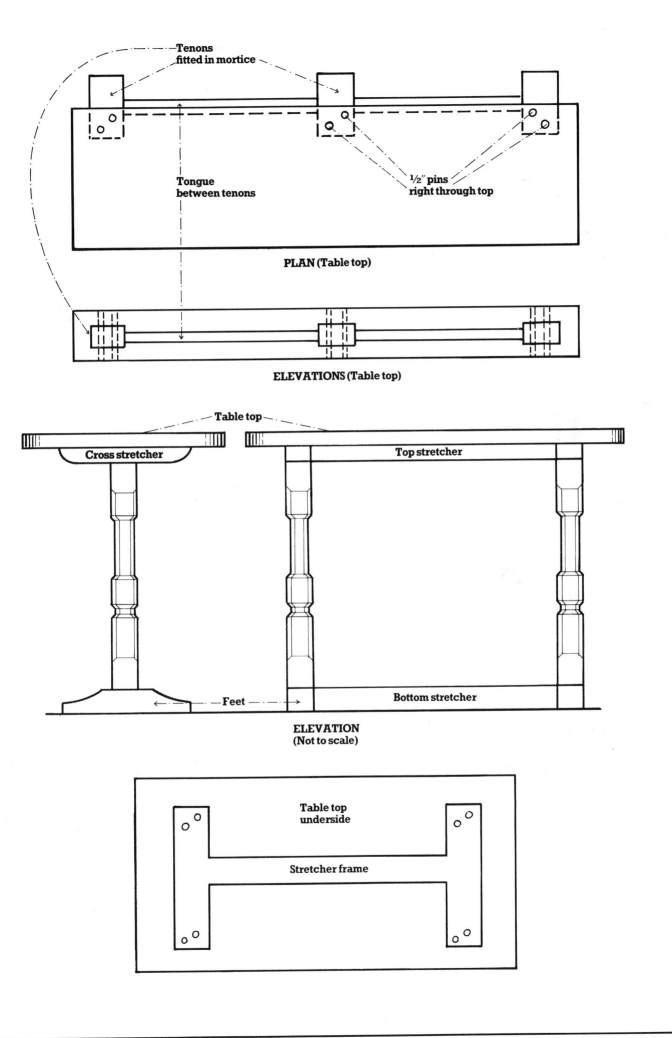

Tenons fitted in mortice

Tongue between tenons

½″ pins right through top

PLAN (Table top)

ELEVATIONS (Table top)

Table top

Cross stretcher

Top stretcher

Feet

Bottom stretcher

ELEVATION (Not to scale)

Table top underside

Stretcher frame

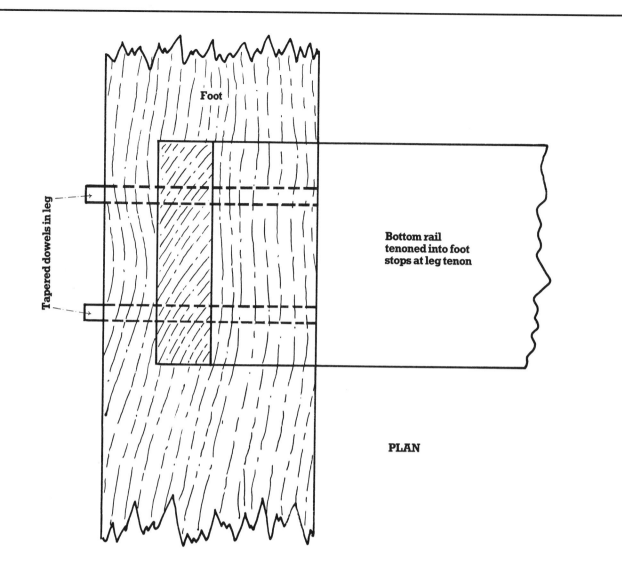

Foot

Tapered dowels in leg

Bottom rail
tenoned into foot
stops at leg tenon

PLAN

Make sure they are bored true so that the table top when cramped is not out of the same plane when tested with a straight edge across the grain. This should ensure, when finally cleaning up, the minimum amount of thickness of the top is sacrificed. It is a good thing to mortice the top before you run the groove so that you stop the groove in the end mortices. These mortices are not used with wedged tenons. The sizes are 4″ × 4″ × ½″. If they are made a little wider it does not matter as the tenons they receive will need a little clearance edgeways.

Making and Fitting the Tongue

A channel is run in the middle of the edge of the top between the end mortices. This should be ¼″ wide and ⅜″ deep to receive a loose tongue ⅜″ wide. You can run it a little deeper, if you like, to allow for depth lost when shooting the joint.

The loose tongue can be made of cross grained lengths of the same wood. As it is difficult, if not impossible to keep a length without breaking it, it is permissible to put it in in short lengths as long as you fill up the whole length of the groove, leaving a slight space between the end of tongue and the mortice and tenon.

There is an easier way using plywood which, having grain both ways, will not break so readily. The idea of the tongue is to give support to the joint across the grain of the two planks which form the table top and give more glueing surface.

Fitting Tenons on Table Top

The three tenons are 8″ × 4″ × ½″ and are fitted into the

two mortices 2″ in from the ends of top and one in the middle. If your mortices are in line, the tenon will hold the top when cramped up absolutely straight across the grain.

Make sure they are a good push fit in the thickness of the mortice with a little clearance at the edges to enable the top to move a little edgeways; ⅛″ is enough. Remember if any joint is too tight it will result in the top twisting when cramped up. This is where a couple of straight edges come is useful to act as winding laths to readily show up any twist. Above all avoid sloppy fitting.

Jointing Table Top

With all grooves and mortices cut, the joints can be shot with a shooting plane. Shoot one edge square with no twist, making sure you have planed the bumps out of the middle. With a 22″ jointer it is difficult to get the edge too hollow, so the main thing is avoiding twisting the plane when progressing from one end to the other. Having got one perfect as can be, shoot the other one. Putting one on the top of the other will show you any bumps as the top one will wobble.

Try a straight edge across the grain of both planks as already described. A sharp plane and plenty of patience, and the smallest shavings you can take, will result in a good joint. Enter your tenons and loose tongue and cramp up dry to make sure tenons are not too long and tongue is not too wide so as to hold the joint off.

Everything right so far you now can separate the planks leaving tenons and tongue in one plank. Bore ½″ holes about 1″ in from the edges of the mortices in the

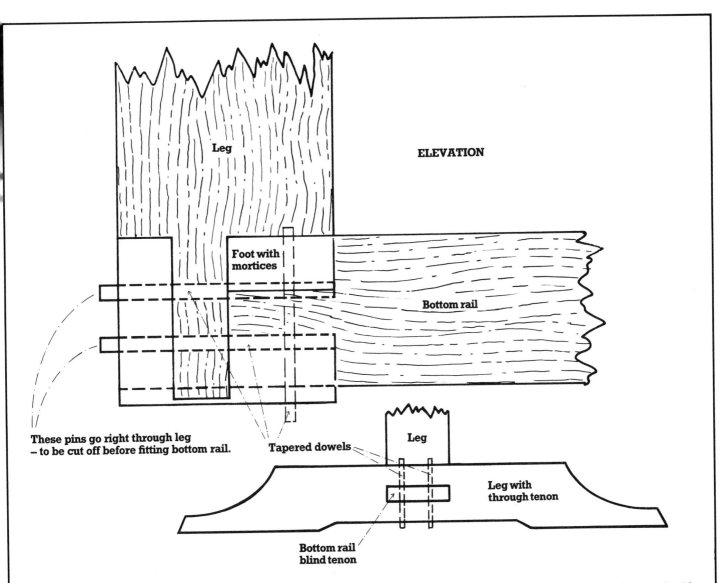

ELEVATION

Leg

Foot with mortices

Bottom rail

These pins go right through leg
– to be cut off before fitting bottom rail.

Tapered dowels

Leg

Leg with
through tenon

Bottom rail
blind tenon

plank where the tenons are entered (see the sketch) right through tenons and mortices. The holes are staggered so they are out of line in the grain of the table top.

These tenons can now be drawn out and coated with glue before putting back and the ½″ pins driven in taking care to drive both pins in one tenon at once.

How do you do *that* you say? Well, you hit one and then the other, taking care to keep them going with a steady rhythm until they are well home. Great care must be taken not to break them off in the pin hole as when cut off they make a pleasant feature and display evidence of your craftsmanship. If broken in, they look awful and need filling.

Draw Boring and Pinning

All the joints are draw-bored except one side of the table top where they are pinned straight through as described in *Jointing the Table Top*. The pins are sawn out of straight grained stuff ⁹/₁₆″ square and twice as long as the thickness of your joint or more. The wood must be like riven timber, with no knots or other imperfections, as it is driven through one hole, through an offset hole and through the last part of the first hole which makes it bend with the tension and keeps the joint up tight.

Take a block of wood about 5″ long, put it in the vice with most of it sticking up and make a U shaped cut on the front edge about ½″ into the block. This is to hold the end of the pin. With the left hand thumb on the other end, keep the pin in the U cut and plane the corners off the pin till it is round. The full ⁹/₁₆″ is kept at the top end and the bottom end tapered so it goes into a ½″ hole for a depth of 1″ or thereabouts.

This trial hole can be drilled right through the block. If it seems easier the taper can be put on in the square,

though I personally find it easier to taper when rounding the pin; it seems to come naturally.

The draw boring pins will need a sharpened point to enable them to enter the draw bored tenon.

Assuming you have drilled all the mortices you now put the brace or drill in the mortice holes and make a backward turn to mark the tenon, having first dry cramped the joint or joints.

Taking the joint apart you can now drill the hole $1/16$ nearer the shoulder. When you are ready glued and cramped up, the draw-pins can be knocked in the tenons through the mortices with a little glue on.

Drive them all at once and keep going at an even rate, if you can get help to keep them all going together, so much the better. Do not break them off with a mis-hit. They can be sawn off after and then cleaned up.

My table has stood near a radiator for thirty years and never moved in the joints at all. The pins should be about 1″ in from the sides and 1″ from the shoulder or joint.

Making Up the Legs
The legs are of $3\frac{1}{2}″ \times 3\frac{1}{2}″$ stuff. Mine are carved, having been rough turned first to remove bulk. (Yours can be carved, turned or embellished with chamfers to taste.) The tenons on them are 1″ thick and right across the width of the leg and wedged into the feet and the top stretcher, which carries the table top which is fastened to the stand with screws through the top stretchers. (See sketch).

(This is an interesting construction. Draw boring the joints is rarely done these days – but it's a good sound method. – Ed.)

Making Up the Feet
The feet are $3\frac{1}{2}″ \times 2\frac{3}{4}″$ cut to shape after morticing. The middle part of the foot is hollowed to lift the bottom stretcher clear off the floor so that only the two extremities of the feet rest on the floor. The top edges are curved and then cut off on a bevel before reaching the floor, thus lightening the effect. The feet also receive the bottom stretcher.

Stretchers
The cross stretchers receive the leg tenons, also the long bottom stretcher, as do the feet in the same way. They are draw-bored and wedged in the through tenons and just draw bored in the stopped tenons. The top stretchers are tapered off as in the sketch and these tapers are where the screw holes are to fasten the stand

to the top as well as two or three counterbored holes along the length of the long top stretcher to enable more screws to hold the top.

Table Top Fixing to Stand
Having pinned up the legs to the feet and joined them together by the top and bottom stretchers, it is time to counterbore the ends of the top stretchers to enable the stand to be screwed to the table top. With the table top upside down on trestles, place the stand, also upside down, upon the top. Measure the ends of stand and position it fairly in the middle of table top. Mark the corners with a special mark on one corner so you can tell which is which end. Do not forget to make sure that you cannot get mixed up or wrong way round. Scribe with a sharp pencil any spot which needs taking down on top stretcher to enable stand to fit snugly on the table top. Dress off any high spots.

Then counterbore $\frac{1}{2}″$ in the taper of the top stretcher to bury the head of a no 10 screw. Bore right through to receive the thread of the screw.

Elongate this to enable shrinkage of the table top to take place when fixed. Screw up when ready and pellet up the holes with the grain the same way.

Finish and Cleaning Up
After each stage of pinning up and jointing, clean off all tenon ends and wedges also pin ends. Do all your planing, scraping and sanding, taking care not to destroy any clean cut edges or dub over corners.

The table top can be cleaned up when fixed to the stand, unless of course you adze it as I did mine, in which case it is done on the floor before fixing.

A sharp plane and scraper applied judiciously, also plenty of elbow grease, should result in a good finish. After being adzed, my top was scraped where necessary with a curved scraper, sanded with care so as not to take out the adzing with M2, damped with a clean cotton rag, sanded again, damped down then the process repeated with fine 2. Fuming then took place in a plywood airtight chamber (you can use polythene sheeting but make sure it does not touch the work) with ammonia.

When the wood was a nice golden shade I wax-polished it. If you wish, you can stain to the colour you want and apply whatever finish takes your fancy.

Cutting List of Finished Sizes

Table Top
Two planks to make $4'0″ \times 2'1″$ when jointed, they need not be the same size.

The Stand
1 Bottom stretcher $2'3″ \times 3\frac{1}{2}″ \times 2\frac{3}{8}″$
1 Top stretcher $2'8″ \times 2″ \times 1\frac{3}{4}″$
2 Cross stretchers $1'11″ \times 3\frac{1}{2}″ \times 2″$
2 legs $2'3″ \times 3\frac{1}{2}″ \times 3\frac{1}{2}″$
2 feet $1'8″ \times 3\frac{1}{2}″ \times 2\frac{3}{4}″$

Incidentals
These can be cut from odd short lengths of straight grained stuff with the exception of loose tongues.
3 false tenons $8″ \times 4″ \times \frac{1}{2}″$
28 Wooden pins 6″ approx $\times \, ^9/_{16}″ \times \, ^9/_{16}$
8-10 Wedges as described in text
2 loose tongues $1'6″ \times \frac{3}{4}″ \times \frac{1}{4}″$ as described in text.

The art of whittling human caricatures

Specialities that once symbolized whittling, like the chain, ball-in-a-cage and fan, are not at all common as projects among present-day Amerian whittlers. They tend instead to produce a variety of animals, ranging from local fauna like rabbits, foxes and bears to domesticated ones like dogs and horses. Or, if they are more ambitious, they carve human representations, traditionally a sea captain on the East Coast, or a cowboy in the Midwest and Far West. All of these figures are basically caricatures (although the whittlers sometimes don't know it), and we have in fact come to contests in which whittlers see who can produce the ugliest cowboy – the one with teeth projecting farthest, greatest grimaces, poorest posture and so on. It is

Skipper Sam'l

perhaps an effort to evade the rather grim truths of everyday life, but classes have been formed to achieve these incongruous results.

The human caricature nowadays rarely is started from a block or a limb as it was long ago; the whittler starts with a bandsawed blank, usually in a soft wood like pine or basswood (Lime). One can, in fact, buy presawed blanks of popular figures (popularized by publication of the pattern in a book or booklet, in most cases). These include caricatures of people, and a variety of animals in a variety of poses. No one seems any longer to consider purchase of a prefabricated blank as unsporting or unethical; it is becoming almost as familiar as buying the wood as precut planks. And all sorts of tools are used to do the rough shaping, depending on size and original condition, from chain saw or bandsaw to rasps and a variety of hand and small power tools. Strangely, the chisel is rarely used for this purpose, unless the whittler is also a woodcarver familiar with more-sophisticated tools.

Typical Figure

To illustrate what I'm talking about, I have chosen a typical human figure – a sea captain which, as far as I know, originated in French Canada a very long time ago, and which I described in *Popular Science Monthly* in the early Thirties. I dubbed him Skipper Sam'l, and the magazine sold kits including instructions, two blanks, a fixed-blade knife, three colours of paint and a brush, all for $1.50 (then five or six shillings). A number of American boys began to whittle with such kits, including the present president of the National Wood Carvers Assn.

A more recent design seems to have captivated our Western whittlers. It is a caricature of a cowboy, with ungainly stance, bow legs, boots with turned-up toes, pants with holes, a slumping posture, and clothes in general that look as if they had been slept in. To top it off, he must be very ugly, unshaven and unkempt, and have buck teeth. Indeed, there seems to be some competition to see who can create the ugliest character. Also, the figures are often carved with separate heads and arms, so these can be later posed and glued in place. It's a strange phenomenon – the ugly carving. I prefer the very proper sea captain.

Note that the skipper has his hands jammed into his pockets. I am uncharitable enough to assume that the reason for such a design originally was not to attain an appearance of nonchalance but to avoid the onerous chore of whittling suitable hands. It is hard to make a hand look caricatured without making it look crude or ungainly. On the other hand (no pun intended) it is possible to do all sorts of things to the face and still have it considered a caricature. And we do it. Huge nose, crossed eyes, distorted and oversize mouth, jutting chin, over-prominent Adam's apple – you name it. And our caricatures tend to have the head overlarge for the body, so that many of our caricatures resemble dwarves. Also, many of our better caricaturists use themselves as models, so their caricatures, regardless of pose or profession, look like their maker making a grimace.

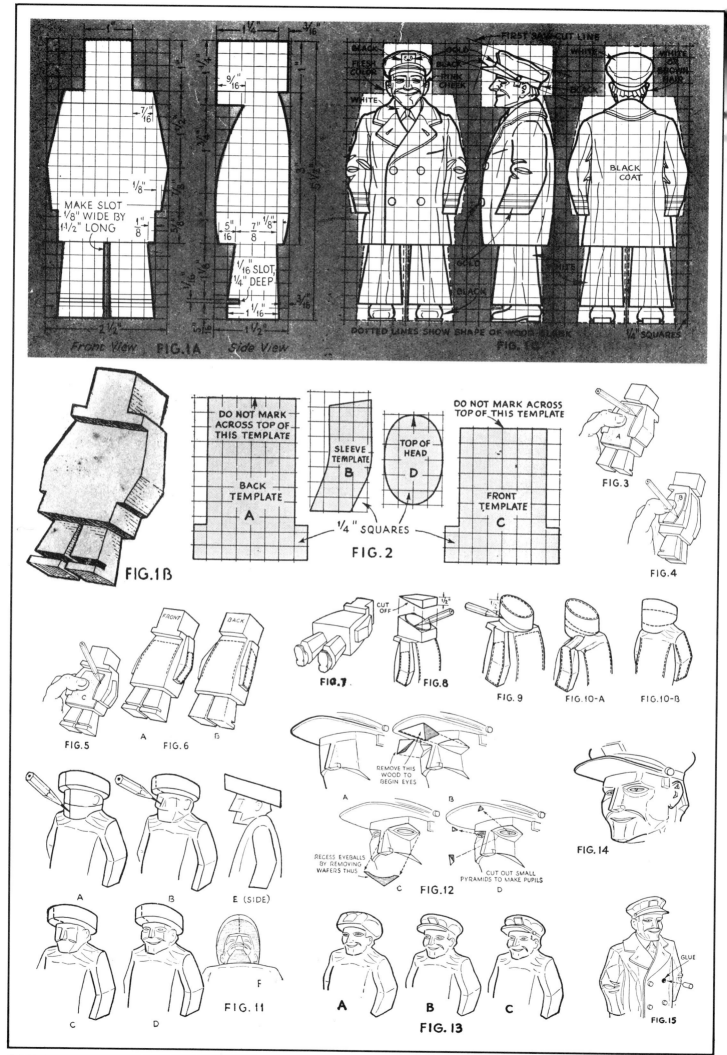

Front View. FIG.1A

MAKE SLOT ⅛" WIDE BY 1½" LONG

Side View

9/16"

1/16 SLOT, ¼" DEEP

DOTTED LINES SHOW SHAPE OF WOOD BLOCK — FIG.1C

¼ SQUARES

BLACK

FLESH COLOR

WHITE

GOLD

BLACK PINK CHEEK

FIRST SAW-CUT LINE

WHITE

WHITE OR BROWN HAIR

BLACK

BLACK COAT

GOLD

BLACK

WHITE

FIG.1B

DO NOT MARK ACROSS TOP OF THIS TEMPLATE

BACK TEMPLATE A

SLEEVE TEMPLATE B

TOP OF HEAD D

DO NOT MARK ACROSS TOP OF THIS TEMPLATE

FRONT TEMPLATE C

¼" SQUARES

FIG.2

FIG.3

FIG.4

FRONT BACK

A FIG.6 B

FIG.5

CUT OFF

½"

FIG.7

FIG.8

FIG.9

FIG.10-A

FIG.10-B

REMOVE THIS WOOD TO BEGIN EYES

A

B

RECESS EYEBALLS BY REMOVING WAFERS THUS

C

CUT OUT SMALL PYRAMIDS TO MAKE PUPILS

D

FIG.12

FIG.14

A

B

E (SIDE)

C

D

F

FIG.11

A

B

C

FIG.13

GLUE

FIG.15

Whittling Skipper Sam'l

Skipper Sam'l is carved from white pine or basswood 1½ × 2½ × 5½ in. On the front and right side, pencil on ¼-in. squares and lay out the patterns sketched in Fig 1A. Saw in all the horizontal lines from the sides – shoulder tops, cuffs, bottom of coat. From front and back, saw in under his chin and at the nape, front and back of coat, and slot between shoes and trouser bottoms. Saw a ⅛-in. wide slot between his legs to his coat bottom. Shave off ¹/₁₆ in. at the back of his head, ¼ in. at the back of his pants. Round up his back and his coat-tail.

None of these cuts has destroyed the pattern, but subsequent cuts will. Saw away waste wood at the sides of the head and outside the arms down to the elbows. Saw up the outside of each leg to ¼ in. from the bottom of his coat, then stop and saw up the front of the legs to the coat bottom. Now complete the side cuts. Saw *up* the sides of the coat to the cuffs, and *down* from elbows to cuffs to avoid splitting. Measure down 1¾ in. from the chin saw cut on his chest, and draw a liberal curve on each side up to the inside end of the chin cut. Saw or whittle this away, and the blank is complete; it should look like Fig 1B.

Cut out the patterns of Fig 2 from heavy paper or thin cardboard. Line up template A at bottom and sides on the back of the coat and mark the sides as in Fig 3 to give the lines of the arms. Do the same on the front, as in Fig 5. Place and trace sleeve template B on each arm in turn, lining up its bottom with the bottom of the cuff and setting the elbow in about ⅛ in. from the back of the block. Score deeply along these lines. Keep forcing the knife point down and cutting away the wood outside these lines until your block looks like Fig 6 A & B. This leaves the arms roughly shaped and standing out from the body (see also Figs 7 to 10).

Study Fig 7 carefully, then form the shoes. Nick out the bottom to create a heel and round it in back. Round off the blunt toe (Careful! This is across grain.) and slope the instep up to the back of your saw cut. Take out a sliver of wood all around each shoe to show the joining of sole and heel to the upper. Whittle off the rough edges of each trouser leg to make an octagonal section tapering *up* from the shoes to the coat, cutting from shoes to coat to prevent splitting.

Next comes the cap. Study Figs 8 to 10. Measure down ½ in. from the top of the block in back and draw a horizontal line across, then lines angling up on each side to the front. Saw away this wedge (Fig 8). Place oval template D on the sloping surface, draw around it and split off the corners to get the cap and head shape, Fig 9. Draw a line around the head oval down ½ in. from the sloping top. Cut in about ⅛ in. along this line and split out the wood carefully underneath, so the top stands out as in Fig 11A. Round and shape the shoulders roughly as in Fig 10A and B.

Locate the nose by drawing a centre line down the face front, Fig 11A, and measuring down ⅜ in. Score straight across the face at this point ⅜ in. deep and cut out the wedge from tip of chin to base of nose, Fig 11C. Cut away wood from tip of nose to joining between face and cap at the same angle. Now you have face slants. Trim up the hair line in back, and your blank should resemble Fig 11E.

Study Fig 11F closely to visualize elevations and angles of chin, cheeks and eyes in your mind. Draw a brow line down ⅛ in. Mark a triangle for the nose, Fig 11B, about ⅛ in. wide at the top and ¼ in. wide at the bottom and cut away wood at each side about ⅛ in. deep up only to the brow line. Slope in the sides of the face to form the chin, but don't cut away wood you'll need later for the ears. From the outer bottom corners of the nose, cut ¹/₁₆-in. diagonal lines downward and outward to define the bottom of the cheek in front, Fig 12A. Cut up to this line from the point of the jaw to form the jawbone and chin. Cut a line across a bit over ¹/₁₆ in .below the nose to define the mouth. It can be straight across to give a stern look, but I prefer it turned up slightly at the outer corners into a smile. (Don't overdo the curve or he'll look like a clown.)

Start the eyes with notches, Fig 12B, about ⅛ in. deep and down about ⅛ in. from the joining of face and cap. They are shallow at the nose and deeper at the outer edges. A simple eye will merely have a slight flat at the bottom of the notch, with a small drilled hole to define the pupil. But the eye of Figs 12C and D is better. Cut out thin wafers to leave the bulge of the eyeball, as in Fig 12C, then cut out a triangle for the pupil as in Fig. 12D. You can now shape the nose and brow lines, leaving nostril bulges and rounded nose ridge – or not, as you prefer.

Shape the cap as in Figs 13A, B and C, sloping in towards the head at the sides and back and forming a visor in front. This must be done very carefully to avoid splitting off the visor, it's a thin section across grain. Shape the ears as in Fig 14 and cut away wood in front to leave Sam's sideburns. Whittle the cap strap, side buttons and ornament and cut a few grooves in back to suggest hair, and the head is done except for any final shaping you want to do.

Draw in the coat lapels, collar and front lap, and locate the buttons. Note that the coat is double breasted and large-collared. (You can have four buttons or the official six.) Force the knife point in along these lines and cut away the *outside* wood only, so the lines stand out to suggest the thickness of collar and buttons. You may want to lower the shoulders a little and round them more to accentuate the collar and lapels. Now follow Fig 1C for putting in creases and rounding up the figure. Sleeve creases are just three notches at the inside of the elbow. The stripes can be whittled or merely painted on later.

Leave some slabbed areas; don't sandpaper the figure to perfection or it will look like plastic or pottery. I'd paint him, however. Coat, shoes, cap visor strap and emblem are black. Trousers are white, as is the crown of the cap. Face is a healthy flesh colour with a bit of red on the cheekbones – perhaps even nose and chin tips as well. Hair and eyebrows are grey or white, pupils of eyes black with a short white line at the left. (Don't put the white inside or outside on both, or the Skipper will be cockeyed.) Put tiny crossed anchors in gold on the cap ornament, and four gold stripes on the sleeve. Buttons on coat and cap are also gold. You can add a pipe or carve Sam with beard or moustache, of course.

Making wooden rocking-horses

Part I – The Woodwork

We build a modest number of rocking-horses each year. If I see some feature on an old rocking-horse in a museum that would enhance ours, I incorporate it. Consquently, in the eight years since I made our first rocking-horse, our ideas and design have changed considerably. The original design was my own – and a very ugly and 'arty' thing that first horse was! But as the design has developed we have moved more and more towards the traditional Victorian style of horse without, I hope, losing that individuality that we seek to impart. A wooden rocking-horse is a delightful thing to build. There are lots of problems, but they can all be overcome. If you have ever fancied having a go at a real rocking-horse I hope this article will be of some use.

A completed small rocking-horse.

We produce three sizes of rocking-horse. The small one is mounted on traditional bow-type rockers, whilst the medium and large sizes are on swing-iron stands (see 1.) The actual construction of the horse is similar for all three sizes, but the horse on bow rockers has its legs splayed out further forward and backward. This enables the bow rockers to be longer – providing a more exciting ride – and safer in that it is virtually impossible for a child to overturn the horse while riding it. (This is not so with some cheap models on the markets.)

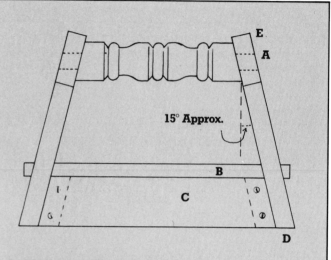

BOW ROCKER ARRANGEMENT

A Turned end pieces glued, etc., and wedged.
B Slatted platform supported by:
C Rectangular framework of rocker assembly.
D Rockers scribed and shaped to level (i.e. floor) though can be left square at extremities E.

Bow Rockers

Bow rockers take up much more space than the swing-iron stand, and tend to move about on the floor while being ridden (gouging lumps out of the wall and crushing toes). So I do not bother with bow rockers for the larger models (unless specially requested). Also, the small bow rockers can be cut from a single plank whereas longer ones need to be joined at the centre. A piece of ash 25½ × 305 × 1448 mm (1 in. × 12 in. × 4 ft. 9 in.) is enough to cut out both rockers with sufficient off-cuts to make the slatted platform [planed down to 16 mm (⅝ in.)] and supporting pieces. The two end pieces are turned 51 mm (2 in.) square ash. The trick with the bow rockers is to make them angle inward at about 15° to give the traditional boat shaped appearance. The drawing should make this clear. The fiddly bit is scribing and notching the insides of the hooves to let them fit snug down on to the rockers, to be fixed in place with a single screw or 6½ mm (¼ in.) carriage bolt at each hoof.

Swing-Iron Stands

The swing-iron stands are quite straightforward to make. I use Douglas fir mostly, for its attractive appearance when varnished. The posts can be turned, or of a tapered rectangular section. The top piece of the stand is finished at 95 mm (3¾ in.) wide to take the swing-irons, which bear on a mild steel strip nailed over the top. Steel strap brackets at each end are bolted through to fix the swing-iron in place.

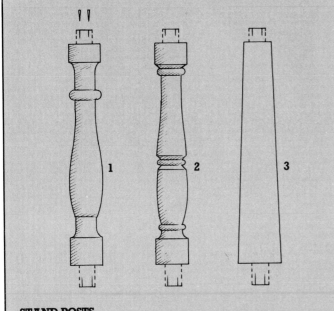

STAND POSTS
Can be turned (1 or 2) or square or Rectangular section (3). Glued and wedged top and bottom. Top wedging may be hidden beneath diamond shaped piece of thin wood.

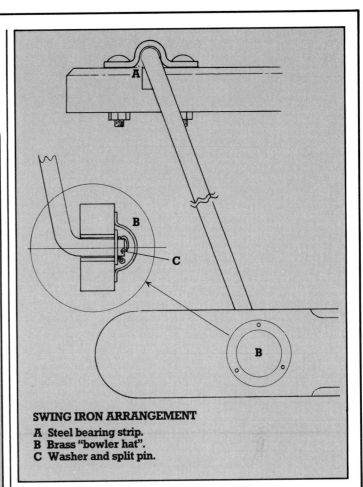

SWING IRON ARRANGEMENT
A Steel bearing strip.
B Brass "bowler hat".
C Washer and split pin.

The lower ends of the steel swing-irons pass through holes bored in the cross-struts, which are 25½ × 51 mm (1 in. × 2 in.) beech. These holes can be lined with short pieces of steel pipe to make a durable bearing – this is particularly important if the horse is for a school or nursery, where it is likely to come in for a lot of hammer. The extremities of the steel swing-irons have holes bored through so a split pin can be pushed through, over a washer. These moving parts should be well greased and the ugly swing-iron end hidden under a brass 'bowler hat' (see drawing).

The main thing with arranging the swing-irons is to ensure they provide a satisfactory rocking motion. They should not be parallel, but should converge as they descend, thus allowing a rocking motion which is enough to be exciting – but safe. The horse should be able to tilt so far – and no further. You may find that when the horse is ridden hard there is a tendency for one end of the stand to lift from the floor. This is acceptable so long as the lift is only very slight, but otherwise can be rectified by lengthening the base of the stand or adjusting the swing-irons. The two small blocks at each end of the stand base prevent it tipping up forwards or back: the two cross pieces beneath the posts must be long enough to prevent the horse from tipping sideways.

Traditionally, rocking-horse bodies were made of yellow pine, but since this is now hard to obtain, and expensive, I use mostly jelutong which is stable, easy to carve, and virtually knot free. The gum holes can be bunged. Any decent close grained carving wood can be used, different types on the same horse according to what you can obtain. But bear in mind that a particularly good strong piece should be selected for the head since the ears and lower jaws are relatively fragile and prone to breakage with use. The legs should be beech

and can be either butt mounted onto the side of the main body section or morticed into the underside of the body in such a way that they splay out at about 10°. I use cascamite powder adhesive throughout, with lots of wooden pegs to help to hold the thing together.

When all the parts have been band sawn out, the first job is to fix the head onto the neck. To facilitate fixing together these two odd shapes, projecting noggins should be left on them when bandsawing, to take the cramps. The head and neck can be fixed in a straight line, but the horse will look far better, more 'alive', if the head is at an angle – about 15° or so – to the neck and body.

You *can* assemble the whole thing before starting to carve, but I find it easier to carve the head and the lower part of the legs before putting it together – they are easier to hold and move about. Also it means I can have a number of part-carved pieces awaiting speedy

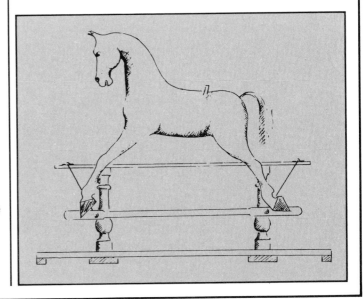

assembly when the orders come in, rather than have my workshop cluttered up with more complete horses than I need at any one time.

The Head

The carving of the head is important because it is the main focus of attention. The expression given to the head will fix the subsequent "personality" of the horse. Some traditional rocking-horses have fearsome heads with great gnashing teeth and an almost vicious glint in their eyes. I prefer a more benign expression – a sprightly but friendly animal rather than a war-like charger.

I believe that with all carving it is best to have a clear idea in your mind of what you are going to do before pickng up the gouge and mallet. It is worthwhile, therefore, to first look at other rocking-horses, to look at real horses, perhaps to make a few "sketches" in plasticene or small practice model heads. The features of a rocking-horse head are normally simplified and the flare of the nostrils and size of the ears are also exaggerated – the ears particularly because these are prone to break and should be left broad at the base and not too pointed. The eyes recesses are cut in – making sure that both eyes are at the same height or your head will really look peculiar.

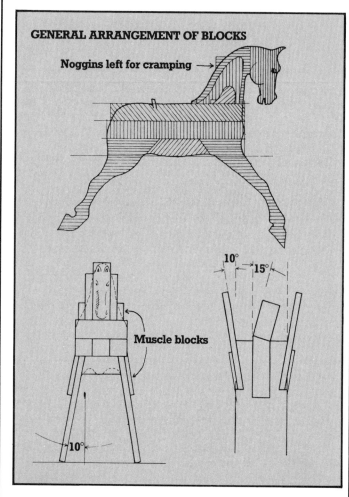

GENERAL ARRANGEMENT OF BLOCKS

Noggins left for cramping →

Muscle blocks

10° 15°

10°

The Body

The body of the horse is essentially a hollow box – 177½ × 177½ × 457 mm (7 in. × 7 in. × 18 in.) for the small model, 222 × 222 ×597 mm (8¾ in. × 8¾ in. × 23½ in.) for the medium, and 248 × 248 × 698½ mm (9¾ in. × 9¾ in. × 27½ in.) for the large. The neck is fixed down to the top section of the body and the noggin (mentioned before) that was left on the neck when bandsawing, is used to clamp the parts together.

Wooden pegs again are driven through the joints. The parts of the body have to be fixed together in stages so that you can ensure the joints are good before fixing the next pieces. The extra thickness and strength required in the neck and at the tops of the legs is provided by glueing muscle blocks onto the sides.

Clamping head and neck.

When this is done you have something beginning to look like a horse, with a fully carved head and lower legs, and a rectangular box for a body. So with your biggest gouge and mallet and perhaps a drawknife if you have one, the chopping out of the main shape of the body and neck can proceed. As the ugly squareness of the body disappears in a welter of woodchips, all your kindling for the colder weather is provided, and you ruminate on the awful proportion of expensive timber that ends up on the fire. I complete the body carving with a surform, which leaves a nice finish to give a key to the gesso coat that will be described in Part 2. But I smooth off the back of the neck and cut the slot for the mane. Having experimented with several different types of mane I have decided that fixing it into a slot is the securest way. The slot starts an inch or so behind the ears and runs back along the centre of the neck for 254 mm (10 in.) or so (less for the small model). It is 6½ mm (¼ in.) wide about 16 mm (⅝ in.) deep.

On larger horses the stirrups are usually hung from giant staples. Small recesses are chopped out or drilled at each side of the body, and the giant staples driven in. The recesses are to allow the buckles of the stirrup straps to lie flat to the horse's sides.

The back of the saddle will fix over a curved block set into the back of the horse, angled slightly rearwards and projecting up about an inch at its highest point in the middle. A slot to receive this block can be sawn across the horse's back and the block glued in place. You *can* leave the horse's back flat but the saddle block provides a more secure seat for the child, and looks better. The 19 mm (¾ in.) hole for the tail should be drilled at right angles to the horse's rump, about 38 mm (1½ in.) deep.

Finally, the insides of the horse's hooves can be scribed and notched to fix onto the cross struts or bow rockers. At this stage I bolt on a pair of temporary cross struts to stand the horse on while it is being painted, etc., and to protect the hooves from getting chipped on the workshop floor.

That completes the woodwork. There is a fair amount of work involved and it constitutes roughly half the making time – the remainder is taken up with the finishing process. The method I have tried to describe is that traditionally employed by most of the old rocking-horse makers, though of course there are plenty of variations. Most notably are the horses you sometimes see which are built up entirely from laminations of thinner timber, some using laminations of contrasting wood colours. The finished horse is varnished, leaving the swirling grain patterns on show. I have built the odd natural wood finish horse by special request, but on the whole am not enthusiastic about it. My feeling is that while natural wood might be appealing to some adults, the "real thing", which is essentially a toy for kids, should be a painted dapple grey. This is, therefore, my standard finish.

I hope that I have covered the main points adequately and that the accompanying drawings clarify what I have tried to explain in words. To anyone considering having a go at a genuine traditional wooden rocking-horse I would say "Go ahead". The delighted pleasure of the new child owner is the rocking-horse maker's best reward.

Head of small rocking-horse.

Part 2 — The Finishing Procedure

The wooden surface of the horse is rough sanded to provide a key for the gesso coat. If you are renovating an old rocking-horse it should be brought to the same condition, ready for finishing. All the accessories should be stripped off, and you should remove or punch in any rusty and broken nails. The stand or bow rockers can be stripped and re-varnished in the usual way but the old gesso on the horse may need to be completely removed and re-done.

Any repairs required to the woodwork can now be done. I recently renovated a little rocking-horse which came to me with three loose legs, the fourth leg falling off completely as I lifted the horse from its stand. Its ears were smashed and the lower jaw broken. These are common faults. I usually renew the smaller breakages with pieces of lime, fixing them securely with screws and cascamite. On one horse whose tenon joint on the leg had become so worn and damaged that it could no longer be made to fit without wobbling, I reset the leg into the body with polyester resin, rather than make a whole new leg, and the fixing proved quite satisfactory.

The purpose here is to make a practicable and lovely toy. Applying gesso over the wood is not to hide shoddy workmanship (definitely not in my case!). When the rocking-horse is finished it will look beautiful – but as a toy it will be abused and damaged in a way that pieces of furniture of comparable craftsmanship and expense will not. This thing of beauty is a joy . . . only until the next time it needs refurbishing.

Gesso

The gesso is made up with animal glue (preferably rabbit skin), broken in bits and soaked overnight, then warmed in a gluepot – a ceramic marmalade jar in a saucepan of water will serve. Gilder's whiting is mixed in, a small quantity initially so that the first coat is thin – the later coats can be thicker. Lay the gesso on with a brush, and over all the joins in the wood, and any knots, lay pieces of plasterer's scrim. Build the gesso coat up – maybe six coats – until it gives a satisfactory appearance. It can be lightly sanded between coats to give extra key but it is not necessary, and can be carved into if required. The final coat should leave the surface smooth. It can be sanded with fine paper if needed, to give a good surface to take the paintwork.

I put on a thin primer first, followed by two or three undercoats, with two gloss coats on top. The paint should be a light grey colour, and since the rocking-horse is a toy, it should be virtually lead free.

The next stage is to apply the dappling which is black gloss. You sometimes see modern horses that have been dappled with a paint spray, discs of masking tape having been stuck over the horse to leave the spotted appearance. But the proper way to do it is this. Make a small pad, about 1″ across, of muttoncloth wrapped round a small piece of foam rubber. Smear some black paint onto a scrap of clean wood which serves as a pallet. Gently touch the pad into the paint, removing any surplus by tapping the pad onto a clean part of the pallet. The paint is then applied to the horse with a gentle dabbing motion – do not smear it or you will make a mess.

You will find that on first application the pad leaves a lot of black, becoming less as the paint is used up. So start at a place on the horse where you want plenty of black and work towards the lighter parts. Dab the pad in circles to leave the distinctive "spottings" of the dappled horse. Precise symmetry of the markings is not necessary but the two sides of the horse should be roughly similar or it will look rather odd.

When the dappling is dry the eye-lashes can be painted in, and the inside of the mouth, the teeth, and the hooves. They eyes are glued into their sockets using a good contact adhesive. Glass eyes are best.

Harness and Saddlery

While the paintwork is drying you can begin to make the harness and saddlery. On my horses, as on most traditional ones, the saddle is permanently fixed in place so that there is no possibility of it moving when the horse is ridden. But I make up a head harness with small buckles so that it can be removed just like a real one. The chest straps are nailed on, so they can be of fairly thin leather. But for the head harness and, particularly for the stirrup straps which bear the weight of the child rider, a good quality 3 mm harness leather should be used.

The bit is forged from ⅛″ mild steel rod with a solid brass harness ring at each end, the various parts of the harness brass-rivetted together according to the size of the head, as in the accompanying drawings. All my harness leather is ½″ wide, while the stirrup straps are ¾″ wide.

There are various ways of making the saddle. The simplest is little more than an oval of leather or velvet nailed over a foam rubber pad. My saddles are a compromise between simplicity and a shape something like a real saddle. The main difference is that on a real saddle the saddle flaps serve to prevent the stirrup straps from chafing against the horse's sides, whereas

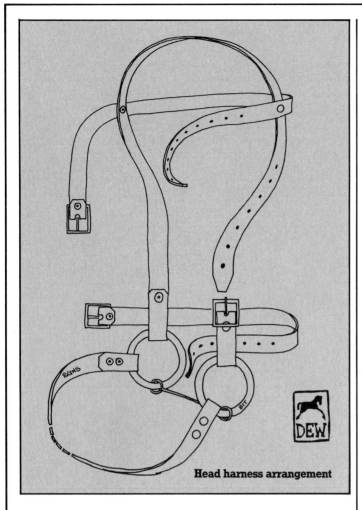

Head harness arrangement

heads of these nails will later be hidden beneath the larger heads of brass dome headed nails.

As mentioned in the first article, most larger horses have their stirrup straps hung from giant staples set into recesses on each sid of the horse. In this case a small piece of the saddle cloth should be cut away to reveal the stirrup strap staple beneath. The other method of fixing stirrups is to have a length of strapping laid over the horse, hanging down evenly either side and nailed in place in the middle. The two ends have a row of holes punched in them. The buckles are attached to a short length of leather strapping and joined directly onto the stirrup iron. I hope the drawings will clarify this since I can barely understand my own verbal ' explanation either!

Next the chest straps can be nailed in place. They go over the horse's shoulders(?) one end to be hidden under the saddle, the other ends meeting in the middle of the chest. A further short strap is lead downwards from this point and fixed underneath the horse. Then the saddle flaps can be nailed on (if you use them), making sure that they neatly cover the stirrup strap staples. A piece of 1½″ or 2″ thick foam rubber is cut about ½″smaller than the saddle top and laid in place. The saddle top is then nailed on. If you find the leather will not conform to the shape you want it to, it can be persuaded more easily by damping it. After damping, however, leather tends to dry rather stiff, so it will need to be softened up with saddlesoap or some other proprietary leather softener.

Mane and Tail

Now the mane and tail. On most old horses the horse hair was left attached to a strip of hide and simply nailed in place along the neck and wrapped round a wedge and hammered into the hole for the tail.

Of course the hide has to be treated and this can be done as follows. First the hide must be stripped from the flesh and all traces of meat removed. Rub it generously with table salt and wrap in a damp cloth for two or more days. Unwrap and remove any shreds of flesh the salt will have dried. Wash and rinse in cold water. Plunge into tanning solution for at least seven days, stirring daily for a few minutes. Then rinse in cold water. The

on mine the stirrup straps run under the saddle flaps and serve to prevent the stirrup strap buckles chafing against the child's leg.

The saddle cloths are shaped pieces of coloured leathercloth, edged with a fancy braid, and go underneath the saddle. They are fixed to the horse first and it is important that they are positioned evenly at either side and in such a way that any rough edges will subsequently be hidden beneath the saddle. I fix these, and the rest of the saddlery, with 1″ wire nails first; the

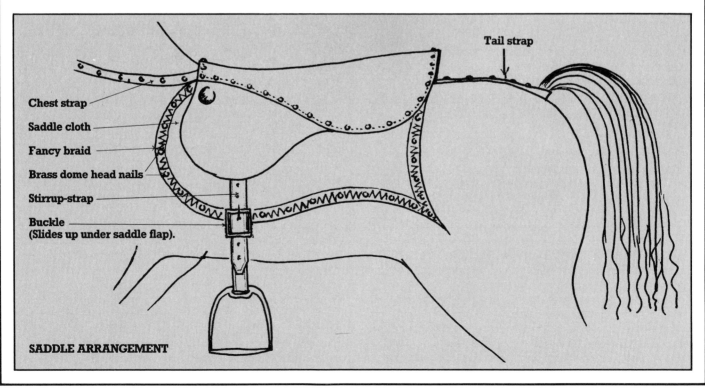

Chest strap
Saddle cloth
Fancy braid
Brass dome head nails
Stirrup-strap
Buckle
(Slides up under saddle flap).

Tail strap

SADDLE ARRANGEMENT

hair will have to be washed thoroughly several times to clean it and to eradicate its strong smell.

Tanning solution is prepared by bringing one gallon of water to the boil and stirring in three pounds of table salt, a half pound of alum and a half pound of powdered borax until dissolved. Add four gallons of water and allow to cool. It can be used several times – until it begins to stink. The tanning solution should be used in a non-metal container and the hide must be totally immersed. This method of treating hide is used by taxidermists and the hair remains firmly embedded in the hide – unlike most tanning processes in which of course the hair is removed.

I use this method occasionally because I like to have a few of this type of tail in stock – but it is a messy business. The tails come from the horse slaughterer (or, as he prefers to be described, a pet food manufacturer). He will not supply manes, because to cut the mane out would damage the hide he wants. He will, however, supply me with any amount of tails at little or no cost. He won't be bothered with skinning them for me so I do it myself but as I say, it is a messy business. Few things can smell as repulsive as a dead horse's tail – particularly if it has been dead for some time. So before visiting the knacker's yard or doing the skinning, arm yourself with a good supply of strong mints to kill the nasty taste left in your mouth, and a nose peg.

An altogether less disgusting way of obtaining horse hair is to buy it ready cut and cleaned. I buy hanks of clean horse hair for tails and have my manes made up for me specially by a wigmaker (wigs for toys, that is). The hair comes in black or grey – the grey being a finer quality and more appropriate perhaps for a dapple grey horse.

The tails are made up as follows. The end of a bunch of hair is dipped in glue and wrapped round a short piece of dowel or a fibre wallplug, held together with some small elastic bands. The tail hole is enlarged until the tail will fit snugly and then, after daubing the hole with glue, is shoved in and a two inch nail driven in through the plug. If it still seems a bit loose a wooden wedge can be driven in under the tail. A short length of leather strapping can be wrapped round the base of the tail and lead back over the horse's rump to the back of the saddle block.

The manes I use consist of long lengths of horse hair seamed down the middle. The mane is wedged into the slot cut into the horse's neck with a thin leather strip and nailed in place. The hair is then pulled over to one side and a second leather strip nailed in place on top. In this way the mane is very securely fixed and will resist much tugging at it. It is worth avoiding manes which are only glued at the hair ends because these do tend to come adrift after a while, and kids will be very rough with them. On old horses the mane and tail is often reduced to the appearance of a tatty toothbrush.

Finally, the chest strap, tail strap and edges of the saddle and saddlecloth are finished off with brass nails driven in at intervals of one to two inches all round. Brass dome headed nails come in various sizes and the half inch ones are also available with a decorative or "daisy" head which I put in at various places for added effect. A colourful rosette is nailed in at the point where the chest straps meet.

The horse is now complete and can be mounted on its stand or bow rockers ready to be ridden.

The continuing fascination in building rocking-horses lies, for me, in the wide range of activities involved. There is straight-forward joinery in making the stands and assembling the horse; there is a bit of turnery and

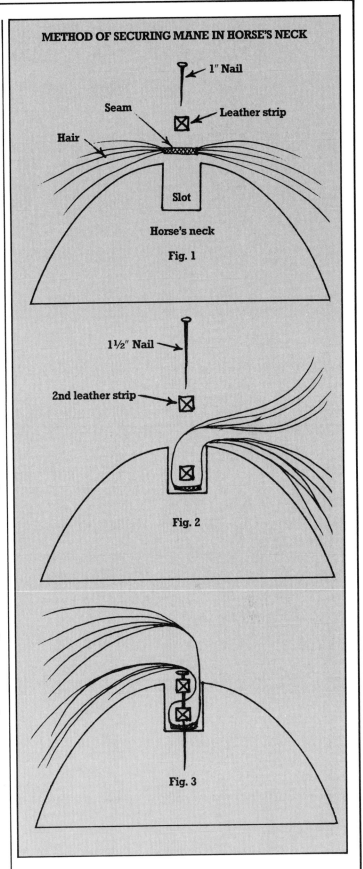

METHOD OF SECURING MANE IN HORSE'S NECK

1″ Nail

Seam

Leather strip

Hair

Slot

Horse's neck

Fig. 1

1½″ Nail

2nd leather strip

Fig. 2

Fig. 3

some interesting carving in the intricate details of the head and the broad curves of the body; there is painting skill; there is a bit of blacksmithing in forging the metal parts; and there is the leatherwork, including tanning and dyeing (I dye some of my leather to the customer's specific requirements).

There is a great sense of satisfaction in conducting the whole process from a pile of dirty timber to a finished rocking-horse, which one hopes, will give enduring delight and pleasure to generations of children.

Barley twist legs

Tools used
3′ Boxwood folding rule
6″ Trysquare
Marking gauge
Jack plane
Smoothing plane
Tenon saw
½″ Firmer chisel
⅜″ Firmer gouge
Half round rasp

Although barley twist legs are usually bought ready machined there are occasions, particularly in repair work, where it is necessary to cut one by hand. A finished table leg is shown in Fig. 1.

Having planed the legs up square, the first operation is to turn the two necks at each end of the spiral making sure that the necks are cut to the same depth as the twists will be (Fig. 2). The twist ends on the opposite side of the leg to which it begins, so that when setting out a leg it is necessary to allow not for a given number of twists, but so many twists and a half. In the example in Fig. 1 the neck of the twist between A and B is ¾× (18mm) wide and there are four and a half twists.

First Stage

The first stage in setting out is to draw four equidistant lines along the length of the cylinder. The number of twists (4½) is multiplied by 4 and the length of the cylinder is equally divided by the result (18). Pencil lines are drawn round the cylinder to join up these points as shown in Fig. 3. The edge of a piece of thin card is now trimmed perfectly straight so that it can be used as a flexible straight edge. By placing the straight edge at A and winding round the cylinder it is possible to draw a line diagonally through the intersections to arrive at B. Two additional lines are drawn parallel and ⅜″ (9mm) on either side of the first line to complete the marking out of a left-handed spiral.

It is usual practice to cut twists in pairs so that a table would have two left-handed spirals and two right-handed. A right-handed twist is marked by starting at point A but wrapping the straight edge round the cylinder in the opposite direction.

Cutting

To cut the twist to an even depth throughout its length a tenon saw is used with a depth gauge secured on either side of the blade (Fig. 4). If the depth of the twist is to be 1 in. (25mm) then the gauge is set ¾ in. (18mm) from the points of the saw teeth.

With the leg held between the lathe centres and slowly rotated by hand, the twists are now sawn. The waste between the saw kerfs is chiselled out, after which the neck of the twist is rounded with a gouge. The twists are now rounded by means of a chisel after which a fine cut half-round file smooths away the chisel marks. Strips of glasspaper complete the final smoothing of the twists. Cutting barley-twists in this manner is slow

work and is only undertaken where machine tools cannot be used e.g. when an unusual twist has to be reproduced for repair work. Where it is decided to make barley-twists, possibly because they cannot be obtained in the wood required, it may be possible to cut them with the aid of a suitably shaped cutter in a high speed router.

Router

The leg is planed square and then turned as in Fig. 2. It is then mounted between the centres of a Router Crafter which enables the leg to be rotated while the router traverses that part of the leg on which the twists are to be cut. A hand wheel at the end of the Crafter is rotated to wind an endless cord from one end of the machine to the other. If the router is detached from the upper cord and fastened to the lower, a twist of opposite hand will be formed.

To achieve a good finish it is necessary to use a sharp cutter and take only light cuts.

The disadvantage of the Crafter is that the pitch of the twist is fixed, it cannot be varied at will.

Further information on the Crafter may be obtained from John Mercer, Sales Administrator, Hagemeyer (London) Ltd., 17-19 Redcross Way, SW1 1TB.

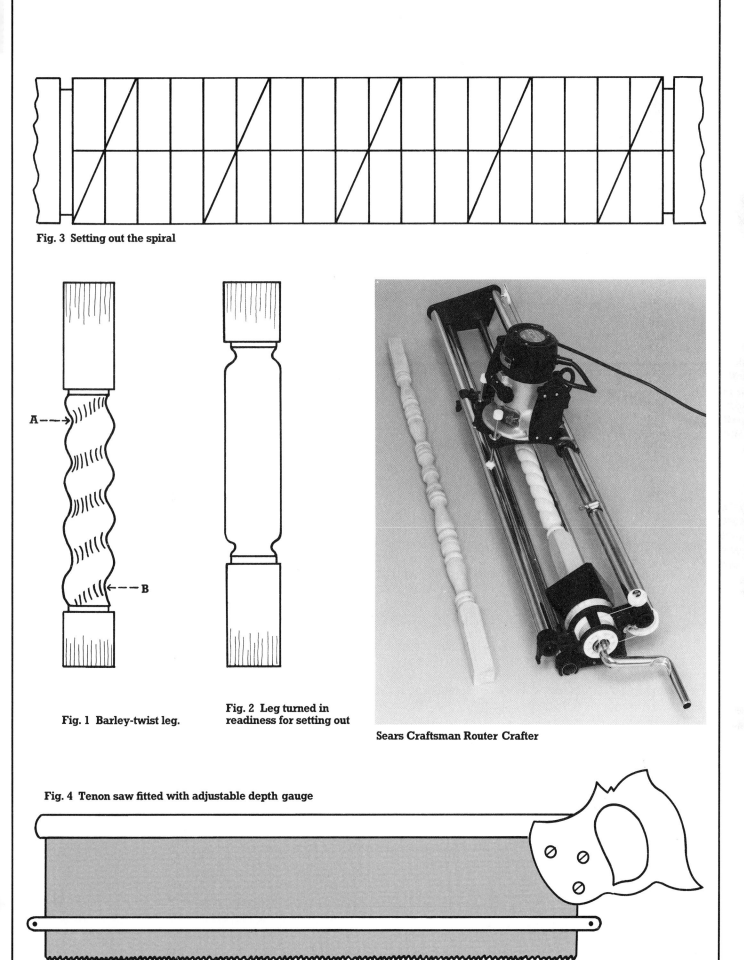

Fig. 3 Setting out the spiral

Fig. 1 Barley-twist leg.

Fig. 2 Leg turned in readiness for setting out

Sears Craftsman Router Crafter

Fig. 4 Tenon saw fitted with adjustable depth gauge

17th century oak cradle

Tools used
Vernier Caliper
Engineer's 4″ Tri Square
Ruler graduated in 12ths
Craft knives
Scalpels
Rip saw, tenon and cross cut saw
Chisel and Gouges
Turning tools, miniature and full size
Unimat 3
Universal fretsaw
K5 Combination machine
Belt sander
Jeweller's saw, needle files, riffles
ML8 lathe
Dremel drill A Press
Mitre box and back saw
British ceramic kiln

Cradles of the 17th century were invariably made from native woods such as oak, beech, elm etc., and were substantial items of furniture. Hoods were often hinged or completely detachable to allow easy access to moving the baby. The body of the cradle was deep to allow a substantial amount of bedding for comfort and also to keep the baby out of the reach of possible attack by mice or rats during the night. Some of these cradles had refinements which included pegs fitted inside and outside the body on which cloth would be suspended. The inside pegs would suspend the bedding and the outside pegs used for a protective cover to be looped across the cradle. The hood itself could be covered with velvet and have a curtain attached to keep the light from the baby's face.

Construction Details
This miniature requires only minimal amounts of wood. The four main corner posts are 3/16 in. square, as are the two hood posts. Rails and fielded panels are made from 3 mm (⅛ in.) thick wood. Rockers detachable hood and cradle bottom are made in 1½ mm. (1/16 in.) thick wood.

There are no complicated joints involved except for a slot or bridle joint where the bottom end of the posts fit over the rockers. All other joints are straightforward butt joints. The tops of all the posts, as shown, are turned to a small bead and ball, and this decorative feature can equally well be carved by hand.

The head and the foot end are made as two assemblies which are joined by the two side assemblies. The hood is treated as a separate assembly, leaving only the rockers and cradle bottom to be added.

Prepare sufficient material to the drawing dimensions for the two side assemblies. Notice that the hood posts are leaved to finish 3 mm (⅛ in.) thick (the thickness of the top side rail). Trial dry fit the details of each side and make any adjustments necessary to ensure both sides assemble squarely and are of identical length, remembering that the sides assemble symmetrically opposite.

Whilst the plan shows fielded panels, you can in fact incorporate in these panels a design of your own choosing to make the piece unique.

On a flat surface and against a straight edge, glue the ends of the two fielded panels to the muntin. When dry, glue the top and bottom rails in position. Leave to dry. Finally, glue the small fielded panel, hood rail and hood post in position on the end of the top rail. The side assemblies are now complete. Proceed to cut out details for front end assembly and foot end assembly, remembering that the posts each have a slot or bridle joint cut in them to accent the rockers.

Glue top and bottom rails to the fielded panels against a straight edge. Glue the corner posts on either end, leaving a gap of 6 mm (¼ in.) between the bottom rail and the bottom of the posts. Glue the assembled sides to the assembled ends. Leave to dry.

Prepare the details for the detachable hood to dimensions shown. Check that the hood rear and hood arch fit easily between their respective posts.

The top ends of the hood sides are bevelled to line up with the top edges of the arch and hood rear. Check the fit of the hood sides between the head posts and the hood posts to ensure an easy fit, and then glue the hood sides, the hood arch and the hood rear together. When dry, glue the hood top in position.

Prepare the two rockers to the profiles shown. Glue in position in the slots in the bottom of the posts. Prepare the cradle bottom to dimensions shown (from random widths if necessary) and glue in position inside of the assembly.

Finishing
It is suggested the finish be traditional linseed oil, followed by wax polishing.

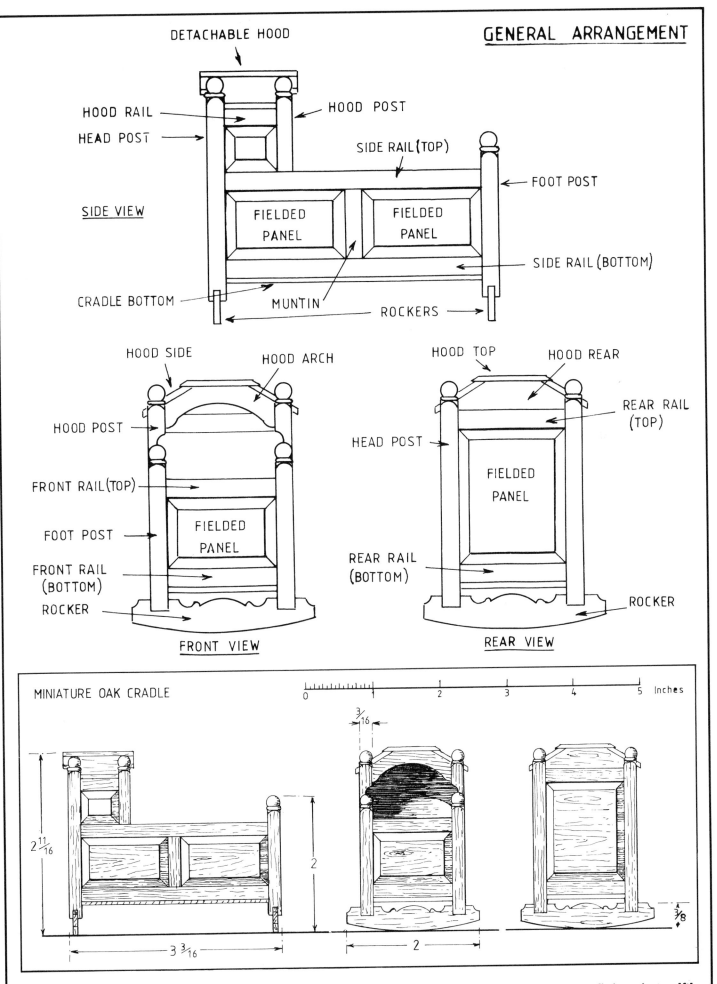

DETACHABLE HOOD

HOOD RAIL

HEAD POST

HOOD POST

SIDE RAIL (TOP)

SIDE VIEW

FOOT POST

FIELDED PANEL

FIELDED PANEL

SIDE RAIL (BOTTOM)

CRADLE BOTTOM

MUNTIN

ROCKERS

HOOD SIDE

HOOD ARCH

HOOD POST

FRONT RAIL (TOP)

FOOT POST

FIELDED PANEL

FRONT RAIL (BOTTOM)

ROCKER

FRONT VIEW

HOOD TOP

HOOD REAR

HEAD POST

REAR RAIL (TOP)

FIELDED PANEL

REAR RAIL (BOTTOM)

ROCKER

REAR VIEW

MINIATURE OAK CRADLE

0   1   2   3   4   5 Inches

$\frac{3}{16}$

$2\frac{11}{16}$

2

$3\frac{3}{16}$

2

$\frac{3}{8}$

All dimensions in inches
Grain direction indicated thus ←→

Photograph by Keith Price courtesy of Northampton Chronicle & Echo.

18th century style Miniature brass fittings in twelfth scale can be obtained from: Margaret Varney (Miniatures) 10 Hardays Lane, West Haddon, Northampton NN6 7AW.

FRONT END ASSEMBLY WITH DETAILS

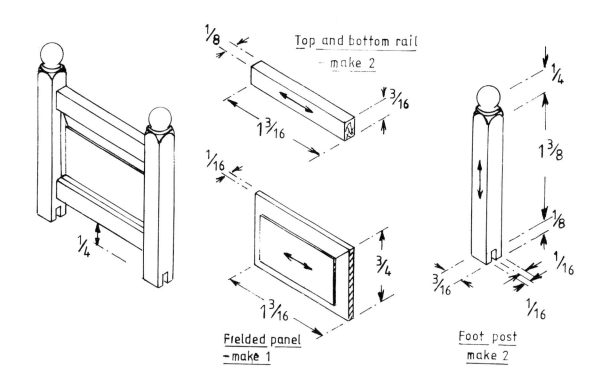

Top and bottom rail
— make 2

1/8

1³/₁₆

3/16

Fielded panel
—make 1

1/16

1³/₁₆

3/4

Foot post
make 2

1/4

1³/8

1/8

1/16

3/16

1/16

1/4

HEAD END ASSEMBLY WITH DETAILS

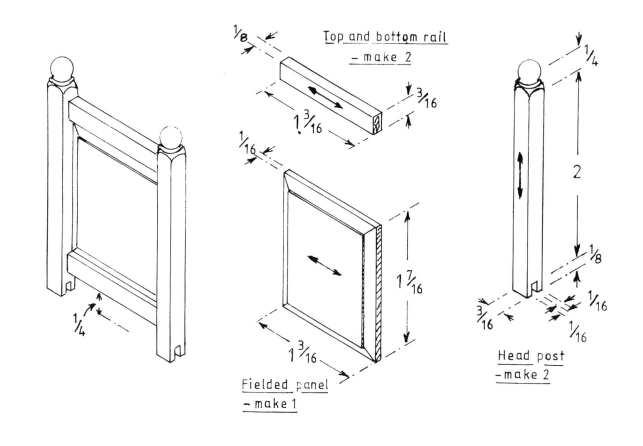

Top and bottom rail
— make 2

1/8

1³/₁₆

3/16

Fielded panel
— make 1

1/16

1³/₁₆

1⁷/₁₆

Head post
— make 2

1/4

2

1/8

3/16

1/16

1/16

1/4

SIDE ASSEMBLY WITH DETAILS

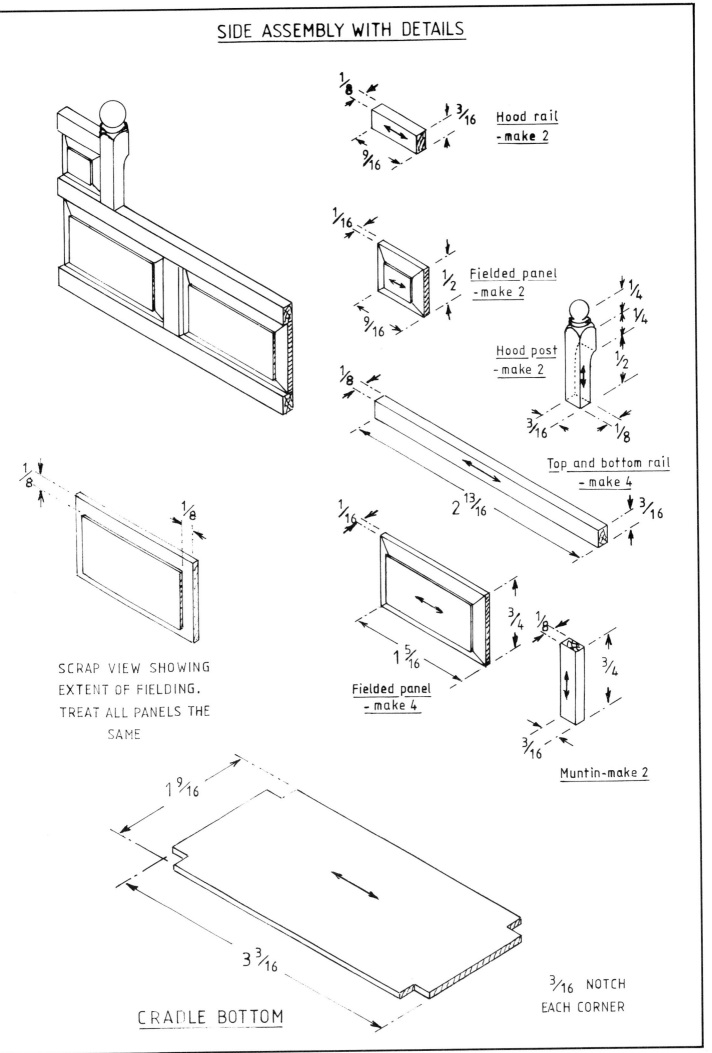

Hood rail
-make 2

Fielded panel
-make 2

Hood post
-make 2

Top and bottom rail
- make 4

Fielded panel
- make 4

Muntin-make 2

SCRAP VIEW SHOWING
EXTENT OF FIELDING.
TREAT ALL PANELS THE
SAME

CRADLE BOTTOM

$^3/_{16}$ NOTCH
EACH CORNER

HOOD ASSEMBLY WITH DETAILS

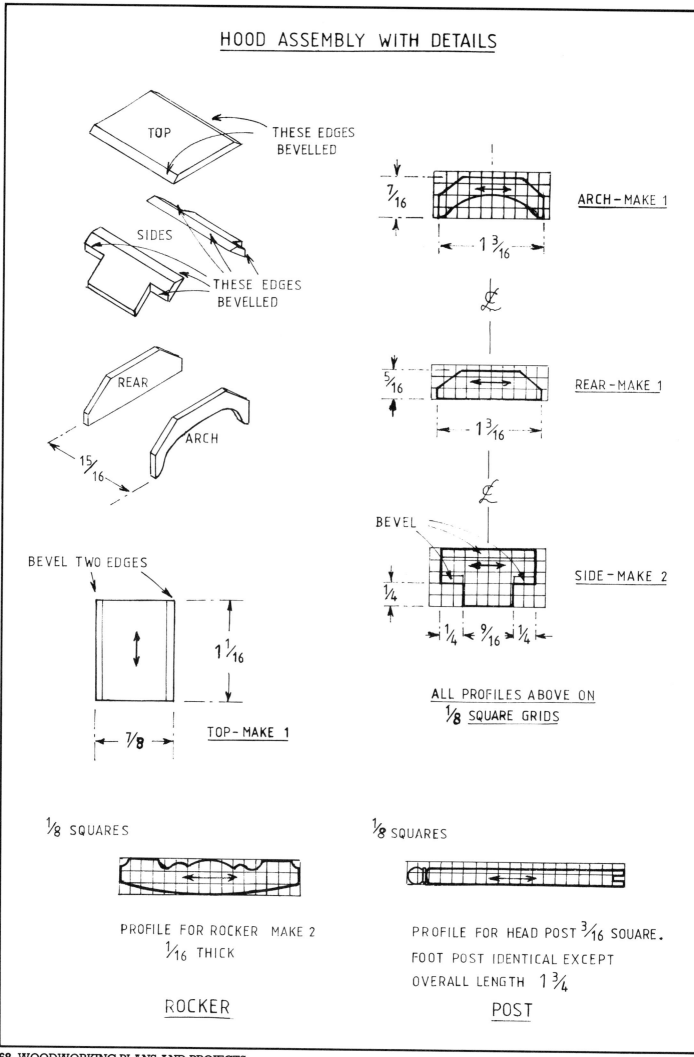

TOP

THESE EDGES BEVELLED

SIDES

THESE EDGES BEVELLED

REAR

ARCH

15/16

BEVEL TWO EDGES

1 1/16

7/8

TOP-MAKE 1

7/16

1 3/16

ARCH—MAKE 1

℄

5/16

1 3/16

REAR—MAKE 1

℄

BEVEL

1/4

1/4   9/16   1/4

SIDE—MAKE 2

ALL PROFILES ABOVE ON 1/8 SQUARE GRIDS

1/8 SQUARES

PROFILE FOR ROCKER MAKE 2
1/16 THICK

ROCKER

1/8 SQUARES

PROFILE FOR HEAD POST 3/16 SQUARE.
FOOT POST IDENTICAL EXCEPT
OVERALL LENGTH 1 3/4

POST

A marble-topped coffee table

Tools used
Early shoulder plane circa 1920 by Tomkinson.
Brass-backed tenon saw (Hibernia)
Wood mallet
Marking gauge (Rosewood)
Wood chisel
2 Mortice chisels

Materials
1″ thick mahogany for trestle legs, etc.
1″ depth hockey-shaped mahogany moulding for
  surrounding marble slab.
½″ Plywood for marble support.
3 grades glasspaper.
Fine grade steel wool.
Wood stain.
Beeswax polish.
1″ approx. Brass screws.

It is a long way from a Moroccan 'souk' to a craft workshop nestling in the shadow of St. Albans Abbey, Hertfordshire. But here on the workbench before me lay a slab of polished marble, reddish brown in colour, studded with fossils, that our customer had carried all the way back under his arm from a business trip. It weighed approximately 20 lbs and measured 28 inches in length by 16 inches in width, and a depth of 1¼ inches. "Could we make something out of it?" he asked. Now we specialize in hand-made picture frames and medal cases, but we always enjoy the challenge of a one-off job. "Leave it with us and we will think about it", we promised, and off he went happy in the knowledge that something would result from his effort.

I had already decided in my mind what to make but I asked my partner, Dena Bryant, who copes with the restoration work and French-polishing, what she thought. "A coffee table, fairly low and sturdy", she replied. That was exactly what I had in mind. The choice of wood to use was easy – mahogany came to mind at once. Partly because our medal cases are made of mahogany, so there is always plenty of that wood in the workshop, but also because of the colouring of the marble. Everything has to tone, and a lighter wood would not have suited the rich colouring. Dark oak would have been too sombre and not set off the marble so well.

The weight was the chief problem. The legs would have to be substantial to take that weight, but should they be short and tapering, or square cut and sturdy? The idea of both did not appeal to us. It should be something elegant and yet graceful, combined with strength. Thinking of the cottage setting where it would ultimately rest, I suddenly had an inspiration. No legs at all, it would have trestle ends!

The trestles would be pinned through with wooden wedges, with a strong stretcher running across to add strength and stability. To make doubly sure that it would not tip over, thick pieces of mahogany would be screwed to the base of each trestle to weigh it down.

The marble slab would be enclosed in a hockey-stick shaped mahogany moulding 2½ inches deep, similar to the top of one of our medal cases. The marble would be dropped in from the top, and would be held securely in position by the shape of the moulding, a piece of strong plywood being used as a base for it.

Everything is hand done in our workshop, in the traditional way, but we needed to take our sheet of mahogany to the mill where it was machined to a thickness of 1″ before we started work.

Trestle Legs
Our neighbour who helps out on special jobs, was called in. "Chris" was given the job of designing the trestle legs. Not too curvy, strong yet graceful, we specified. The shape was drawn out on squared paper to suit the measurements of the slab. We decided the height would be 24 inches and the width of the marble was 16 inches, which determined the size of the trestles.

The template was then cut out and laid on the slab of mahogany which was carefully cut by hand using a fretsaw. Two slots were marked, one on each trestle, large enough to take the head of the stretcher. A hand drill was used to drill the width of the hole required, then a chisel to square it off.

Stretcher wedges were cut to suit. The stretchers have to fit exactly, so care must be taken when cutting out and fitting the heads. Holes were made each end of the stretcher in the same way, to make a slot for the wedges. The two end pieces for the trestle legs were cut from an oddment of mahogany to give the bases stability. Another two were cut for the top of the trestles. Three screw holes were drilled in the base pieces to take 2½ inch brass screws, whilst the top pieces had eight screw holes drilled in each, one in the centre of each end and three each side along the length.

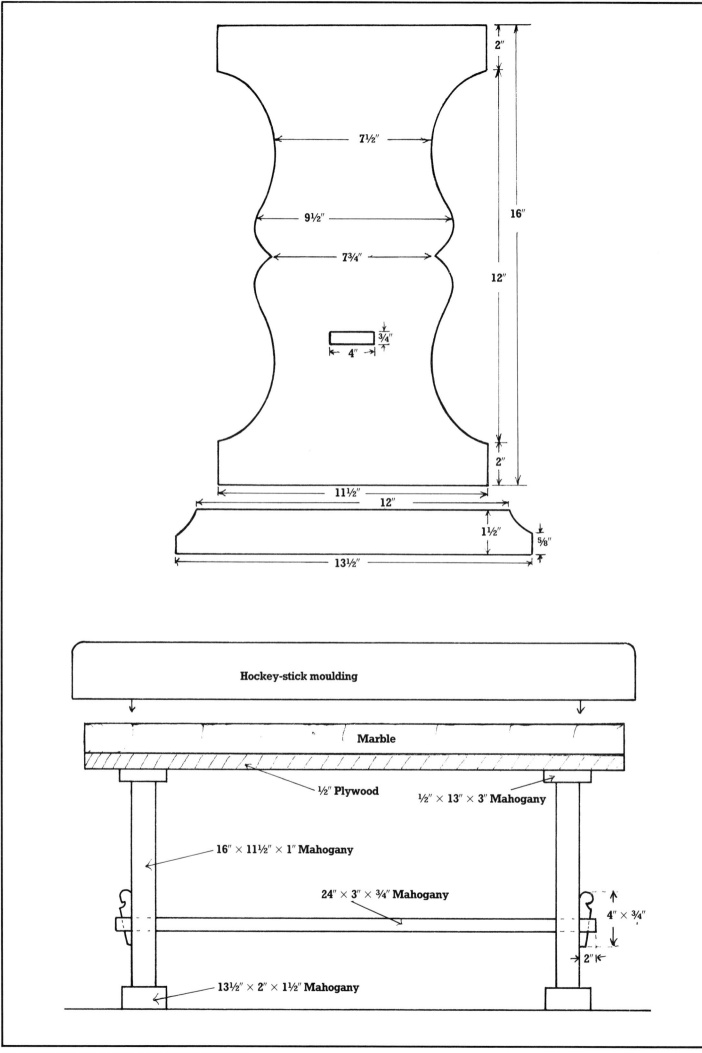

2″

7½″

16″

9½″

12″

7¾″

¾″

4″

2″

11½″

12″

1½″

⅝″

13½″

Hockey-stick moulding

Marble

½″ Plywood

½″ × 13″ × 3″ Mahogany

16″ × 11½″ × 1″ Mahogany

24″ × 3″ × ¾″ Mahogany

4″ × ¾″

2″

13½″ × 2″ × 1½″ Mahogany

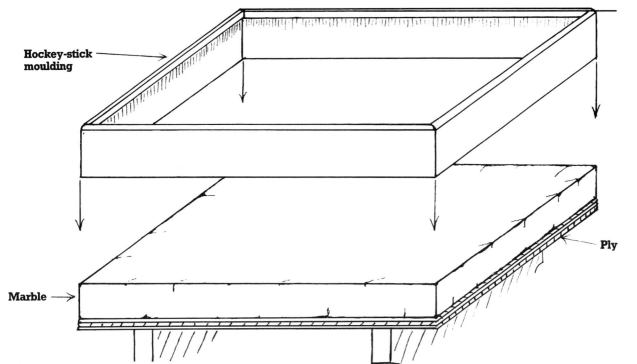

Fig. 1 How the top section is dropped over the marble.

When all the cutting had been done, and the pieces laid out on the bench (Photo. 1.) everything was given a very thorough sanding, starting with a coarse grade, working through medium and fine grade and finally ending up with a rub down with the finest grade steel wool, so that everything was smooth as silk. We were not using any glue in this table, so that it could be taken apart and taken back to Morocco if necessary.

A piece of plywood, ½ inch thick, was cut the exact size of the marble top. This would act as a seating for the marble top, a 'frame' was made of the hockey-stick shaped mahogany moulding, 2½ inches deep. The corners were cut on the mitreing machine, but a satisfactory job could be done usisng a 45 degree mitre block and hand tenon saw. A cabinet maker would no doubt use a butterfly or dovetail joint. The frame was then pinned and glued with Evostick resin glue for extra strength. This was the only part permanently fixed, as no one would want the task of re-doing the corners! The frame was again carefully sanded using three grades of glasspaper and being very careful to keep the corners true. When absolutely smooth, the frame was dusted off, ready for staining. (Photo 2. plus Fig. 1 and 2).

Stain

We decided to use Indian Rosewood stain from Colron, the Ronseal manufacturers, and easily obtainable from D.I.Y. stores. Peruvian mahogany made by the same firm would be an acceptable shade. All the work was dusted off, and several coats were applied by brush, finishing off with a rub with a soft rag, until the required depth of colour was obtained. After it had dried, a final light rub with fine glasspaper ensured that the grain had not been 'raised' with the stain. Each item was then lightly brushed over with a thin coat of shellac to seal the grain and when hard, again lightly rubbed over. A second coat was treated in the same way. Finally each piece was thoroughly waxed with beeswax polish and rubbed until gleaming, with soft dusters. (Photo. 3.)

Assembly

Next, the screws were driven home into the base plates on the trestles. The stretcher and wedges were

assembled. Wedges were placed in position but not tightened at this stage. (Photo. 4; another view to show ends Photo. 5.) The plywood top was attached to the top plates by turning the whole table upside down on the bench with the ply resting in the correct position underneath. Screws were placed, eight on each plate, one at each end and three along each side, to make a very firm job and support the marble.

Once the ply was in position, we turned it back again so that the table stood upright, and tightened the wedges by tapping with a mallet. The marble was then laid on top, right way up, level all sides with the plywood support. (Photo 6.) The outer frame made of the hockey-stick moulding was dropped over the top like a picture in a frame. This was made to be an exact fit over the marble and the plywood base, to leave half an inch covering the plywood. (Photo. 7.)

Small wooden blocks of scrap mahogany were cut and stained, ½ inch square, and screwed into the side of the frame and into the plywood back. This was to eliminate unsightly screws and caps.

And that completed the table. Everything was very simple, easily made, using tools available to any handyman. I have not given plans in this article, but the photographs should give all the information needed. The main thing is to measure up your prospective top – whether it be marble, ceramic tiles, plate glass, or whatever – make sure all is in proportion, and finish everything off well.

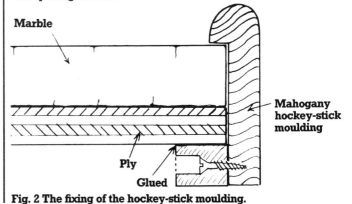

Fig. 2 The fixing of the hockey-stick moulding.

An apothecary's box

Materials used

If no off-cuts available you will need:

4 ft. length of Brazilian mahogany ⅜ in. thick × 6 in. wide for box exterior.

2 pieces of plywood 12 in. × 9½ in. to make the base.

12 ft. length 3/16 in. thick 2½ in. wide to make the small boxes.

Plus

Approximately 1 yard velvet, brocade, baize, etc. to line sides, drawer and padded interior of box. Oddments will do.

A piece of foam rubber, padding or wadding 12 in. × 9 in.

9 brass drawer knobs, ½ in. size.

3 brass drawer knobs, ¼ in. size.

1 small brass jewel box lock and key.

1 small piece mother-of-pearl (optional).

1 in. veneer pins.

"Evo-stick" Resin W Wood Glue.

Pair of 2 in. brass hinges. (Piano hinges are best if obtainable.)

½ yard strong Petersham ribbon to tone with material.

Abrasive, coarse, fine and medium.

Fine steel wool Grade 000.

Springs out of a couple of old ball point pens, plus small metal bar and clip as shown in drawing, to fix secret drawer.

Wood stain, to tone.

Wood sealer (optional).

Beeswax polish.

When a lady in long flowing robes, carrying a basket of strange-smelling herbs, climbed up the old wooden stairs to the workshop the other day, I was rather apprehensive. Was she a gypsy, selling her wares, or was she a w——? No, a quick glance out of the window reassured me that she had not parked her broomstick on the yellow line.

She wanted a box made. A very special box to take her herbs. This lady turned out to be a very well-known herbalist, who travelled a great deal about the country giving talks and demonstrating the use of herbs to cure modern ills in the age-old way.

Warming to this request, I decided to make a box similar to those used by the apothecaries of old. A box she could be proud of, made in the traditional way, with all the skill and craftsmanship I was capable of. But cost? As low as possible. The herbalist departed, confident that I would come up with something special, and I sat down and sketched out a few ideas.

To save cost, the box would be made entirely from off-cuts of wood from the workshop. We always have plenty of small pieces of Brazilian mahogany to use up. It would consist of an exterior hinged cabinet with lid. The lid would lift up to reveal interior boxes, all fitting neatly round a larger central box. All the lids would fit

tight flush, and have small brass knobs to lift them by. The interior of the lid would be padded out and finished with blue velvet, and I would add 'hinges' of matching blue Petersham ribbon to hold the lid open, rather in the manner of a Victorian workbox. The customer would be able to put a good selection of herbs in the air-tight boxes, and for a finishing touch. I would add a 'secret' drawer which could be opened only by releasing a hidden spring. With the tightly fitting interior boxes and the padded lid, the whole box could be taken anywhere in the world without danger of the contents falling out. A lock and key would give added security.

To Make the Main Box

The box is cut out in one whole piece to start with, then cut to form the base and lid later.

Cut out two pieces of wood measuring 12″ × 6″ × ⅜″ thick, and two pieces measuring 9½″ × 6″ × ⅜″ thick. Mitre the corners. Glue with Evostick Resin 'W' and pin with 1″ veneer pins for added strength. Allow to harden. When thoroughly hard and set, scribe down 1″ deep from the top all round, then saw accurately to the mark to make a lid, using a tenon saw. Next, mark the front base, scribed in the same way, to make the drawer. Mark 1″ up from the base, turn the box upside down, and cut down the mitre at the corner from the base, then cut along the line in the front only. You can use the tenon saw again, or if you have one a very fine fretsaw and blade would be easier. Cut a piece of plywood 12″ × 9″ to fit the base, and glue into position.

The plinth base is made of four pieces of mahogany, mitred at 45° in the corners, and fitted and glued together. Allow the base to overlap half an inch all round to give the plinth effect. Screw the base to the underside of the box.

The lid of the box is assembled from cuttings to form a pattern. See photo. (1).

Two brass hinges 2″ in size are countersunk into the appropriate places at the back of the box lid and base.

The drawer is assembled and made as shown in *diagram 1 with photograph.*

To finish the outer part of the box, chamfer the lid with abrasive to take the edge off all round. Note from photo. 1. how the corners are kept true, and the same depth maintained all round. Use from coarse through to very fine abrasive, by hand. This will take a great deal of time and effort but the success of the whole box depends on the hand finishing. Go over the whole box and plinth until absolutely satin smooth, then give a final rub-over with finest grade steel wool.

Remove any dust, and stain with Indian Rosewood or Peruvian Mahogany stain if you are using mahogany wood. When sufficient colour has been obtained, allow to dry. The next day, seal and polish.

To Make the Small Boxes

Measure up the available space inside the large box, and decide how many boxes you are going to have. I made twelve in mine. (Photos. 2 and 3).

Calculate the sizes and cut out each individual box from the 12 ft. length of 3/16 in. mahogany, or any suitable off-cuts. The small boxes are made in the same

Photo. 1 Lid of the box. Note how the corners are kept true.

Photo. 2 Twelve boxes and a drawer.

Photo. 3

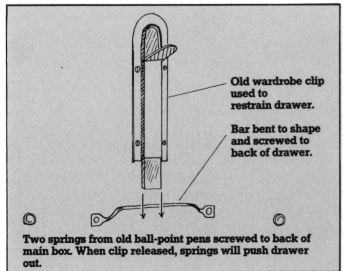

Old wardrobe clip used to restrain drawer.

Bar bent to shape and screwed to back of drawer.

Two springs from old ball-point pens screwed to back of main box. When clip released, springs will push drawer out.

way as the large box, with mitred corners, and all the same width. They are glued with Evostick Resin 'W', then held together with cellotape or elastic bands to dry. No pins are used in the small boxes. This is so that no pins will catch when the boxes are fitted tightly together.

The boxes are then very well papered until they will all slide in gently, yet be a tight fit. Bottoms are cut to the centre and glued in position. Cut a 'U' shaped portion from the centre back of the small box in front of the spring so that the mechanism will operate freely. The lid of the larger, centre box consists of oddments mitred and fitted into a pattern. (See photo. 3). Pieces of plywood are cut to fit inside the small boxes, and the mahogany lid fitted on top to overlap the ply, to be flush with the interior. Chamfer the lids to make a rounded edge, to give a 'cushion' effect. Stain and polish in the same way as the large box. Screw in the brass knobs in the centre of each lid, using ½ in. ones on the 9 larger boxes and ¼ in. on the remaining three.

Lining and Padding

Having finished the main woodwork and staining of the box the final touches are added by lining the interior of the large box, and the secret drawer, and by padding the lid.

Measure the depth and length of the interior, and cut a piece of velvet, brocade, or baize to fit. Glue into position. If there are any raw edges on your material, you must allow in addition ¼ in. to turn down to conceal them. Line the drawer in the same way.

To pad the lid, cut a piece of foam rubber, or whatever you are using, to the exact size of the interior of the lid. Press it down on to the brass knobs on the boxes, so that you have an impression. With a sharp knife or scalpel, cut small circles out of the padding to correspond with the impression of the knobs. This is to make a really tight fit on to the tops of the boxes so that they will not move in transport. Having carefully noted their position, glue a piece of velvet or brocade etc. to cover the entire top and sides of the padding. When dry, glue the entire pad into the lid interior, pressing down well, and making sure you have the little cut out portions for the knobs, now hidden by the velvet, in exact position to close down over them.

To Make the Ribbon Hinges

Try out the box first. Open the lid to the upright position and measure the distance of the angle formed by the box and lid. It may vary according to your individual work. I used two lengths of ½ in. Petersham 9 in. long. Cut the ribbon to size, slanting each edge by cutting off a portion. Then turn a small piece under each end to prevent fraying. Glue as shown in photo. 3.

Lock and Key

Take the small jeweller's lock and key, and mark the centre of the box top and bottom front. Look at the box to see the best position for the lock. Then insert in the usual way, cutting the wood from the back to fit exactly round the lock. Do the upper lid in the same way. As an added refinement, I like to use a mother-of-pearl inlay round the key hole. Cut a suitable pattern, such as a hexagonal, out of the mother-of-pearl. Mark the surround of the lock, and cut away a thin layer of wood the exact shape and size of the inlay. Glue the inlay into position.

Give a final polish and rub over with a soft duster. You should then have a box any apothecary would be proud of!

Pistol case

Introduction

About two years ago when I took up competitive target pistol shooting, I found I needed a suitable case to carry not only my pistol but also the additional small items necessary at a competition. Thinking of the old tradition of pistols being kept in wood cases I decided to design and make a case suitable to my own requirements.

Although the sizes given are appropriate for this project, there is of course no reason why they cannot be modified to enable cases and boxes to be produced for other purposes.

I am sure most people will be aware, but it is still probably worth mentioning, that wood cases and boxes are not made in two pieces but as one, being sawn into the two halves that form the lid and base after the sides, top and bottom have all been glued together.

The reason is to ensure that the top and bottom will be a perfect match when the hinges and catches are fitted.

The case (Photos 1 & 2) is made in mahogany with block foam inside cut to house the various objects, there is also a false hinged panel incorporated in the lid, this is to hold targets, gun mat, entry forms etc.

Construction

My need for the case was urgent and therefore I sought quick methods to produce a functional as well as

Photo. 1

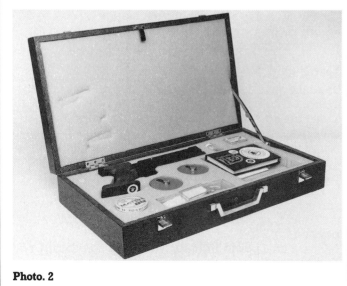

Photo. 2

aesthetically acceptable item. I decided to make the basic case with the assistance of limited machinery, namely a combined Barrus drill stand and Shapercraft table with a Ceka-Zenses heavy duty mill and a combi-cutter used in an electric drill mounted in the drill stand. By this method I was able to produce mitred corner joints to the case without having to resort to secret mitre dovetails (a very time consuming operation).

Photo. 3

Work commenced by cutting the mitres at each end of the four sides. This was accomplished by mounting them in a jig (Photo 3) – already existing from a previous project – and passing them in turn along the fence of the drill stand table to be cut by the heavy duty mill. One should remember not to take off too much at the first pass; three or more are required to obtain an acceptable finish.

When all the mitres have been cut, the mill is re-placed by the combi-cutter and the height of the drill adjusted so that the stopped grooves in the mitres can be cut to accommodate the loose tongues.

The next task is to produce grooves on the inside faces of the four sides. These grooves are to take the top and bottom and are formed by again using the Shapercraft table, but on this occasion a Barrus HSS router bit is used. For this operation the case sides are rested flat on the table. The drill containing the router bit is then lowered into the timber, the amount of penetration being controlled by a depth stop on the drill stand column, the timber is then passed along the table to allow the cutter to produce a groove. This procedure is followed until all four sides have had two grooves cut into them. To complete the joint between the top and the sides a rebate is produced on the four edges of the top, this operation is duplicated for the jointing of the bottom. The case should now be cleaned up and the whole glued together in one operation.

Cutting the Case Open

When the glue is dry, with the use of a marking gauge, a line is scribed around the sides of the case 1⅝ in. from the top edge. The case is then cut in half. I found this was best achieved by using a backless tenon saw. (*A fine bladed saw or a thin circular saw might also be used. – Ed.*) When the case is in two pieces the sawn edges should be cleaned up with a plane, making sure the two halves fit together without any gaps.

Lid – False Panel (See photo. 4)

A 1 in. × ⅜ in. mahogany block is cut and glued along the inside of the lid against the opening edge and ⅜ in. square blocks along the two sides; these form the support for the false panel when in its closed position. The two hinges used on the false panel are cut from a blank piece of brass piano hinge. The required holes should be drilled as necessary, bearing in mind that screws are only used to fix the panel to the case, the panel itself being secured to the hinge with pop rivets.

When the false panel has been fitted, an appropriate size hole is drilled in the centre of the 1 in. × ⅜ in. block, into this is inserted a small round magnetic catch. On the inside face of the panel and opposite the magnetic catch a leather tag is fixed with a small steel countersunk screw in such a position as to permit the screw head to engage the magnet. This will keep the panel closed but will also allow it to be pulled forward by means of the tag. Once the fitting of the panel is complete the 2 in. brass butt hinges can be cut and fitted to the main case, along with the brass catches and the stay. My case was also fitted with a box lock for added security.

As I stated at the beginning, throughout this project I have looked for quick methods of production, therefore having decided to enhance the appearance of the case with a form of inlay, I thought I would try an experiment. What might appear from the photograph to be a traditional satinwood or boxwood inlay is in fact white "Brummer" stopping. I produced, with the aid of a scratch stock, two 1/16 in. square grooves in the top and one ⅛ in. × 1/16 in. deep groove in the bottom, as shown on the working drawing. This was followed by the carving of an initial in the centre of the lid. Sufficient white stopping, with a little water added to turn it into a smooth paste, was then applied to the grooves and the initial, taking care not to spread the filler too far beyond their edges. Once the filler was dry the top and bottom were carefully glass papered using a very fine paper in a power sander, a final finishing being carried out by hand using a cork block and flour grade paper.

Handle and Feet

Although the design includes the handle and feet, my skills do not extend to producing this type of hardware in solid brass. I was however fortunate enough to have a friend in engineering who produced them for me.

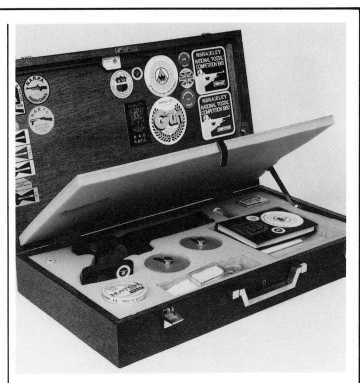

Photo. 4

Finish

On completion of final cleaning up, apply 3-4 coats of a clear polyurethane satin finish lacquer, each coat being allowed to cure and then lightly glass papered using flour grade paper, before applying the next. After the final coat cut the surface back by rubbing lightly in the direction of the grain with 000 steel wool dipped in soft white wax, then buff with soft duster to obtain an extra smooth satin finish.

Fitting the Foam

The foam is fitted in three pieces. Commence by cutting the ½ in. thick piece to size, and glue to the false panel in the lid, then cut the two 1 in. thick pieces and push them into the bottom section of the base.

Having decided the postion the various items will occupy in the case, make and cut a cardboard template with overall dimensions the same as the internal sizes of the case. Place the template in the case on top of the foam and draw round the shapes transfering them to the foam. A fibre tipped pen is ideal for this task.

All that remains is to cut the profiles out of the top piece of foam, this can be accomplished with the judicious use of a power jigsaw containing a knife blade. Once all the shapes have been cut apply glue to the underside of the foam and replace in the case.

Cutting List

All measurements given are finished sizes but include allowances for joints etc.

Description	No. Reqd.	L × W × Th. (inches)			L × W × Th. (millimetres)		
MAHOGANY							
Sides	2	22	4½	½	558	114	013
Ends	2	12	4½	½	305	114	013
Top & bottom	2	22	12	½	558	305	013
False panel	1	21	11¼	⁵/₃₂	533	286	004
FOAM							
For false panel	1	21	11¼	½	533	286	013
For bottom section	2	21	11¼	1	533	286	025

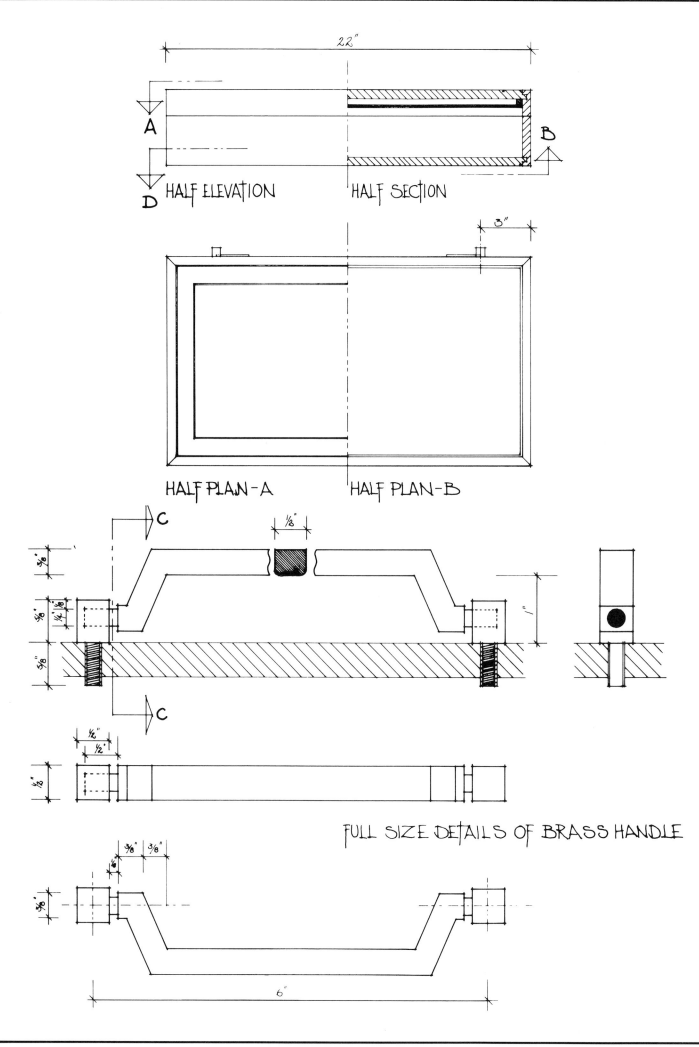

22"

A

B

HALF ELEVATION   HALF SECTION

D

3"

HALF PLAN-A   HALF PLAN-B

C

⅛"

⅝"

⅝"

1"

½"

⅝"

C

½"
½"

⅛"

FULL SIZE DETAILS OF BRASS HANDLE

⅜"   ⅜"

⅜"

6"

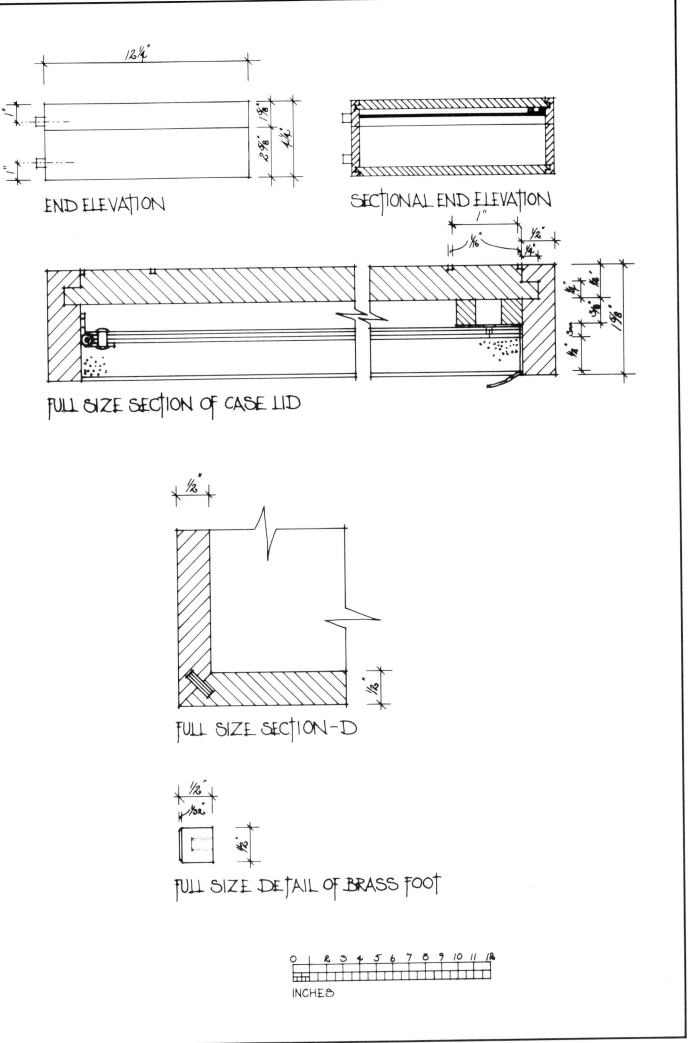

END ELEVATION

SECTIONAL END ELEVATION

FULL SIZE SECTION OF CASE LID

FULL SIZE SECTION-D

FULL SIZE DETAIL OF BRASS FOOT

0 1 2 3 4 5 6 7 8 9 10 11 12

INCHES

Roll-top desk

I have always been fascinated with roll-top desks. After rebuilding an old one, and using it for several years, I decided to build one myself. I used the new one for a while and then, when offered a price I could not refuse, sold it. So I then changed my design, incorporated some improvements, and built the desk that I have now and which is featured here.

The joints on my first desk were held together with dowels, but on the new one I used for greater strength the more traditional mortice and tenon joint. Most of the old roll-top desks around here are made of oak, but I chose black walnut for mine because it is native to this area. My lumber comes largely from trees that I have bought and sawed myself. The crotch wood panels in this desk were given to me by a neighbouring farmer. The drawer sides were made of ½″ oak, while the drawer bottoms are of ¼″ plywood.

Base

I started construction of the base by making the raised panels which are ½″ thick except for the two middle panels of the back section which are ¾″. Since they are raised on each side they have to be thicker as they will show in the kneehole. I used a Rockwell panel raising cutter on my shaper to make the bevel edges. These raised panels are fitted into ¼″ × ⅜″ grooves in the rails and styles.

I cut the ⅜″ × 2″ haunched tenons on the ends of the rails by using the outer two blades of a dado set with a ⅜″ spacer in between them. This will cut each side of the tenon at once and each one will be the same thickness. The stiles in between the panels fit in the same ¼″ × ⅜″ groove as do the panels. They are fastened with a dowel and the panels are left loose. Do not glue in these joints as you need to allow for movement caused by changes in humidity.

Next I made the drawer dividers which form the framework to hold the drawer units together. After they're completed and checked, make sure they are parallel and square. Screws are used to screw into the stiles. I made the stiles about ⅛″ oversize so that when assembled they could be run through a jointer and then cut on the table saw to exactly 12″ width. This ensures that both sides are straight and parallel. Since the front stile is made of one inch and the rest are ¾″, I put ¼″ strips on the sides of these drawer dividers. They will serve as drawer guides.

After the two drawer units are assembled the panels are put together to complete the base unit. A skirt (¾″ × 3″) is then made to go around the unit with mitre corners held together with splines. This joint is a great deal stronger than a plain mitre joint and should not come apart over the years.

Once the top is glued up, it is fastened to the base by screws into the top rail of the outside unit and then, from underneath, through the drawer guides for the kneehole drawer. The screw holes should either be slotted or counter-bored from bottom sides to help prevent splitting of the top when it expands and contracts with moisture. The kneehole drawer guides are glued together from two pieces which are screwed even with the top inside edge of the kneehole panels.

Drawers

In the centre kneehole drawer I made a cove-cut pencil trough. I ran the piece of wood at an angle to the blade of my table saw, taking very shallow cuts until reaching the desired depth. I used my router and dovetailed jig to dovetail all the front joints of the drawers. The back of each drawer is dadoed into the sides. In two of the drawers I made small grooves in the sides and fixed partitions for file folders and other papers. Drawer fronts should have a slight clearance at top and both sides. In the kneehole drawer I used a french dovetail joint to fasten the sides to the front.

To make the drawer pulls, I used the split turning technique with ⅝″ waste piece in the centre, making four six inch pulls at one time. I then used my dado head and radial arm saw to hollow out the finger grooves.

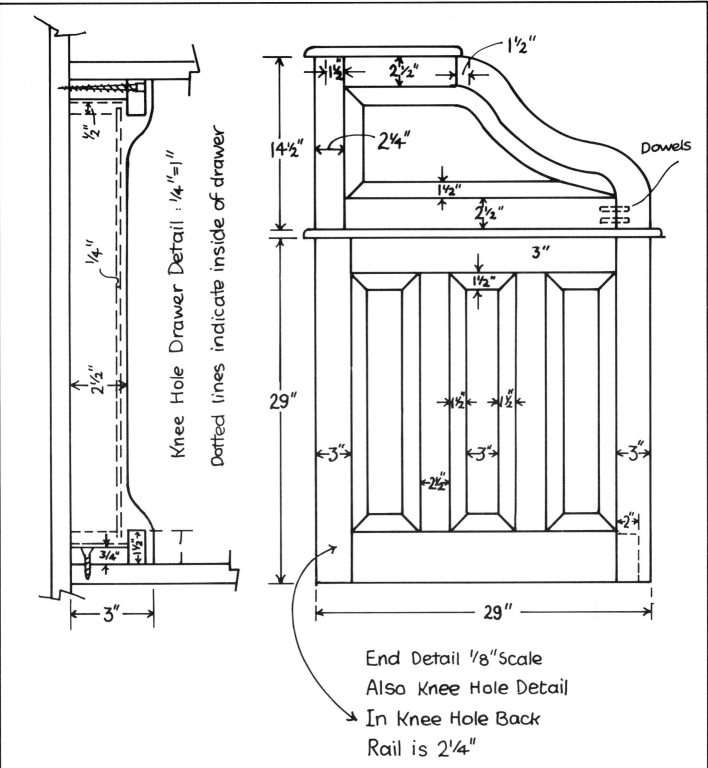

Knee Hole Drawer Detail : ¼"=1"

Dotted lines indicate inside of drawer

Dowels

End Detail ⅛" Scale
Also Knee Hole Detail
In Knee Hole Back
Rail is 2¼"

Writing Boards

For the pull-out writing boards, I used a ⅝" piece of particle board with veneer glued on both sides. This veneered panel has 1½" × ¾" strips along both sides and front. The whole unit is then fastened with ⅜" dowel pins. The writing boards of the old desk were constructed with the grain of wood liable to come apart with changes in humidity. I felt the particle board I used would help correct this problem.

Roll-Top Section

With the base of the desk completed, we are now ready to start on the roll-top section. Constructing the end panels with tambour grooves is the most difficult part of the entire desk. There are several ways to cut the raised panels for the ends, but since I have access to a large shaper, I used a horizontal panel raising cutter with a ball bearing guide. I made the grooves for the tambour

in the end panels with a template and router. When the framed end panels were finished I constructed the framed back panel in the same way as for the lower desk. The back was then fastened using ¾" × ¾" cleats and screws.

Ten ounce weight canvas backing may be purchased at an art supply store or you can use, as I did, a good quality denim cut to 24½" × 44½". The finished tambour strips will be 46¼" long overall, and when the shoulders are cut the distance between the shoulders is 45½". I first fastened the canvas ½" from the ends of the tambour strips and then allowed a two inch overhang of canvas beyond the first tambour strip to be fastened on the lifting bar. I used Titebond glue to fasten 4 or 5 strips at a time to the canvas. Be sure the glue does not seep out in between the strips. I used a roller or veneer hammer to smooth the canvas and spread the glue. The tambour should dry for 24 hours before being removed

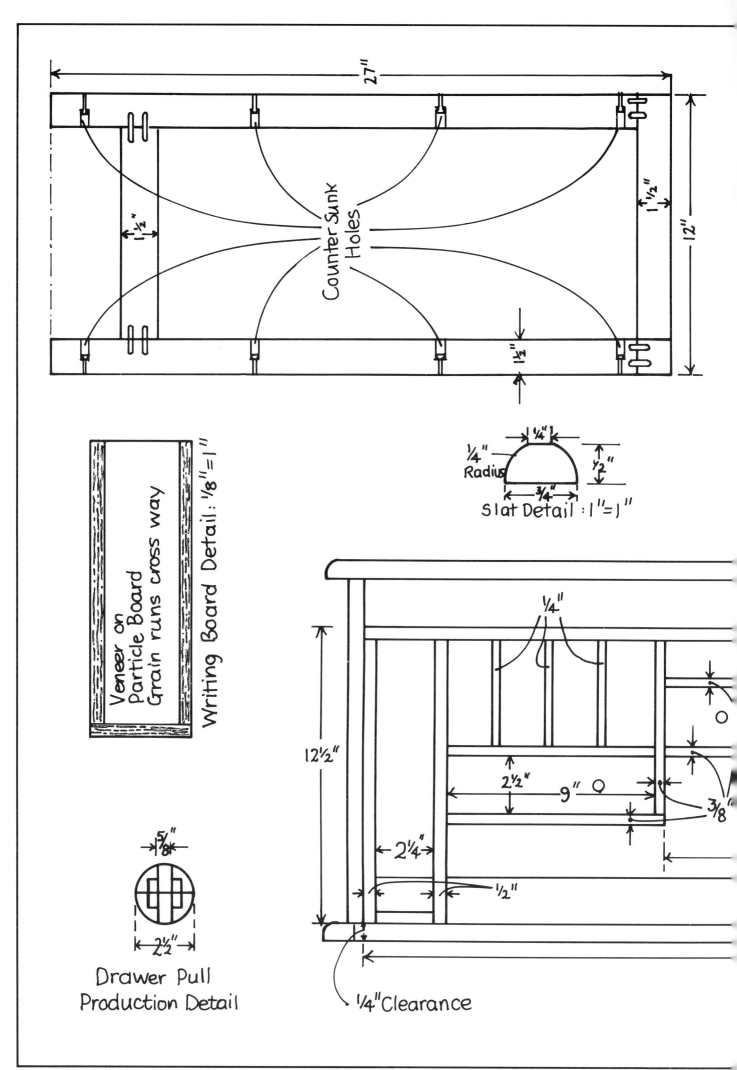

27"

1½"

1½"

1"

12"

Counter Sunk
Holes

1½"

Veneer on
Particle Board
Grain runs cross way

Writing Board Detail : ⅛"=1"

¼"
¼" Radius

½"

¾"

Slat Detail : 1"=1"

¼"

12½"

2½"

9"

3⁄8

2¼"

½"

5⁄8"

2½"

Drawer Pull
Production Detail

¼" Clearance

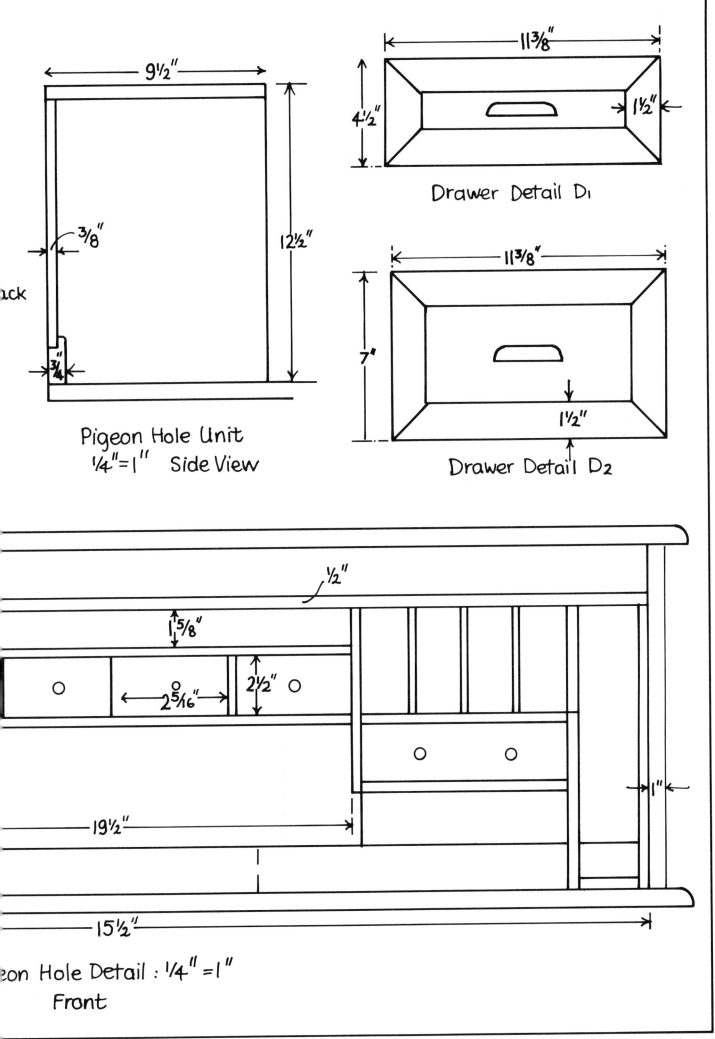

9½"

3⁄8"

12½"

ack

3⁄4"

Pigeon Hole Unit
¼"=1" Side View

11³⁄8"

4½"

1½"

Drawer Detail D₁

11³⁄8"

7"

1½"

Drawer Detail D₂

½"

1⁵⁄8"

2⁵⁄16"

2½"

1"

19½"

15½"

eon Hole Detail : ¼"=1"
Front

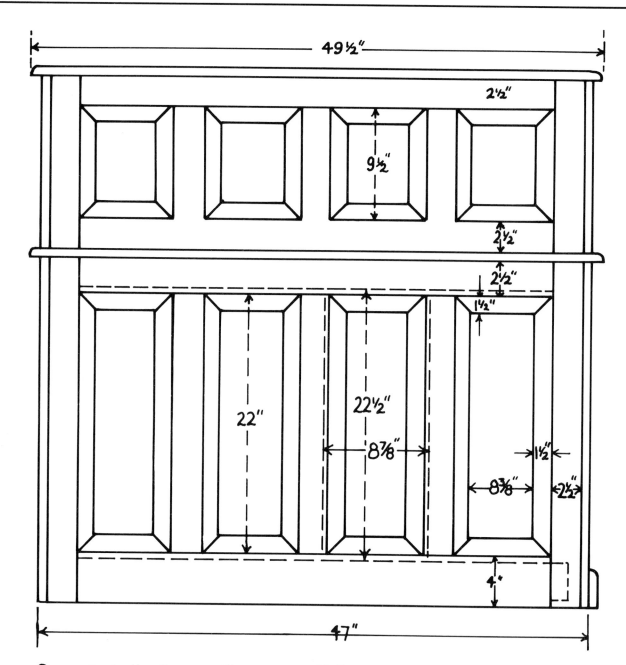

49½"

2½"

9½"

2½"

2½"

1½"

22"

22½"

8⅞"

8⅜"

1½"

2½"

4"

47"

Rear Detail : Panels float with ¼" inset into grooves.

Dividers also float. Panels are ½" thick with edges tapered to ¼".

from the jig. Trim it with the router, and a clamped guide strip, to the finished length of 46¼".

After trimming, cut a strip of ⅜" wood to fasten the two inch tail of the canvas to the lifting bar, using countersunk screws through the strip and canvas and into the bar. The bar is fitted with a ⁷/₁₆" dowel pin at each end to allow it to track into the grooves. A little sanding may be necessary to fit the tambour into the grooves. When the tambour slides easily, take it out and apply finish without touching the canvas.

Pigeon Hole

The pigeon hole case is constructed separately with a slide fit as a unit between the end panels. Dados and rabbets are used to fasten various partitions and shelves and shaped with a jig saw. The drawers are made with ⁵/₁₆" sides, ½" fronts, ¼" dovetail for the joints, and ⅛" or ¼" plywood bottoms. The ¼" plywood back with matching veneer is rabbeted onto a ¾" by 2 × 44" rail fitted into notches in the case uprights.

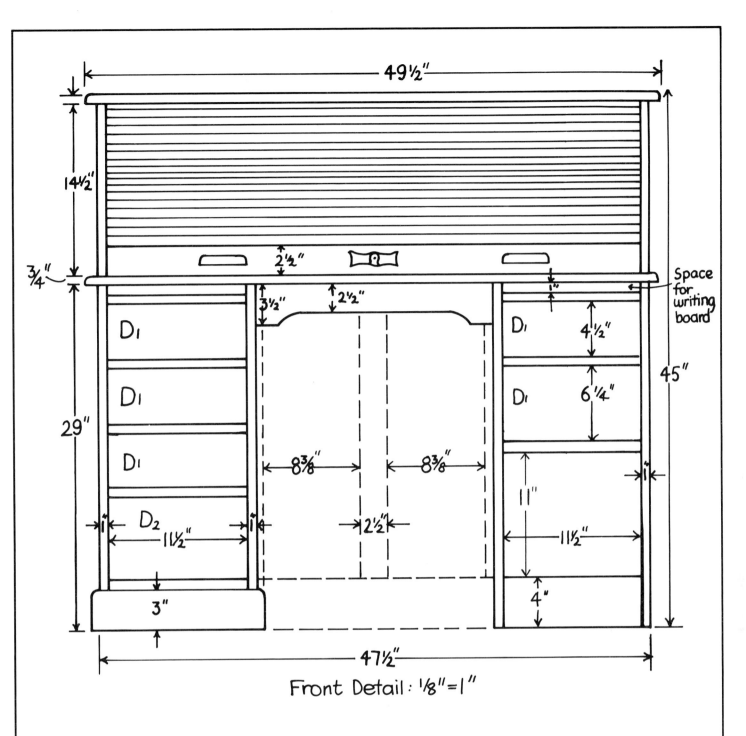

49½"

14½"

¾"

2½"

29"

3½" 2½"

D₁

D₁

D₁

D₂

11½"

3"

8⅜" 8⅜"

2½"

1"

Space for writing board

D₁ 4½"

D₁ 6¼"

11"

11½"

4"

45"

47½"

Front Detail: ⅛"=1"

I ordered the roll top lock from The Wise Co. 6503 St. Claude Ave., Arabi, La. 70032. It is made of brass and iron construction and finished with two keys and a trap door catch. The model number is L31. The matching escutcheon (Model No. E22) is made from 16 gauge solid brass. Both the lock and escutcheon are of excellent quality. Drill and mortise the desk top and lifting bar as required for installation. Also select an appropriate drawer lock and escutcheon for the kneehole drawer and install.

Choosing a final finish will depend to a great extent upon the type of wood used for the desk, as well as individual taste. No matter how you decide to finish the project, it should be done with patience and care. The sanding should be thorough, and any planer marks removed completely.

Since my desk was made with walnut, I chose to finish it by brushing on three coats of polyurethane wood finish, sanding lightly between coats. For the final coat I used a spray which leaves a fine brush-free finish.

Making the drawer pulls using the split turning method

Sharpening and care of your saw

In use most handsaws and panel saws wear hollow in the middle. Topping corrects this and takes out any unevenness. This is not a common fault with the tenon saw, mainly due to its short blade length.

The saw is placed in a vice which should be very firm as any movement or vibrations will result in problems occurring when filing. (The correct pressure on the teeth will be impossible to achieve causing them to be uneven, especially the last two inches below the handle). Pass a 10 in. flat millsaw file down the saw on top of the teeth keeping it at a 90 degree angle to the saw from the handle end. This way you are flatting with the teeth and the file will run much easier. Do this several times to make sure that the saw is flat and there are no uneven teeth. If there are teeth that are standing higher than the rest grind a bevel across the end of the file as this will help it to run over them and fetch them down much faster, restoring a straight flat cutting edge on which to start filing.

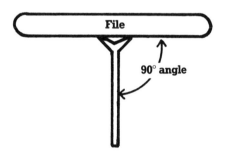

File

90° angle

Now select the correct file for the size of the teeth. We can begin to file. Make sure that the file covers the teeth by about two-thirds of its width leaving a third overhanging.

Place the file at right angles to the saw in the gullet between the teeth. Gently file each gullet until the teeth are all the correct shape. For a crosscut, the front of the tooth should be about 5 degree negative with alternate bevelled top on the teeth and for a ripsaw, a 5 degree positive angle with a flat top, although it is best to turn the saw over and file from both sides even when filing flat tops. This will help to keep the saw even.

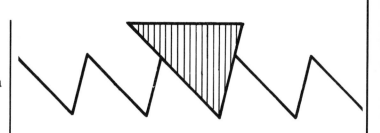

File 1/3 wider than tooth

Most saws appear to be a mixture of both these types with very uneven teeth as there are not many ambidextrous people about. To correct this fault hold the file, firmly using your index finger for guidance, and make a clockwise turning pressure almost as though you are screwing a screw in as the file passes down the tooth face. This will correct too much positive hook on a crosscut tooth pushing it backwards. To correct too much negative hook an anti-clockwise pressure should be applied, pushing the file hard into the gullet of the saw to bring the cutting point forward so that all the teeth are at the same angle. This must be done with a slow filing action with the file pressed very firmly in the gullet, hence the very firm vice with the saw not more than ¼ in. out of the top.

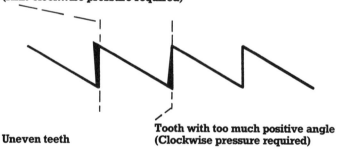

Tooth with too much negative angle (Anit-clockwise pressure required)

Uneven teeth

Tooth with too much positive angle (Clockwise pressure required)

If some teeth are just wider than others and the fronts are all the correct angle, then file with a sideways pressure only. This operation should be carried out working from left to right along the saw on the face of the wider teeth, not putting any pressure on the downward movement until all the teeth are even.

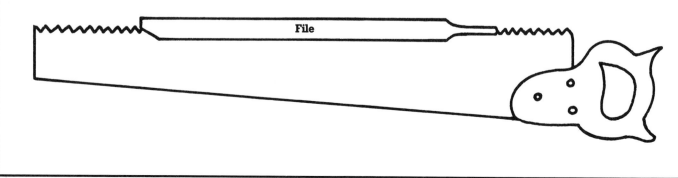

File

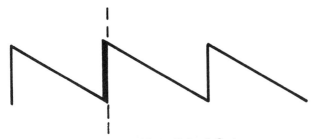

File wide tooth back first

After this, the saw requires setting. All saws are set to give a cut slightly wider than the thickness of the blade to allow clearance for the body of the saw to follow through the cut. Each tooth is bent outwards alternatively and equally, not more than half the thickness of the body of the saw, to cut about one times the width of the blade. For re-setting of saw teeth, setting pliers have been specifically developed for the job. These are very popular and will set most wood saws 4-12 points per inch, with the exception of hard point saws, in one smooth, progressive movement. The tool first grips the saw then accurately sets the tip of each individual tooth without subjecting the full length of the tooth to unnecessary strain.

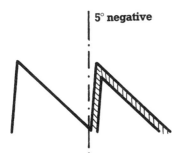

Crosscut teeth with bevel top and face

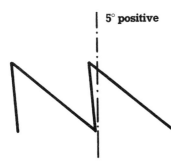

Ripsaw teeth with flat top and face

Most of the hard work has now been completed, all that remains is to top the saw again very lightly and file the teeth. Fix the saw firmly in the vice and, working from the opposite end to the saw handle, place the file on top of the first tooth away from you, with the handle of the file at a 70 degree angle away from the handle of the saw. This gives a front bevel on the tooth, with the set pointing towards you for crosscuts. Keep the file at a 90 degree angle to the blade of the saw for ripsaws as these require square faces and flat tops as when ripping timber the waste should fall away in stringy threads, rather than sawdust as is the case with crosscuts.

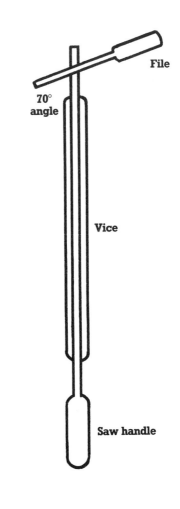

When you have given each tooth light strokes, reverse the saw and repeat the operation down the other side, holding the file at a steady angle throughout and filing with light pressure only. All the hard filing should have been carried out during the shaping operation and four light sharpening strokes at this stage give better results than two heavy ones. It is a timely reminder that the saw needs re-sharpening when the teeth are dulled as this is the first sign of wear. It is best carried out at this stage to avoid too much re-shaping.

A wheel for a horse-drawn vehicle

When I worked for a Wheelwright he was very careful to draw a distinction between that trade and what he called the Cartwright. By his definition wheelwrights made wheels, Cartwrights made carts and Coachbuilders made floats, gigs and traps. I later found that this distinction did not apply elsewhere, and that the Wheelwright made farm vehicles and drays. (Actually so did my boss and he was a Smith as well.)

For my own part I had come into a trade which was already almost extinct at the end of an era. I made wheels only for farm carts ("muck carts") which were converted with racks or shelvings to cart hay in summer time. It was usually done under supervision other than in the case of repairs, which I did a lot of, to both this type of heavy wheel and to those lighter ones for floats and traps. It certainly was exacting work (though I loved it) and I stood in utter awe of the seemingly limitless knowledge of those older men who tried their best to pass on to me what was in fact a lore. Sadly, they had not the time left in which to initiate me fully.

No Wheelwright, it ought to be said, could ever make a wheel without the right timber. The production of timber of the superb and rare quality required to make a wooden wheel is a subject in itself. Suffice it here to say that the final selection was so meticulous, at least one third of that which had originally been put aside for the purpose was rejected somewhere along the way. Age and curing were of the very essence.

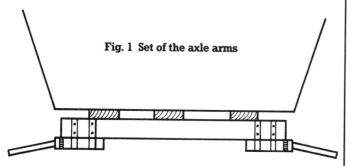

Fig. 1 Set of the axle arms

Component Parts

Let me recall for you the process of making a wheel, beginning with the component parts. The 'rim' was made up of several sections each an arc and, joined together, forming a circle. The sections were known as the fellies and were invariably made of ash which absorbed the massive pressure in 'closing' the wheel and the terrifying jolts to which the wheel would ultimately be subjected on a rough farm track.

The spokes were of oak, always with some heart, which would accept the vertical thrust to which each in turn would be subjected as the wheel 'came to the bottom' and one spoke was vertical to the ground, taking the punishment from the weight both of the cart and of the load. Spokes, however, were cut in a certain way to give them an ovoid shape and were made from oak which had been seasoned for at least one year for every inch of thickness 'and another for luck'.

The hub (or 'stock') was called the nave and this was made from a solid stock or butt of elm. Good timber, this, for taking a lot of mortising (which it certainly had to!) and extra special care was taken with its selection.

Mathematics

The reason why wooden wheels did not collapse the first time out is because they were dished. Not only that but they were 'off-set hung' as well. I have tried to show the effect of this in Fig. 2 and 2a.

The mathematics are important. The need for the adjustment arises, in the first instance, because of the peculiar gait of the horse. If you examine carefully any horse-drawn vehicle you will notice the distinctive shape of the shafts. They are not made like that 'for fancy' but, literally, to accommodate the moving body of a horse. You could not as a rule reverse a horse into the shafts; you had to position him and then lower the shafts over him because as he walks he sways from side to side. So there has to be room for movement at his rump yet not too much play at his shoulders. Therefore, if the rim is not chamfered, only one thin edge of it will run on the ground.

The angle at which the spoke entered the felly was usually 3 degrees, so the down-angles from horizontal on the axle and felly were also 3 degrees. The tread of a muck cart wheel was often as much as 5″, the track 60″ and the diameter of the wheel 4′ 6″. Since the naves were anything between 10″ and 12″ in diameter and the fellies 3″ or 4″ thick, it follows that the spokes were normally of the order of 18″ between nave and felly, a further 4″ or so at either end of that taking the form of haunched tenons. Two spokes were fitted to each felly; 5 fellies to 10 spokes, 6 fellies to 12 spokes.

Assembling the Parts

It is important to note that no nails, screws or glue were used in a wheel. To begin to assemble the component parts you will require quite a few tools, some of which cannot now to my knowledge be bought. The diagrams attempt to show the unusual ones such as boxing cramp, spoke closer, traveller, tyring plate. You also need a felly horse (which can be made quite easily) and a closing table (which can also be made). In addition you will be lost without the adze, sliding bevel, chipping axe, draw-knife, jack- or trying-plane, spoon and twist augers, inside and outside calipers and a large three-cornered chisel which we used to know as a 'bruzz'. Finally you will need a smokeless fire – and a good eye.

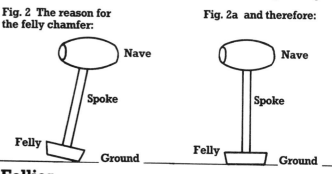

Fig. 2 The reason for the felly chamfer:

Fig. 2a and therefore:

Fellies

Having decided on the size wheel required, work out the extreme circumference minus the hoop (iron rim) and divide by five for the fellies. Make the fellies of the required breadth and thickness using a traditional draw-knife and frame-saw or today's band-saw and sander. True it up face side to face edge and work out roughly the angles at 'C' in Fig. 4 by geometry. Mark them with sliding bevel, and cut. Having *roughly* cut the fellies to shape and size they now have to be bored. Set them on the felly horse and mark dead centre of thickness of the felly at two points, each one third of its length on the concave side. Bore the holes with a 1½" twist auger from the concave side out, and at 3 degrees from cart side to outside. Don't worry if the angle is slightly out because wedges can and will be used to great effect later when the wheel is on the closing table.

Spokes

With suitably cleft (or sawn) oak calculate the length of each spoke complete with its tenons and shape each into an ovoid with a sharpish narrow side. The wide side of the ovoid will be against the cart when the wheel is finally fitted; it is on this side that the heart of the wood should be used. The tenons at the nave end of the spokes must be square and such a size as to leave a good shoulder, since they will eventually be hammered into the nave. A good dimension overall for a spoke, therefore, is three inches longways and two and one half inches at the belly, leaving nice room for 1½"/1¾" tenon. At the felly end the tenons will be round like dowels and these 'dowels' must be in the region of 1½" diameter, again leaving a good shoulder or haunch. The length between each shoulder must be the same in every case for obvious reasons, but the square tenons must be cut to length suitable for the eventual nave. They can, in fact, come through to the centre of the nave and be taken out when the nave is ultimately bored for the axle box, but I found it better to cut them at source and mark my auger with a bit of tape to drill the right depth. It is a useful tip to chamfer the ends of both square tenons and 'dowels' but only very slightly and at the very tips to give them a start when the time comes to wield the hammer.

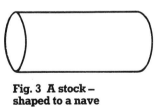

Fig. 3 A stock –
shaped to a nave

Nave

Now we turn out attention to the nave. You start with a stock of elm which you have made into a cylindrical block of 10"/12" dia. (your choice, depends on the weight of the cart). Most axle stubs were 12" long and that would be the length of the nave. Shape it as in Fig. 3. This is not, again, 'just for fancy'. Much of the craft of the Wheelwright was devoted to 'trimming' – which is to say trimming away any superfluous timber to reduce the ultimate work load of the horse.

The centre of the nave where the spoke tenons enter must be 'flat'. Score your centre line round the circumference of the nave and mark out 10 (or 12) equidistant mortices to suit your square spoke tenons and cut them out to the requisite depth at an angle of 3 degrees. Once the first hole is cut you will know which way they all have to follow. And here is where you need that good eye of yours! The only way I know of doing this job with any degree of accuracy is to use a swinging rod with a fixed pointer to sight along and pinned to the nave temporarily to give the angle. A round hole is best to start with, then clean out square with the bruzz. These mortices, however, must be of such construction that when the spokes are later hammered in it will be impossible to remove them other than by splitting .

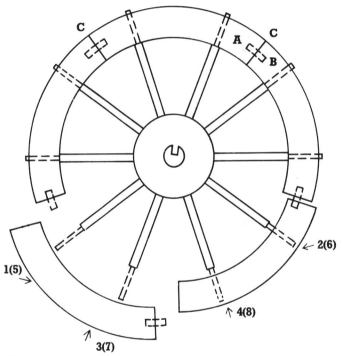

Fig. 4 Closing a wheel (with striking sequence)

Assembling the Wheel

Now to assemble the wheel, starting with the spokes into the nave. Take the nave over to the fitting horse (which is more or less an open-topped stool) and lay it outside up. Take spoke number one and start square tenon into mortise. Continue with the other spokes all round until they start to resist under fair hammer pressure. Incidentally, by 'hammer' I mean cob or even sledge. At this point you need a mate to hold the spoke closer, while you start to belt them home. You must make sure that they are going in at pretty well the right (and similar) angles. Much can be done to rectify wanderings as you go by the very point at which you strike the other end. (I ought to mention that the dowl-ends of spokes were not normally cut until the other ends were firmly into the nave.) With your chipping axe put a piece of oak heart against your leather apron (if you have one!) and cut small, hard wedges to correct any tendency of a spoke to stray from the way you tell it to go. There's no need to worry – you won't split a nave that came from the right wood. Finally, cut the 'dowel' tenons, keeping the exposed part of the spokes exactly the same throughout.

Now, to close the wheel with the fellies, you want the whole thing over at the closing table. This is more robust than the fitting table and is secured to the floor. Lay the wheel, spokes 'starting at the ceiling', on the table and close a cramp over the nave to keep it rigid. Place the fellies in the vice and drill the ends as shown in Fig. 4 to receive the felly dowels. These need be only ½″ thick and travel 1½″/2″ into the felly ends. Be sure the holes match as though this were a piece of furniture. Set the dowels into either end of the first felly and tap it on to two spokes. *Do not take it home.* Insert the dowels into the further ends of the next two fellies and lay them gently on each side of the first. You are going to be glad now that you took the trouble to chamfer slightly because you need a 'start'. And only a start, because now you need the help of your mate again. He must use the spoke closer to pull them together while you hammer home the fellies right up to the shoulder, closing the dowels in at the same time.

Fig. 5 Boxing cramp

Having now closed three fellies home, the wheel is at last becoming pretty rigid. The fact that the felly mortices are nearer on the inside than the outside causes some problems with the spoke closer. These problems become even more pronounced when you come to fit the last two (possibly three) fellies; but there is a trick that helps overcome the difficulty. If the last two fellies are dowelled up and laid very lightly to rest against the tips of the round tenons, and the striking sequence shown in Fig. 4 is faithfully followed, then the wheel should close completely, screeching its way home under the persuasion of the sledge.

Rudimentary

What we now have is a rudimentary wheel, dished as planned, tight and firm as a drum, but with the fellies untrimmed, the nave unbored and the spoke tenons sticking through the rim. There is still much to do.

At Tom's we had a short stout plank buried into the walls at either end and with a false wheel axle (always made of iron) fastened to it at the mid-point. This axle had a slot for a lynch-pin and that was the next destination of the wheel. The next step, therefore, is to drill the nave dead centre for the axle box, which was a hollowed-out circular iron box whose inside diameter was, I think, usually 2″ at the cart end tapering to 1¾″ at the other (lynch-pin end). Therefore if a 1¾″ hole is drilled it must also be reemed out slightly at the cart side to take the box. After that the nave must be slotted to match the lynch-pin slot in the box. When the box is hammered home (axle boxes were made in the Midlands, like axle-arms and cart irons) it should be left to protrude ever so slightly from the cart side because it will in use continually collide with the shoulder of the axle arm – Fig. 1.

Fig. 6 Spoke close

Having done all this, set the wheel on the 'trying arm' and insert the lynch-pin through its slot. Slowly spin the wheel and see how far out of vertical it is at the floor. As the axle arm is shaped to come off the 'bed' at a slightly downward angle, you now have a simulated cart and the wheel must be trued out of any eccentric motion (of which there will be plenty at this stage). This is done by driving little iron wedges into the back of the nave wood around the axle hole, 'lifting' or 'lowering' as required. It is a tedious and skilled job but the result is rewarding. When the iron wedges have trued the wheel they are removed and replaced with wood.

Truing

The next process is concerned with truing the rim and it is now that the protruding tenons are cut flush, the face-sides of the fellies *roughly* smoothed, the face edge smoothed into a perfect circle and slowly and diligently chamfered throughout with the plane until the whole face touches the ground 'flat' as the wheel revolves.

Blacksmith

When the wheel has been finally trued, a smoke-free fire and a very good blacksmith are needed for its completion. The latter makes the tyre or 'hoop' between

Fig. 7 Draw knife

eccentric rollers, which have been set to match the inside and outside circumference he has already measured with his traveller (Fig. 8) he makes the iron tyre and closes it in heat. It is then carried to the tyring plate (Fig. 9), laid 'staring at the ceiling' again and screwed down solid. The tyre is heated in the fire until the Smith shouts 'ready' – only he knows when that is – and on that command two burly men with huge callipers

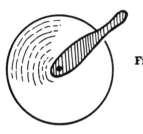

Fig. 8 Traveller

grab it from the fire and run with it to the wheel where they drop it very accurately and concentrically over the felly rim. Meantime several young lads are stood around with buckets of water to quench the iron and prevent too much scorching, while the Smith and the Wheelwright together force the thing home with sledges. For the next quarter of an hour or so there is much screaming and groaning and cracks as loud as rifle shots as the wheel settles in the vice-like grip of the cooling tyre.

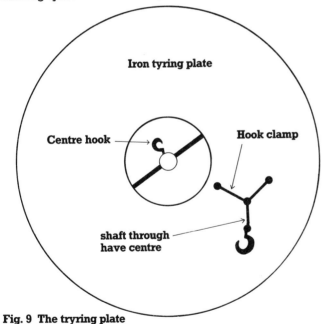

Fig. 9 The tryring plate

And then the moment of truth as the Smith and the Wheelwright pick up the wheel, take it to hard ground and drop it – yes, DROP it – to make sure it is 'reet tough'. It always was. There is nothing I know of that is so many-featured and yet so strong as a cart wheel.

Finally, the felly edges are trimmed round to smooth them to the tyre and the wheel is complete. Although it is difficult to put into words something that really only experience can teach, I hope this attempt will prove useful to somebody somewhere, sketchy though it may be.

Sound

In parenthesis it may be of interest that I knew many men who could tell a good wheel by the sound of it as the cart travelled. With the forward-back motion of the horse the wheel is alternately rammed first against the lynch-pin and then back to the axle-arm shoulder, causing a characteristic click-clack sound. They knew from that what sort of a wheel it was. Another interesting point is that the lighter the wheel the less it was dished. So, the lighter the vehicle, the swifter the horse and the less the dish. Indeed I used to drive a pony in a trap whose wheels were hardly dished at all and, with the pony at the trot, the cart swayed very little. There is far more to this subject than meets the eye!

Garden trough and tub

These containers must be of necessity 'heavy-duty' garden furniture, while at the same time they are expected to enhance the general scene. This means tough, high resistance to moisture and pleasant-to-view timber while the design should be easy on the eye. Thinking of ships' decks, it suggests teak as the most reliable material.

In addition to exterior weather forces the drainage factor needs adequate consideration. This implies that the timber should be capable of resisting, as far as may be possible, the dampness both within and without. There is no doubt that teak wood will give long service and, at the same time, look right in its surroundings. It pays to use preservatives when surface appearances indicate their necessity. Jointwork should be put together using waterproof glue.

Opinions differ with regard to the right kind of containers best suited to a particular setting. One can see clay, plaster and other substances in use for tubs, urns and troughs nowadays but to many people wooden containers make a homely choice for the garden.

Garden Trough

Using measurements taken from the drawing make out a Cutting List. The four long horizontal pieces are simple to assess. Add together, end to end, the four vertical corner posts after allowing ½ in. on to the end of *each* piece. Add together the four cross rails of the trough ends; making one long piece. Add together the four vertical intermediate pieces. It will be a simple matter to saw off the required lengths; each of which should be ½ in. longer for squaring off later.

Unless circumstances regarding timber supply dictate otherwise, or the constructor prefers to plane up the wood from the rough, the finished width and

thickness of the pieces will be ordered P.A.R. (planed all round) and joint making can start immediately. Consider the trough ends first.

Use a protractor on the drawing to read off the less than 90 degree angle of the shoulders. Mark this angle on the true edge of a spare piece of wood and set a sliding bevel to this angle. Cut the shoulder lines with a knife, mark out and cut to shape the tenons. Chop out mortises, work to a fit and try the frame together. Test for accuracy by comparing diagonals and scan the frame surface for twist. In the interests of drainage it should be noted that no grooves are cut in the vertical direction on either corner posts or the intermediate vertical pieces; only horizontal grooves are used to retain the infilling boards.

Lay out, full size if possible, on a large sheet of paper the opening you expect to have when the complete frame becomes a reality. Use the drawing as a guide and space the number of narrow boards you will need to completely close the eight open spaces. A rough sketch plan of the end view of two or three boards will reveal the need to add a board thickness to each width in order to allow the 45 degree edges to be formed. Where the boards meet verticals in the frame a butt joint occurs. On the appropriate edges of the rails plough the grooves, form stop chamfers where shown on the drawing, and work to a shape the top corners of each post. Assemble the end frames, measure and cut to the lengths and shapes required.

It is possible to go ahead and complete the skeleton frame, if one so desires. However, the original trough was made by first of all finishing out the two ends and gluing the joints, with waterproof glue, checking for correct angles and surface twist.

Be sure sufficient time has been given to completely allow the glue to harden before marking off and cutting the long rail tenons and their mortises, the tenons and mortises for the upright intermediate pieces. Assemble the whole frame, measure for and cut sufficient infilling boards.

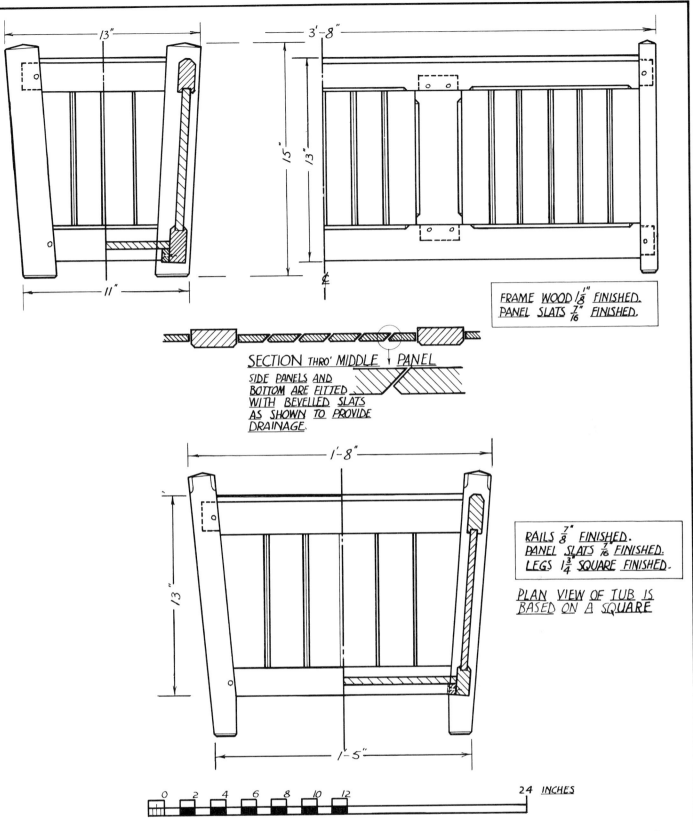

13"

3'-8"

15"

13"

11"

FRAME WOOD 1⅛" FINISHED.
PANEL SLATS 7/16" FINISHED.

SECTION THRO' MIDDLE PANEL

SIDE PANELS AND
BOTTOM ARE FITTED
WITH BEVELLED SLATS
AS SHOWN TO PROVIDE
DRAINAGE.

1'-8"

13"

RAILS 7/8" FINISHED.
PANEL SLATS 7/16" FINISHED.
LEGS 1¾" SQUARE FINISHED.

PLAN VIEW OF TUB IS
BASED ON A SQUARE

1'-5"

0   2   4   6   8   10   12   24 INCHES

The bottom of the trough also is made of loose boards resting on a hip strip; which should be very securely screwed in position. The boards are fairly static when a layer of ¾"-1" gravel is laid on them before horticultural compost mixture is used to fill up ready for use. Remember to apply a coat of, say, raw linseed oil before the trough is filled.

Garden Tub

Preparation by hand from rough timber to finished sizes seldom is seen nowadays. The availability of power driven saws and planing machines enables one to make an early start on jointwork and projects quickly begin to take shape.

First of all a cutting list must be prepared to give the timber merchant a clear idea of your requirements. From the drawing take careful note of widths and thicknesses of the various parts. Short lengths may be added together to make lengths worth while passing through a machine. Therefore, after adding the ½ in. on each length your list will state, e.g. the tub corner posts; one piece (4 × 17½ in.) 5 ft. 10 in. long P.A.R. (planed all round) to 2¼ in. × 2¼ in. Next, add together the four top rails in length, also add together in length the four bottom rails, which are narrower.

On a large surface of paper draw, full size, the opening made by joining up two corner posts and two rails. On the sketch set out the board widths occupying

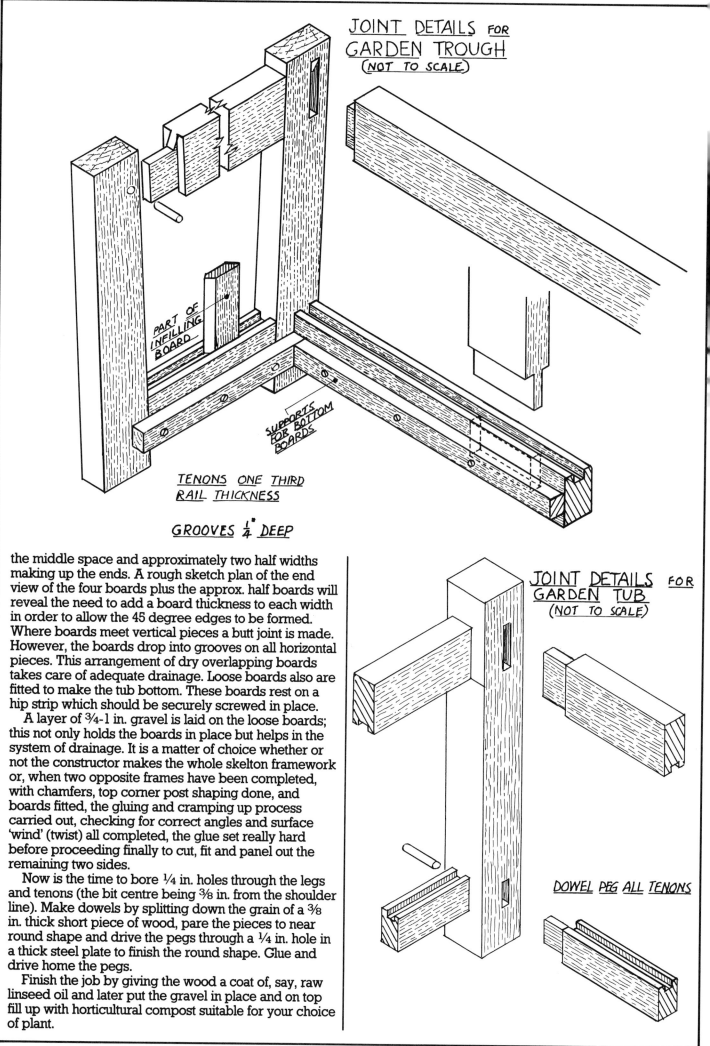

JOINT DETAILS FOR
GARDEN TROUGH
(NOT TO SCALE)

PART OF
INFILLING
BOARD

SUPPORTS
FOR BOTTOM
BOARDS

TENONS ONE THIRD
RAIL THICKNESS

GROOVES ¼" DEEP

JOINT DETAILS FOR
GARDEN TUB
(NOT TO SCALE)

DOWEL PEG ALL TENONS

the middle space and approximately two half widths making up the ends. A rough sketch plan of the end view of the four boards plus the approx. half boards will reveal the need to add a board thickness to each width in order to allow the 45 degree edges to be formed. Where boards meet vertical pieces a butt joint is made. However, the boards drop into grooves on all horizontal pieces. This arrangement of dry overlapping boards takes care of adequate drainage. Loose boards also are fitted to make the tub bottom. These boards rest on a hip strip which should be securely screwed in place.

A layer of ¾-1 in. gravel is laid on the loose boards; this not only holds the boards in place but helps in the system of drainage. It is a matter of choice whether or not the constructor makes the whole skelton framework or, when two opposite frames have been completed, with chamfers, top corner post shaping done, and boards fitted, the gluing and cramping up process carried out, checking for correct angles and surface 'wind' (twist) all completed, the glue set really hard before proceeding finally to cut, fit and panel out the remaining two sides.

Now is the time to bore ¼ in. holes through the legs and tenons (the bit centre being ⅜ in. from the shoulder line). Make dowels by splitting down the grain of a ⅜ in. thick short piece of wood, pare the pieces to near round shape and drive the pegs through a ¼ in. hole in a thick steel plate to finish the round shape. Glue and drive home the pegs.

Finish the job by giving the wood a coat of, say, raw linseed oil and later put the gravel in place and on top fill up with horticultural compost suitable for your choice of plant.

How to make your own toolcase

The tool case we are about to make is the type that has been used by carpenters and joiners for generations as they go from one firm to another, or one site to another, or even from one room to another in their own home as they fit cupboards, etc.

It is designed to feed you just the tools you want, because you get to know exactly where everything is placed and at the same time the tools are protected. It serves you like a faithful assistant. It can be kept in the dry and when required carried to where the work is to take place. It will have button turns that clip the saws into place, protecting the teeth from having their points damaged by knocking against some other steel tool. The three-section drawer will hold the chisels, screwdrivers, rules, pencils, bradawl, punch, files, coping-saw blades (which get so easily broken or lost because of the small thin size), drills and so on. The centre section of my drawer contains pieces of steel,

odds and ends that I improvise with when I have perhaps to rout out a special channel in wood or round off a slot or curve in inaccessible places which the designed tool will not reach.

In the lower section of the case we can place our jack-plane, smoothing plane, brace and bit roll, hammer, coping saw, sharpening stone, square etc.

A case like this makes the work almost exciting. It will be constructed as soundly as any piece of furniture and take pride of place wherever it is set down. The joints will be dovetailed, a proper lock and handle or handles fitted, and the case finished in a nice wood stain and varnished.

Well, let's get started: The best wood to use is Ramin, which is knot-free and a semi-hardened. The appropriate size of the case is 762 × 457 × 152 mm (two foot six long by eighteen inches high by six inches deep).

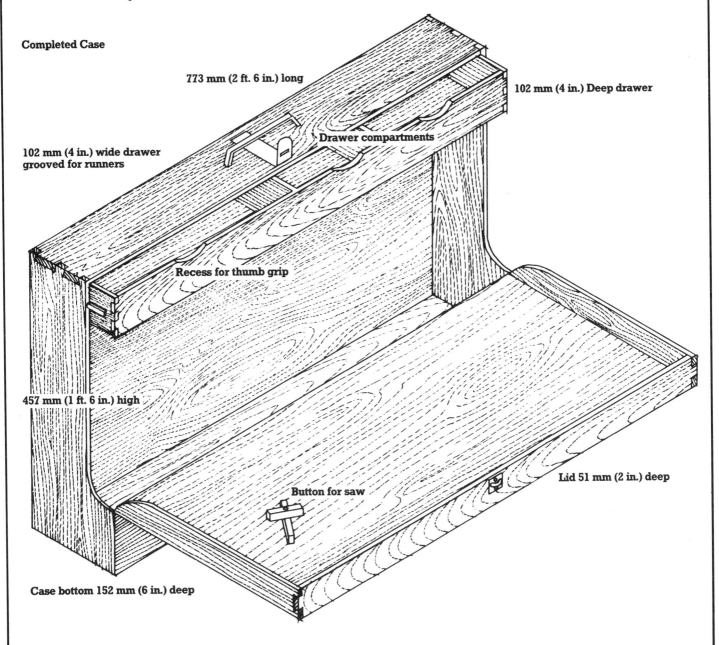

Completed Case

773 mm (2 ft. 6 in.) long

102 mm (4 in.) Deep drawer

102 mm (4 in.) wide drawer grooved for runners

Drawer compartments

Recess for thumb grip

457 mm (1 ft. 6 in.) high

Button for saw

Lid 51 mm (2 in.) deep

Case bottom 152 mm (6 in.) deep

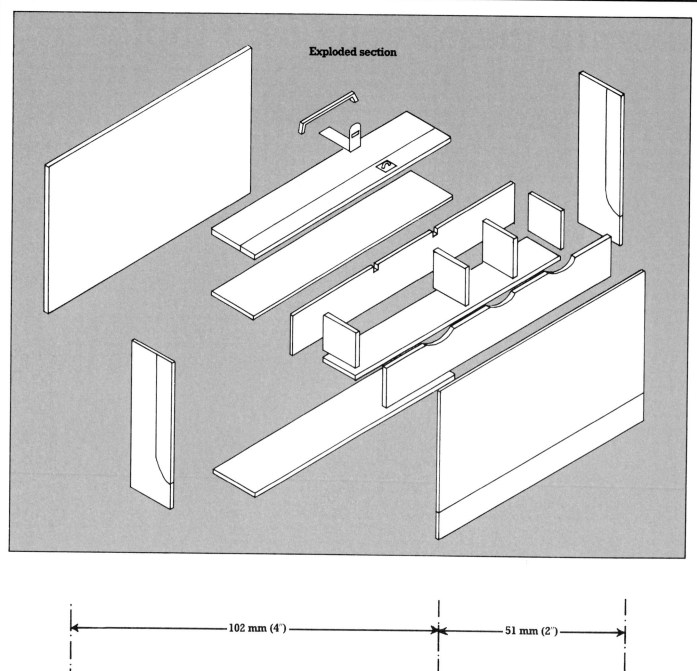

Exploded section

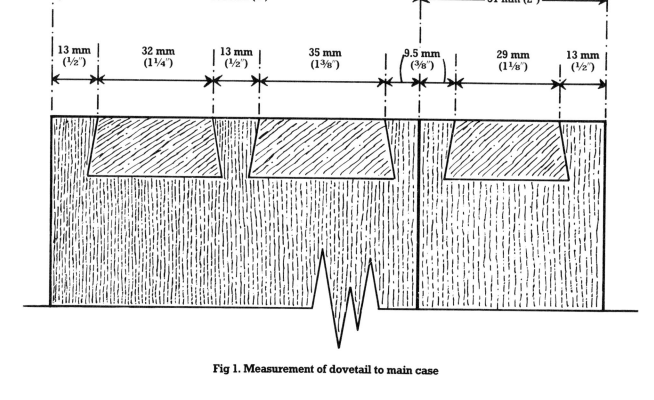

←——————— 102 mm (4″) ———————→ ←——— 51 mm (2″) ———→

| 13 mm (½″) | 32 mm (1¼″) | 13 mm (½″) | 35 mm (1⅜″) | 9.5 mm (⅜″) | 29 mm (1⅛″) | 13 mm (½″) |

Fig 1. Measurement of dovetail to main case

Cutting List

Your cutting list of planned finished wood is: 2 × 787 × 152 × 16 mm (2 ft 7 in. × 6 in. × ⅝ in.). 2 × 483 × 152 × 16 mm (1 ft 7 in. × 6 in. × ⅝ in.). 2 × 762 × 102 × 5 mm (2 ft 6 in. × 4 in. × 3/16 in.) ply for the drawer. 1 × 457 × 102 × 5 mm (1 ft 6 in. × 4 in. × 3/16 in.) drawer bottom. 2 × 102 × 102 mm (4 in. × 4 in.) dividers. 2 × 762 × 457 × 5 mm (2 ft 6 in. × 1 ft 6 in. × 3/16 in.) ply sides to case. 2 × 102 × 102 × 16 mm (4 in. × 4 in. × ⅝ in.) Ramin ends to drawer, which will require grooves for runners. 2 × 16 × 14 mm (⅝ in. × 9/16 in.) runners. Also you will require: l pair of brass butt hinges 38 × 10 mm (1½ in. × ⅜ in.) countersunk with screws. 1 small brass hasp and staple. 1 handle. Wood glue.

Special care will have to be taken when dovetailing the corners of the case and drawer. The joint must be made as illustrated in Fig. 1 to take the strain of lifting when the case is loaded with your tools.

Main Case

We will construct the main case first. The lengths of timber have been ordered slightly longer to allow offcuts to be taken off the ends to ensure they are squared off correctly. Place your square across the end of the first piece at 762 mm (2 ft. 6 in.) and, with a finely pointed pencil, strike a line against the square as you hold it firmly in position with the stock pressed against the wood with the blade about half an inch from the end. Remove the square and saw off the excess to give you a clean square edge, standing over the saw and allowing the teeth to do their job without too much pressure. You should see only the top edge of the saw blade and not either side. This way you will get a nice cut for jointing later on. Measure the length at 762 mm (2 ft 6 in.) long marking it with your pencil. Again go through the process with your square, striking a pencil line against the blade, and cut. Repeat the operation with the second long length of timber. You can place the cut piece on top of the one you are about to cut to length. But for future reference, in the event of many pieces of wood being cut to the same length, always mark your first piece with a pattern mark and use it as you would a measuring rod. Because if you are careless, and use each cut length of timber as you go along to mark the next one, the thickness of the mark, plus any deviation with the saw, will increase the length from your first and last. Consequently your assembled article will be cut out of square.

The same operation as above follows with the 457 mm (1 ft. 6 in.) pieces.

Case Dovetails

Now we are ready to make the dovetails using the common or box dovetail joint that will strongly join the sections together. As already mentioned, it is important in setting out the dovetails that we think about where the most strain is in carrying the case. Mark the first dovetails on the side pieces 457 mm (1 ft. 6 in.) long and allow for the lid section, Fig. 1, so that the dovetail is not sliced in half when we come to cut the lid section.

In marking out the dovetail it is preferable to use a marking knife. This acts as a stop for the chisel to a smaller degree. Measure the length of your dovetail to the exact thickness of your timber from the edge, using a sharp pencil at all times. You should at this stage mark your timber with a face mark on one flat side and joining to an edge mark on one edge. Now you square your mark around allowing only the stock of your square against the sides that you have marked. This way your pencil lines should meet.

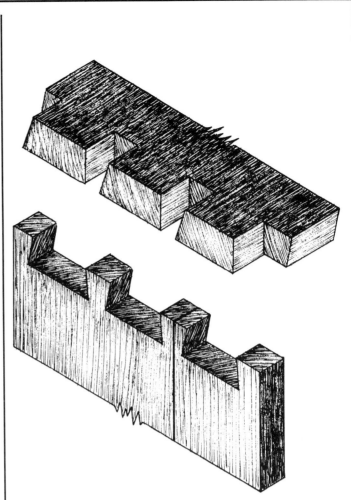

Fig 2. Method of marking dovetails before cutting

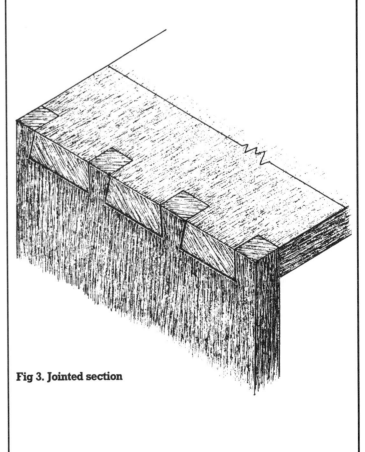

Fig 3. Jointed section

Set out your dovetails as shown in Fig. 2. Using a bevel, set the angle of your dovetail. Judge the angle sensibly; do not make it too acute or it will be weak at the base, or too shallow so that the joint comes apart under strain. Note the wider section where the lid is to be cut through. When you have marked out your lines, scribble through the sections of the joints that are to be cut away as waste. This will avoid cutting by mistake the parts to be left in.

The first setting out takes place on the side pieces 457 mm (1 ft. 6 in.) long. Number each end on both pieces from 1 to 4. Also mark top and bottom. This is especially important for when the lid is cut. Cut out the waste sections of the ends using a fine dovetail or tenon saw. After making the cut, preferably with the boards held in a vice or Workmate cramp, place your boards on a flat bench.

(Be careful, whenever you lay boards down to work on in this manner, to make sure all previous workings are swept clean. Any wood chips, nails, screws, etc., should be removed as they cause small indents into board and are hard to sandpaper out, with the result that often the do-it-yourselver has to plane the wood again to remove the blemishes.)

Now gently chisel out the cut sections of the waste areas from either side. Go down to a small depth at a time as you will be unable to work your chisel from the front end as you go deeper, as you would when cutting a mortice end, because of the angle of the dovetail.

Lid

When you have finished the chiselling out of all your dovetails and cleaned them out, mark out on the bottom of the end sections the curve of the lid at 152 mm (6 in.) high and 51 mm (2 in.) wide. You can judge the curve you want using a round object and mark around. Cut through with a coping saw the curve only, leaving the main saw cut until after the case has been glued up. Now mark through the cut out dovetails, with the ends resting on the edges of the top and bottom pieces, placing the top and bottom sections upright in a vice as you mark through. Cut out as before.

Here you must remember to make sure that the top

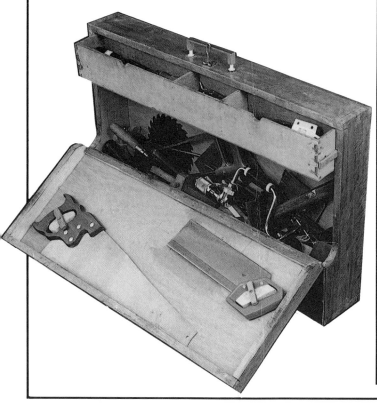

and bottom sections are numbered to the corresponding one. It would be wise to place all the boards on edge on the floor as they are to be joined together, then mark as mentioned. This way you will get the lid and ends in the right place when it comes to joining.

After chiselling out the waste, test the fitting of the case. Now take the end sections and cut a groove 38 mm (1½ in.) from the top inside and cut one groove to each end 6 mm (¼ in.) deep and the width of your runners. Having done that, glue up your case.

Next, glue and pin the plywood back and front, plane around the edges to take away any excess overlap and remove ragged edges. The fixing of these plywood panels will square up the case. You can now complete the saw cut after marking out the lid from the centre of the curve cut, because your saw cut must meet at this point.

With this case as with everything, always examine your timber and put the best side outwards when marking and making up. After you have made your lid cut and it comes away from the main case, lightly plain the saw marks from the edges.

Drawer

Now make up your drawer which should be 102 mm × 102 mm (4 in. × 4 in.) deep. Groove out your dividers getting your measurements of the lengths of the compartments by measuring your longest chisel or screwdriver to one side and the folding rule and such like for the other. For the centre compartment (to house your tape rule, punch, drills, plumb-line etc.), groove out the ends outside, at 6 mm (¼ in.) deep 37 mm (1 7/16 in.) from the top, for your runners. You may now wish to place your drawer into position and mark through.

For the end sections of the drawer you will need the 16 mm (⅝ in.) thick sections which allow for the grooves. These are the sections you mark through first for the dovetails as you did with the case. Fit and glue the runners to the insides of the case with the fronts projecting out an extra 19 mm (¾ in.) Then when you pull out the drawer it will rest open clear of the case to enable you to gain access to all the contents.

Hinges

In hinging the lid, it will be necessary to glue and pin one 10 mm × 25 mm (⅜ in. × 1 in.) batten to the plywood edges. Cut and fit two brass butt hinges to the depth of the flange to lid side. Then place against the case, mark across and cut out for the hinge flange that side. Screw and fix the hinges. Fix handle.

Handle

In my case I used a bolt-through aluminium door handle with extension spacer sleeves around the bolts to enable my knuckles to slip through. But you may prefer to make a leather handle of your own or substitute one from an old case or bag. You will have to cut away a small recess from the back section of the drawer where the drawer will slide past the screw or bolt ends of the handle. While you are cutting these recesses the same can be done to the front of the drawer. Here the recesses will serve as thumb grips to make it easier to pull the drawer out.

All that is now left to do is sandpaper your new tool case, stain to whatever colour you prefer – i.e. walnut, oak, teak, mahogany – and varnish. For so much care and pride to have gone into the making of a case to hold one's tools will leave all who see it in no doubt as to the quality of anything else its maker may produce.

William Sinott comments as an alternative:

The method of setting out the dovetails, shown below is generally accepted as being correct and is favoured by most tradesmen.

The way I have shown the lid cut gives added strength when the case is closed and the dowel gives strength to the weakest part of the ends, where it is most likely to split.

Quite often the drawer slides are glued and screwed to the inside of the case and the grooves cut in the drawer slides. The drawer slides are allowed to project by 1″. This allows the drawer to be drawn out a bit further without falling out and helps to keep the lid in line when the case is closed.

A leather handle which goes flat when not in use, I think is best, and a desk lock is preferable to a hasp and staple. It is also much nicer when the plywood is set in to frame.

The method of finding the angle I have shown is correct for softwoods and should be a little less for hardwoods.

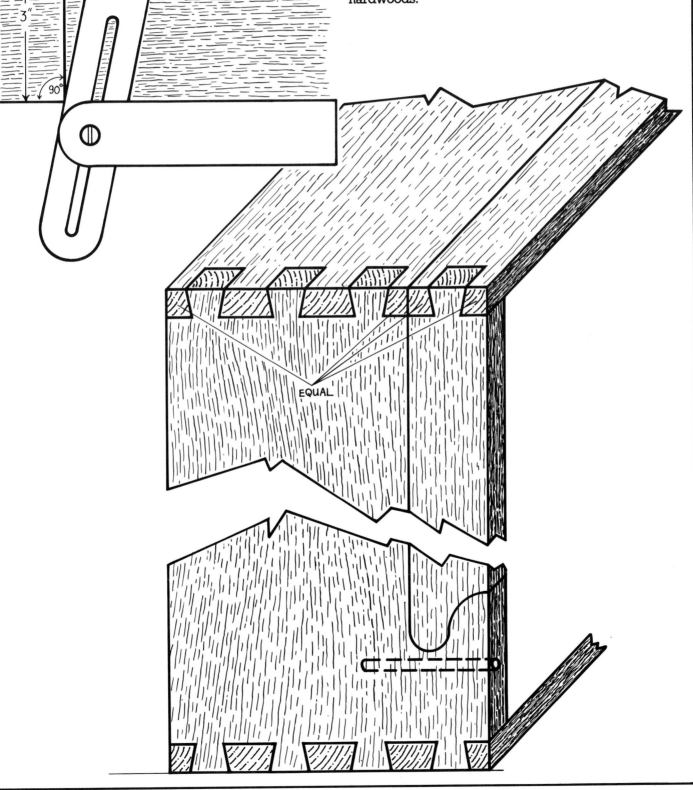

Making a telephone table

Instead of being solid the legs of this table are built up of two lengths of material as shown at 'B' in the 'Leg Construction' sketch. In appearance the tongue and groove joint looks simple enough but the quality of craftsmanship must be of the highest order to guarantee a permanent and lasting union. In addition to the outside surface moulding of the legs the play of light and shade on the inside surfaces promotes extra interest in the piece.

Take four pieces of wood 27″ long and finished to 2″ by ⅞″ and four pieces 27″ long and finished to (2″ minus ⅞″) + ¼″ for groove depth, leaving 1⅜″ width finished. At ⅝″ from one edge on the four wider pieces plough a groove ⁵⁄₁₆ths wide and ¼″ deep. Leave the tongues slightly oversize in thickness and finally bring them to make a press-in-tight-fit in the grooves. Check each rebate adjoining the tongues for accurate squareness. When all is ready arrange sufficient 'G' cramps and/or sash cramps with protection slips for each cramp position. After a dry trial glue up, tighten the cramps and leave with the inside surfaces making an exact right angle.

Prepare the long back and front rails 2′ 6″ long 4½″ wide and ⅝″ thick finished. One end rail 14½″ long 4½″ wide and ⅝″ thick finished. Cut and fit the rail joints. Use the drawing and the scale provided to determine length and width of the top and bottom flat-lying rails forming the shelf opening. Where stop

dovetails are shown for the top rail there are stop tenons in the bottom rail. Assemble the frame and work out sizes for the dovetail housed intermediate rail. Plough a groove on the inside edge of the bottom flat-lying rail. Mark out and cut the stopped mortises for the wooden buttons. When all the jointwork is finished make a final dry assembly and correct any faults.

The moulded shapes on the outside of the legs are achieved by first of all planing each outside surface to make a taper from the outside corner to ⅝″ thick at the inner parallel edges. Without using round planes the prototype was moulded by using a scratch-stock and home-made blades from a broken hand-saw blade or an old cabinet scraper. Work the mouldings to a finish and finally shape some 'former' blocks to use covered with suitable grades of glasspaper. N.B. The two surfaces facing outwards at the directories end of the table are not treated as indicated above. Instead, work a concave channel where letter 'A' is given on the end elevation, then proceed to shape the remainder of this surface below the letter 'C' on the 'Leg Construction' sketch to match the six surfaces elsewhere. Finally taper all leg inner surfaces from 2″ at a point level with the under edge of side and one end rail to 1¼″ on the ground.

Check all meeting parts, glue and cramp up end frames. When dry, bore screw holes in top flat-lying rail and proceed to glue end frames to the side rails. When dry and hard, cut and finish the shelf.

'The built-up back edge of the table top.' To some eyes a little superfluous perhaps but its presence, well carried out, adds to the table's quality and general acceptance; especially to the maker!

Referring to the sketch on the drawing, the strip required is as long as the table top and 1¼″ by ½″. Be sure the meeting surfaces are quite true in two directions. When satisfied with a try-out of the strip in place prepare adequate cramping and stiff blocks to spread the pressure throughout. Glue up and cramp up

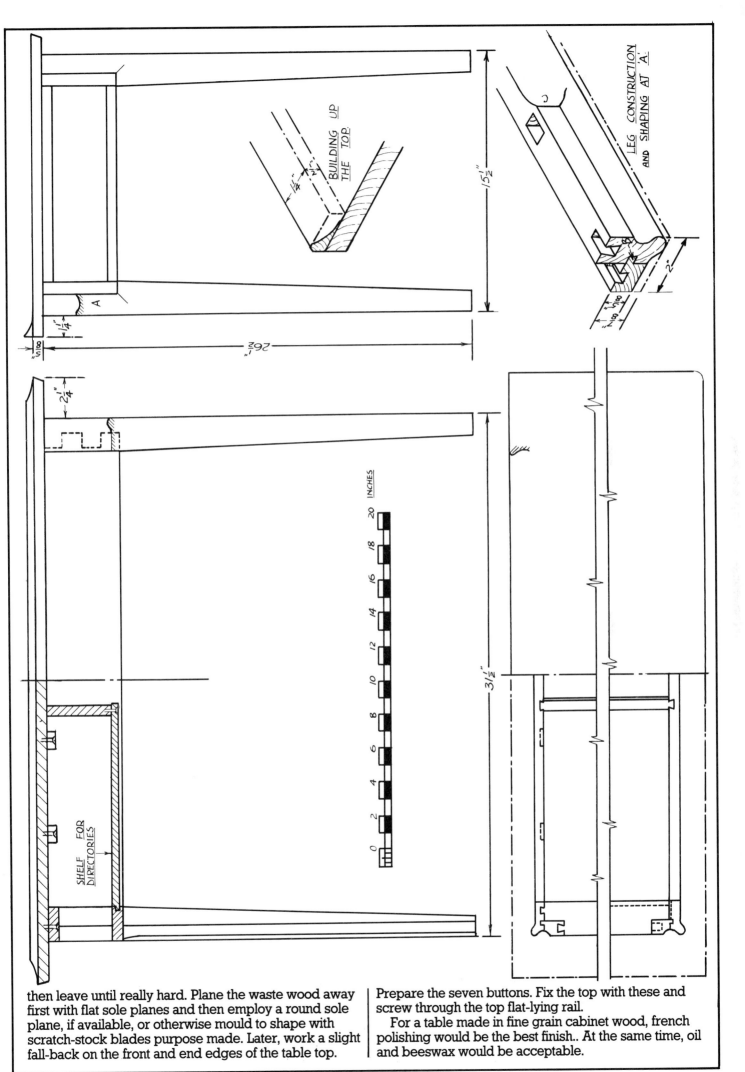

BUILDING UP THE TOP

LEG CONSTRUCTION AND SHAPING AT 'A'

15½"

2"

26½"

2¼"

31½"

INCHES

0 2 4 6 8 10 12 14 16 18 20

SHELF FOR DIRECTORIES

then leave until really hard. Plane the waste wood away first with flat sole planes and then employ a round sole plane, if available, or otherwise mould to shape with scratch-stock blades purpose made. Later, work a slight fall-back on the front and end edges of the table top.

Prepare the seven buttons. Fix the top with these and screw through the top flat-lying rail.

For a table made in fine grain cabinet wood, french polishing would be the best finish.. At the same time, oil and beeswax would be acceptable.

Wall mounted bookcase

Photo. 1

Introduction

For many years now I have favoured the design of period furniture, but as I am sure many readers will have experienced, the dimensions of modern houses can restrict both the sizes and quantity of this type of furniture that can be tastefully accommodated in their homes.

A couple of years ago I had a problem regarding the storage of books. I found I had insufficient space for a floor standing unit and there was nothing available on the market that would provide adequate wall storage whilst at the same time being in sympathy with the existing reproduction furniture. It was for this reason that I decided to design and make a pair of wall hung bookcases.

The bookcases are made in mahogany, the design being loosely based on the top section of an 18th Century Welsh Dresser. I felt by incorporating a small top cupboard and two drawers it not only enhanced the design but provided very practical additional storage (Photo 1).

The Carcase

Both bookcases were made at the same time and commenced with the marking and cutting of the ends and frieze rail profiles. These require accurate templates which are easily produced from a 5 in. wide piece of 4mm plywood, the shapes being cut using either a coping saw or a fine blade in a power jig saw. One edge of the plywood is used for the frieze rail shape and the other for the carcase ends (Photo 2).

The profiles are cut in the mahogany using high speed steel blades (14 teeth per inch) in a power jig saw. With care, the finish obtained is clean, accurate and requires the minimum of cleaning up.

Being of solid timber the corners are all hand cut lap-dovetails so that no traces of the joints appear on the ends.

The next and most time consuming task is the marking and cutting of the stopped housing joints (14 for each bookcase) used for the shelves, drawer partitions and cupboard sides, these also being cut by hand. The whole carcase is then cleaned up and assembled.

Cutting and Fitting Back and Frieze Rails

The appropriate back and wall support rails (see parts drawing) should have the holes drilled for wall fixing prior to being fitted to the carcase.

The use of a drill stand is recommended for this task and will ensure all 13 screws go in at 90° to the carcase, thus making the task of mounting the bookcase on the wall much easier.

The back rails are lap-dovetailed into the carcase ends and glued and screwed to the rear of the shelves.

Photo. 2

Photo. 3

However before fixing the back and wall support rails to the carcase a rabbet should be worked on them as shown in full size detail 'D'. Finally the frieze rail is glued into position and held with cramps until set.

Cornice Moulding

On completion of the main carcase assembly a 1/16 in. deep rabbet, to accept the cornice moulding, is formed on the carcase ends and the front of the frieze rail (see full size detail 'E'). The moulding is then mitred at the front corners and glued and cramped into position, the side mouldings being trimmed to length after the glue has set.

The Drawers

The drawers (Photo 3) are of traditional construction with each drawer component being planed to fit its respective place and numbered for identification.

A groove to take the drawer bottom is then cut into the sides and the front followed by the marking and cutting of the joints, these being lap-dovetails at the front and through dovetails at the back.

Prior to assembly the fielded feature is worked onto the drawer front using a rebate plane with the bevel produced using a shoulder plane.

The Door

The door carries $2 \times 1\frac{1}{2}$ in. brass butt hinges and is held closed by a mini automatic latch thus obviating the need for a handle (Photo 4).

To make the hanging of the door easier the timber is first cut and planed to fit its appropriate opening. The brass butts are fixed and the door hung in position; it is then removed and the fielded detail produced on the front using the same technique as with the drawers. The door is then re-hung and the latch fitted, the final position of the door should be as shown in the full size section 'F'.

Finish

On completion of cleaning up apply 3-4 coats of a clear polyurethane satin finish lacquer, each coat must be allowed to cure and should be lightly glass papered using flour grade paper before applying the next. After

Photo. 4

the final coat cut the surface back by rubbing very lightly in the direction of the grain with 000 steel wool dipped in soft white wax and buff with a soft duster, this will produce an extra smooth satin matt finish.

Fixing Bookcases to the Wall

A solid fixing to the wall is essential as the unladen weight of each bookcase is approx. 89 lbs. The wall support rail should be fixed first, with the aid of a spirit level.

If the bookcases are to be placed in a restricted opening or close to a wall one should bear in mind that the wall support rail is 1¾ ins. shorter than the overall width of the bookcase and allowance should therefore be made for the ⅞ in. difference at each end. With the wall support rail fixed in position the bookcase can then be located on the rail and fixed back to the wall in the usual manner.

Having marked, drilled and plugged the wall, rub a little paraffin wax on each screw thread prior to inserting into the plug, this will ease the tightening of the screws and also their removal at a later date.

Cutting List

All measurements given are finished sizes but include allowances for joints etc. The quantities indicated are for two bookcases.

Description	No. Reqd.	L × W × Th. (inches)			L × W × Th. (millimetres)		
Ends	4	42	12	⅝	1067	305	016
Top	2	53½	11⅜	⅝	1359	288	016
Bottom	2	53½	12	⅝	1359	305	016
Shelves	6	53½	11⅜	⅝	1359	288	016
Back rails	6	53½	2	⅝	1359	051	016
Back support rail	2	53½	2¾	⅝	1359	070	016
Wall support rail	2	52¼	1½	⅝	1372	038	016
Top frieze rail	2	54	2½	⅝	1327	063	016
Cupboard sides	4	12⅝	12	⅝	321	305	016
Drawer partitions	4	4¾	11	⅝	121	279	016
Cupboard doors	2	10	8	⅝	254	203	016
Drawer fronts	4	17⅜	4	⅝	441	102	016
Drawer sides	8	10⅜	4	⅜	263	102	009
Drawer backs	4	17⅜	3¾	⅜	441	095	009
Drawer bottoms (plywood)	4	17	10³⁄₁₆	³⁄₁₆	432	258	004
Top front cornice moulding	2	55½			1410		
Top side cornice moulding	4	12¾			349		

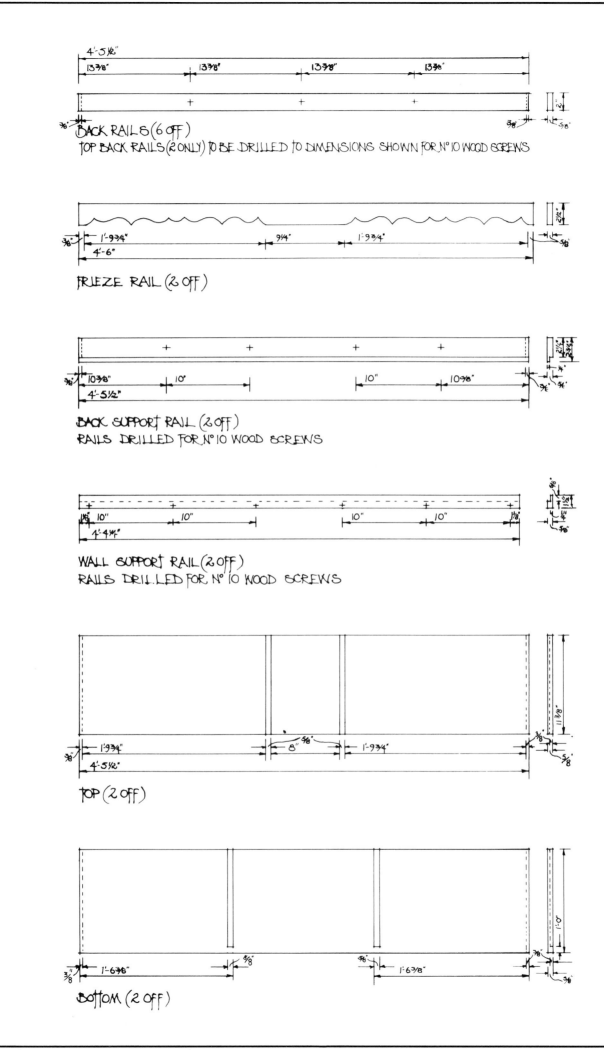

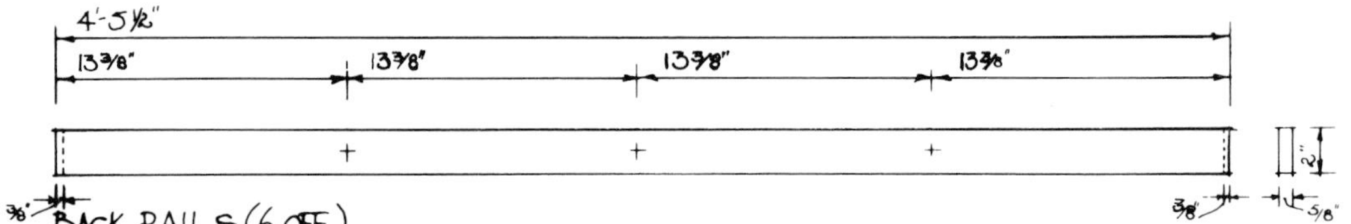
4'-5½"
13⅜"
13⅜"
13⅜"
13⅜"
2"
3/8"
3/8"
5/8"

BACK RAILS (6 OFF)
TOP BACK RAILS (2 ONLY) TO BE DRILLED TO DIMENSIONS SHOWN FOR N° 10 WOOD SCREWS

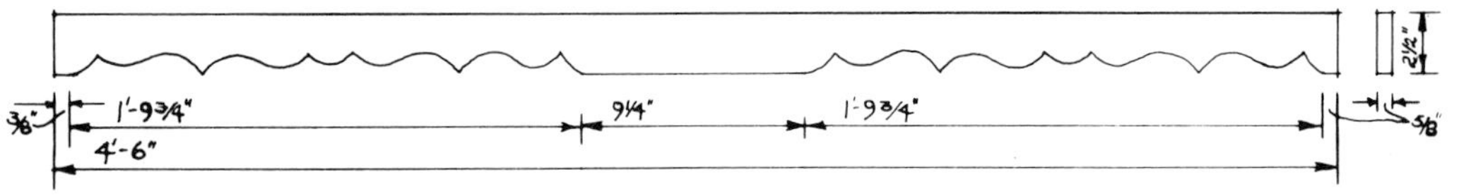
2½"
3/8"
1'-9¾"
9¼"
1'-9¾"
4'-6"
5/8"

FRIEZE RAIL (2 OFF)

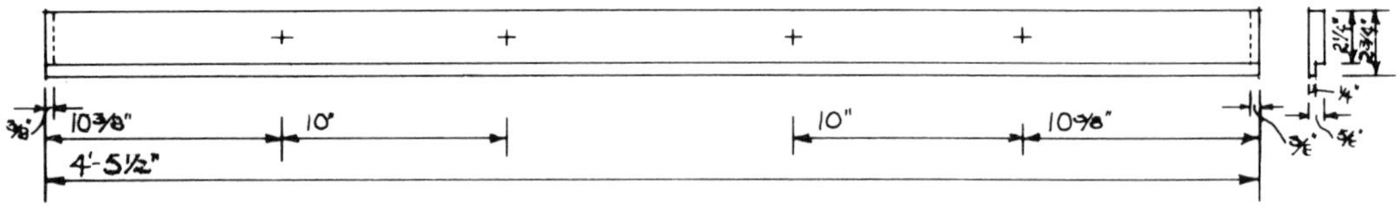
3/8"
10⅜"
10"
10"
10⅜"
4'-5½"

BACK SUPPORT RAIL (2 OFF)
RAILS DRILLED FOR N° 10 WOOD SCREWS

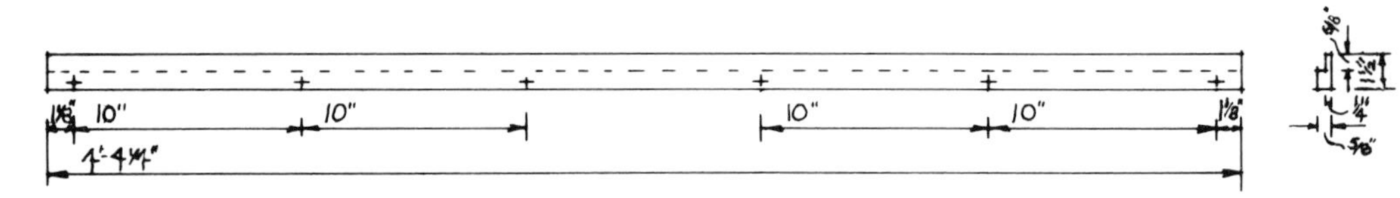
1⅛"
10"
10"
10"
10"
1⅛"
4'-4¼"

WALL SUPPORT RAIL (2 OFF)
RAILS DRILLED FOR N° 10 WOOD SCREWS

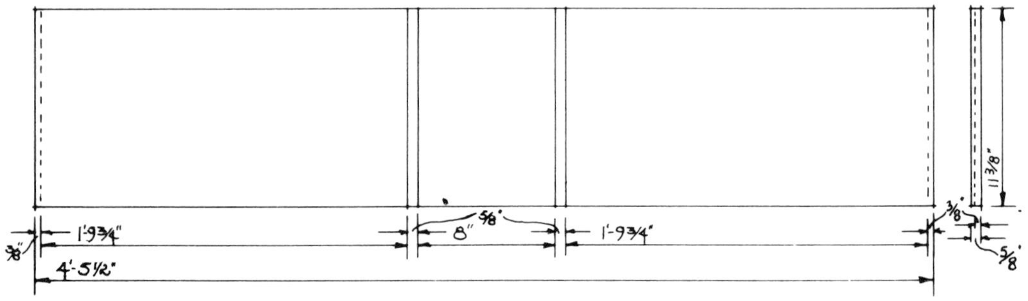
11⅜"
3/8"
1'-9¾"
5/8"
8"
1'-9¾"
3/8"
5/8"
4'-5½"

TOP (2 OFF)

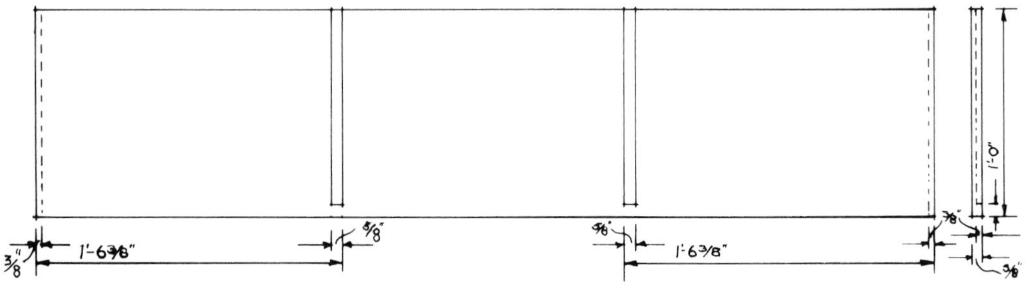
1'-0"
3/8"
1'-6⅜"
5/8"
5/8"
1'-6⅜"
3/8"
3/8"

BOTTOM (2 OFF)

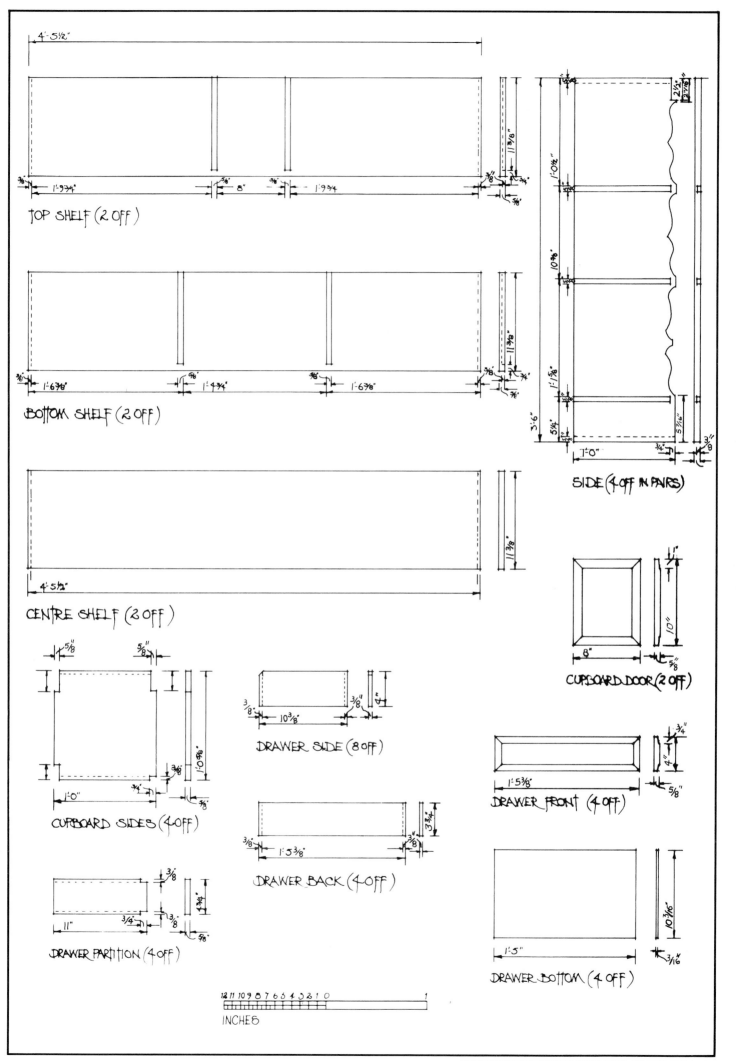

4'-5½"

1'-9¾"   5/8"   8"   3/8"   1'-9¾

TOP SHELF (2 OFF)

1'-6⅜"   5/8"   1'-4¾"   5/8"   1'-6⅜"

BOTTOM SHELF (2 OFF)

4'-5½"

CENTRE SHELF (2 OFF)

1'-0½"   10⅞"   1'-5⅞"   5¼"   3'-6"

2½"

SIDE (4 OFF IN PAIRS)

1'-0"   ¾"

8"   10"   5/8"

CUPBOARD DOOR (2 OFF)

5/8"   5/8"

1'-0⅞"   1'-0"   ¾"   5/8"

CUPBOARD SIDES (4 OFF)

3/8"   10⅜"   3/8"   4"

DRAWER SIDE (8 OFF)

3/8"   1'-5⅜"   3/8"   3¾"

DRAWER BACK (4 OFF)

1'-5⅜"   4"   ¾"   5/8"

DRAWER FRONT (4 OFF)

3/8"   1¾"   3/8"   11"   ¾"   5/8"

DRAWER PARTITION (4 OFF)

1'-5"   10³/₁₆"   3/16"

DRAWER BOTTOM (4 OFF)

12 11 10 9 8 7 6 5 4 3 2 1 0   1

INCHES

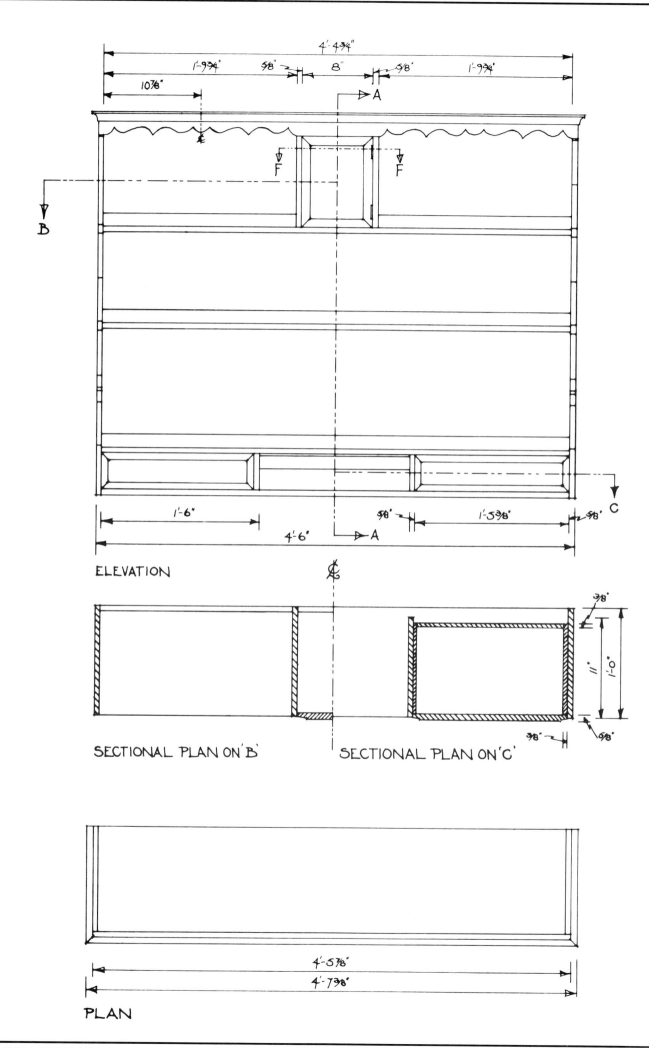

ELEVATION

SECTIONAL PLAN ON 'B'   SECTIONAL PLAN ON 'C'

PLAN

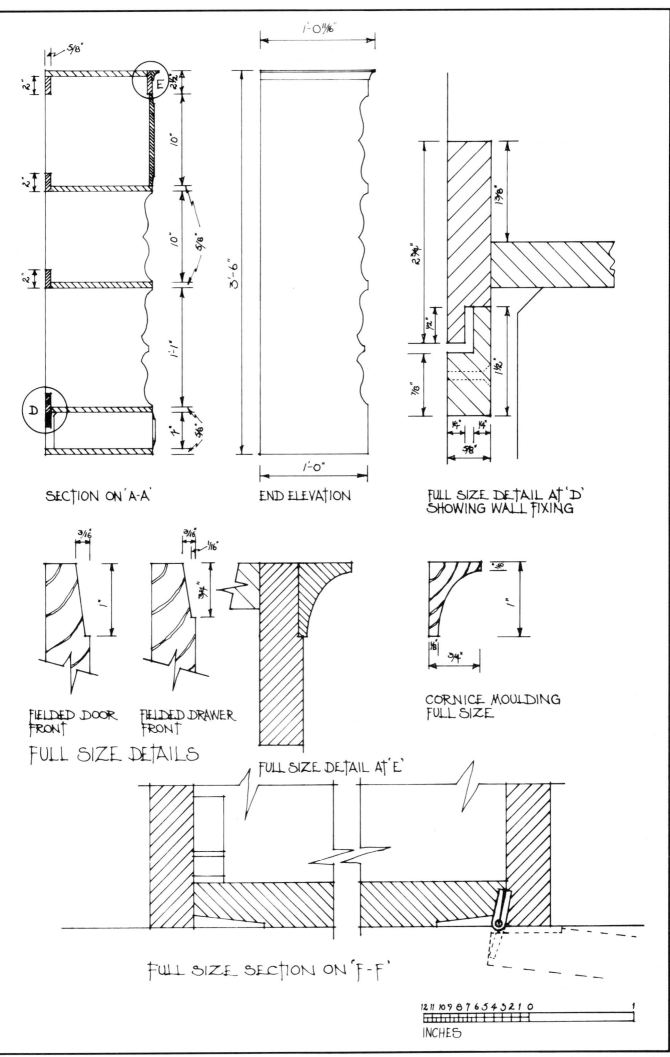

SECTION ON 'A-A'

END ELEVATION

FULL SIZE DETAIL AT 'D'
SHOWING WALL FIXING

FIELDED DOOR
FRONT

FIELDED DRAWER
FRONT

FULL SIZE DETAILS

CORNICE MOULDING
FULL SIZE

FULL SIZE DETAIL AT 'E'

FULL SIZE SECTION ON 'F-F'

INCHES

Constructing a circular table utilizing the wooden lathe

Tools used
Trammel Points
Outside Callipers
Tenon Attachment
Tool Rest & Stand
Dado Head
Clamps
Faceplate
Lathe Tools

Materials
Black Cherry
Black Walnut
¼" Plate Glass
A/C Int. Plywood
Adhesive – Tightbond Glue

Equipment
Wood Lathe
Bandsaw
Combination Sander – Stationary Disc Sander
Circular Saw – Tilting Arbor Saw
Portable Belt Sander
Finishing Sander

Additional equipment used
Jointer
Drill Press
Spindle Sander
Radial Arm Saw

Figure 1

Figure 2

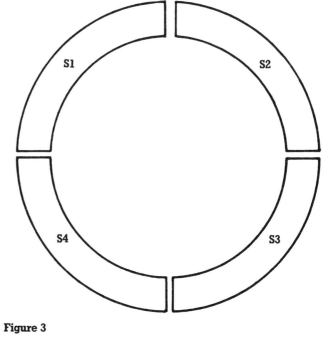
Figure 3

Many features are found in woodworking publications on articles which can be made on the wood lathe, but the "art," or use of, outboard faceplate turning in today's reading material is rare indeed.

The basic set-ups and tooling methods employed in outboard turning are the same as utilised in conventional (inboard) faceplate turning. The biggest distinction between the two processes is the precision required in preparing the wood components because of the large diameter size of the turning. In addition, the preparation of a faceplate of larger than normal size is critical and not commonly employed.

In this article I will endeavour to illustrate the procedures required to turn an exceptionally large object. Discussion of the selection of wood, tools, equipment and processes needed to construct a rather useful household activity will be covered. I have chosen a simple, yet useful table which is circular in design and made up of two tiers or levels. Fig. 1. The top tier, or upper level, is the largest diameter of the two levels and will be highlighted by the use of clear quarter inch plate glass inlayed in the inner circumference. A bottom tier, or level, of a lesser diameter provides an added opportunity to use the process of inlaying to further enhance the beauty and richness of the table if desired. Fig. 2.

The Top

I have chosen a thirty-inch outside diameter top to be made out of the always popular black cherry. The top will measure three inches in width and have a thickness of five-quarters.

To begin, use a large piece of kraft paper scribing the thirty-inch diameter (outer edge of the top) with trammel points and a pencil. Using the trammel points, inscribe a second circumference of twenty-seven inches which will then provide the desired three-inch wide top tier for the table. Now divide the top into four equal segments, being as accurate and precise as possible, and cut four templates. Fig. 3.

Select good sound wood and be sure to select stock wide enough to facilitate one complete segment. A word of caution at this point; be sure the grain of each segment will be at right angles to each intersection, or joint. This will help to ensure a good, strong joint where the segments are to be joined later during assembly. Fig. 4. Using templates trace the shape of each segment onto the selected stock and number each segment consecutively. Fig. 5.

Cut the four segments out on a bandsaw, cutting on the outer edge of each line. This will enable you to retain the desired finished width of three inches when outboard turning your top tier.

Now that the stock is roughed out for the top, select a sound piece of three-quarter inch A/C plywood. The (A) side of the plywood sheet will provide an excellent substrate for mounting the two pieces to be turned. Be sure to select a piece that is not warped. In addition, if encountering a piece of plywood which is not flat, it can be straightened out with several one by fours fastened to the back side. We now have a smooth, and solid backing for our faceplate. Proceed to inscribe a 36-inch diameter circle for the top tier on the (A) surface of the faceplate. Take segment one and square each end taking off as little as necessary just in case more must be removed from the other end later. The squaring process is best accomplished on a stationary disc sander, being sure the table is square to the disc and the mitre gauge at ninety degrees to the disc. Place S-1 in the inscribed circle, and with a pencil, mark each end of the segment on the faceplate. At this point in layout, accuracy is exceedingly important when placing and marking each segment. The reasons for this are to ensure proper joint fits between segments and to aid in the balancing of the total unit. Proceed with S-2 and continue the process of aligment through segment four. Fig. 6.

Dry clamp four segments in place on the faceplate and check the total alignment of the segments and quality of each of the four butt joints. Be sure to use wooden culls between your clamps and the top surface of your segments to keep from marring the surfaces.

Next, cut the slots for the splines on each segment end. The most accurate way of doing this is with the tenon attachment of the circular saw. Use a dado head for a quality slot. Cut the slots one-fourth of an inch in height and three-quarters of an inch deep. When doing this be sure the slots are cut from the back side of each segment. This will insure that all four segments lay flat and even when splined.

Select a wood for the splines which is the same as the top, or for a contrast, choose a contrasting wood such as rock maple. Consider the density and strength of the

Figure 4

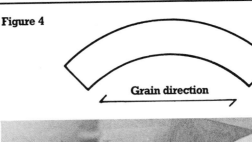

Grain direction

Figure 5

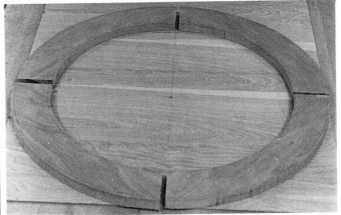

Figure 6

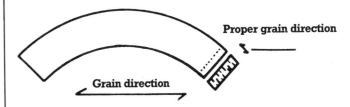

Proper grain direction

Grain direction

Figure 7

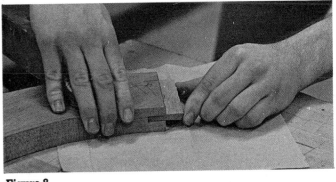

Figure 8

wood since this is the top tier and must provide stability for the legs and bottom tier. When cutting the splines be sure the grain is running perpendicular to the joint, helping provide a stronger joint between segments. Fig. 7. Cut the splines slightly smaller than the slot to compensate for the swelling of the wood fibres when the liquid adhesive is applied. This is indeed critical! Certainly, pride in your ability to match the splines is the key to good workmanship at this point, since the joints are completely exposed from both sides of the top tier. Fig. 8. Again dry clamp, but this time with the inserted splines. If everything is satisfactory you are ready to glue the top tier together.

Using a good strength adhesive proceed to glue two segments together at a time and allow each to dry overnight. I have found that gluing on a flat surface provides the fastest and easiest method of holding the two segments in place as shown in Fig. 9. Simply clamp one segment to the table, or bench top, and apply the adhesive to the segment slot. Now put adhesive on the spline and insert it into the slot of the first segment. Take segment two and apply glue to the slot pushing the segment into place and clamp securely. If each joint has been prepared properly each will pull up snugly with only direct arm pressure. After overnight drying take the two sections, using the same procedure, and glue the two together allowing them to dry overnight.

Take your circular top and sand the splines flush with the segment on the outer side only. Align the top on the front surface of the faceplate. Securely fasten the top to the plate from the back side with two one and one-half number ten wood screws using two per segment. Also, at this point in assembly, mount a six-inch or larger metal faceplate to the back side of the plywood faceplate with stove bolts, flat washers, lock washers, and nuts. Fig. 10. It is very critical that the metal

Figure 9

faceplate is tight and centred as accurately as possible. This becomes exceedingly important because of the large diameter being turned. The top is now complete and ready to be turned.

The Legs

A well designed leg will certainly enhance the total appearance of the table. The legs, three in number, make a smooth curve outward from the top tier downward to the bottom tier. The legs are designed to attach to the top and bottom tiers with wood screws and adhesive. Draw a suitable design on kraft paper and cut the pattern. Fig. 11. When selecting stock for the legs keep in mind that the grain should be running parallel to the length of the legs. Trace the leg design on the selected stock and proceed to cut the legs out on the bandsaw, cutting to the outside of the lines. Sand the legs being sure all three are of equal size and shape. To best ensure sanding uniformity fasten all three together for this operation.

Since the bottom tier fastens to each leg, approximately at midpoint, it is now necessary to counter bore each leg from the outside to the depth which will adequately house the woodscrew using a half-inch machine bit. A three-inch, number eight flathead steel wood screw is recommended for this assembly procedure. In addition, counter-bore the top tier, with the same half-inch bit, where the three legs are to be secured in place. Drill the appropriate shank and pilot holes in the top tier and legs to facilitate two-inch number ten flat head wood screws. Use the wood screws to fasten the top to the legs; do not glue at this point.

The Bottom

The final part of the table is the layout and construction of the bottom tier, also to be outboard turned. Measure the distance between the legs and establish the required diameter for the bottom. For the bottom, a solid piece of five-quarter black cherry is used and a four-inch diameter of half-inch black walnut is inlayed in the centre. The inlaying of other woods makes an attractive design as one looks down through the glass on the top tier and certainly, design choices are unlimited.

Select stock from a board with an outstanding grain pattern since it will be highlighted through the glass. To eliminate warp use several pieces gluing them edge to edge. Inscribe the diameter on glued-up stock and be sure to indicate the location of the centre. Proceed to cut the bottom out on the bandsaw cutting to the outside of the line. Fig. 12. Remember the legs must meet the specified diameter. Anything smaller will take away from the alignment of the legs.

Outboard Turning

In review, we now have constructed the top, the bottom and the legs. We must now prepare the lathe for turning the bottom and top tiers.

The recommended RPM for faceplate turning of this type is 150 or as close as can be provided. This may necessitate reducing the pulley sizes but will provide the turner with a safe and stable turning speed. Remember, you are working with a large diameter which automatically increases the centrifugal force.

Hone each lathe tool to a keen edge which certainly is one of the most important secrets to good quality lathe turning.

Place the top tier on the lathe and secure it into place. Turn it by hand several times checking balance and

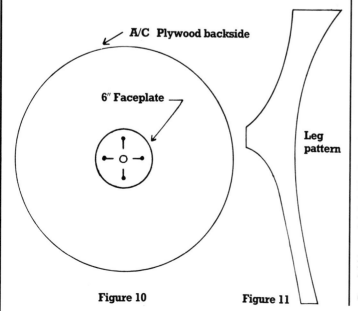

A/C Plywood backside

6″ Faceplate

Leg pattern

Figure 10   **Figure 11**

trueness. Select the proper tool rest stand and place it one-fourth of an inch from the work. Check to be sure the tool rest edge is free of nicks or rough spots. Once again turn the faceplate by hand being sure the work does not come in contact with the tool rest holder.

The first step in turning will be to square the outside edge and to repeat the same with the inside edge in order to obtain the desired three-inch width of the top tier. Fig. 13. For this procedure select a skew chisel and do the cutting with the point holding the tool flat and securely on the tool rest. The tool rate of feed should be deliberate but the operator should avoid over-heating of the point. Now shape the outer edge to your desired specification and cut your glass recess on the top inner edge. You are now ready for the sanding process which should not take long if your turning is of good quality. Finish sanding with a two-eighty grit abrasive and remove from the faceplate, which will complete the making of the top tier.

Finally, mount the bottom tier on the plywood faceplate and turn the blank down to the desired design on the outer edge and sand as needed, to a two-eighty grit. Cut the required recess in the centre of the bottom tier to facilitate the walnut which will be inlayed after the bottom is completed. Fig. 2. Now that the top and bottom tiers are completed, through the process of "outboard turning", the only remaining component to be made is the black walnut disc, four inches in diameter and one-half inch thick. Select an attractive piece of walnut stock and cut a four and one-quarter inch disc out on the bandsaw. Mount the walnut disc on a three-inch faceplate and turn it to size on the inboard side of the head stock. Check the diameter often with a pair of outside callipers until the four inch final diameter is obtained. Take the faceplate off the head stock and see if the disc fits snugly into the recess. If so, remove the disc from the faceplate and glue it in place.

Use a belt sander with an eighty belt and level the bottom tier. Proceed through grits ending with two-eighty.

Final Assembly

Now, final sand all the components individually. The top tier, bottom tier, and the three legs using a straight line finish sander with two-eighty grit abrasive or finer. Fasten the top tier to the three legs with the two screws and snug the top to the legs. Keep in mind no glue is being used until it is certain everything fits together perfectly. Slide the bottom tier into place and drill the shank and pilot holes which will accommodate the three inch, number eight screws. Fasten the bottom tier in place and check the alignment of the table. If everything is acceptable number the legs and indicate on the top and bottom tiers the matching numbers. Disassemble the table, apply the adhesive and screw the components back together again, being sure the numbers match. The table is now complete and only lacks the protective finish and the inserting of the plate glass. Since this article is dealing with the actual construction of the table only, we will not get involved with the application of a suitable protective finish.

In Conclusion

As a result of our design and outboard lathe turning we have produced a very charming and delightful circular table which could be used in a corner or just about anywhere in the living area of one's home.

Hopefully your encounter with outboard turning will prove to be an enjoyable one and you will pass this "art" on to someone else. Fig. 14.

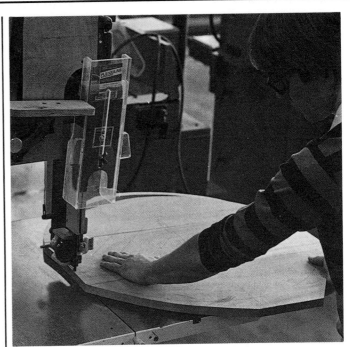

Figure 12

Figure 13

Figure 14

Wall mounted display case

440mm

350mm

Drawing 2   Plan   Scale 1:2

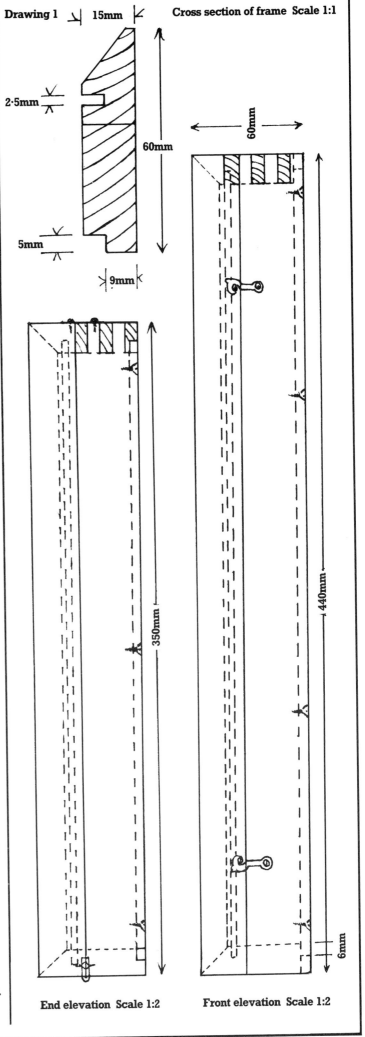

Drawing 1

15mm

Cross section of frame Scale 1:1

2·5mm

60mm

60mm

5mm

9mm

350mm

440mm

6mm

End elevation Scale 1:2

Front elevation Scale 1:2

Some while ago my son and I were asked to design and construct a set of wall cases for the display of Lepidoptera. Each case to be virtually a deep picture frame with a hinged front for access and as dust-proof as possible.

During the initial design exercise it became apparent that the basic display case could be used in a number of ways. With one or two shelves it is ideal for displaying small collections of china, glass, fossils or geological specimens etc. Without shelves and with a suitable background it can be used to display medals, coins, or a single item such as an antique pistol. (Examples in illustrations numbers 4 and 5.)

The choice of timber can be influenced by cost, availability, or the desire to fit in with existing decor.

The construction can span the whole range from glued and pinned butt joints, through the range of decorative joints, i.e. combed or dovetailed, or for the high-flyers, the Queen of all joints the secret mitred dovetail. There is an application for all levels of ability.

Dimensions can be varied to suit individual requirements and the finish can be tailored to individual taste, from paint, stain and varnish, through sealed and wax polished to a full French polish.

The following is an account of the method of construction with mention of alternatives as appropriate.

Drawings numbers 1 and 2 show dimensions and are for illustration only; the proportions and dimensions can be varied to suit individual requirements. Drawing number 3 illustrates the stages as described in the text.

Rebate
Having decided the main dimensions the selected timber is prepared and planed to a good finish. Two dimensions must be decided at this stage, firstly the inside depth of the case from the inside face of the glass to the back of the case, and depending upon the type of background to be used, the dimension of the rebate to accept the back.

The rebate for the back is put on a spindle moulder, an operation which can also be carried out with a plough plane, a hand held electric router or two cuts with a saw. The glass rebate is then cut; a tipped saw gives a snug fit to picture weight glass:- drawing number 3 (stage 1). With the glass rebate cut any desired edge treatment can be worked on the top edge. This is best kept very simple, a chamfer is ample. Remember that the function of the case is to display the

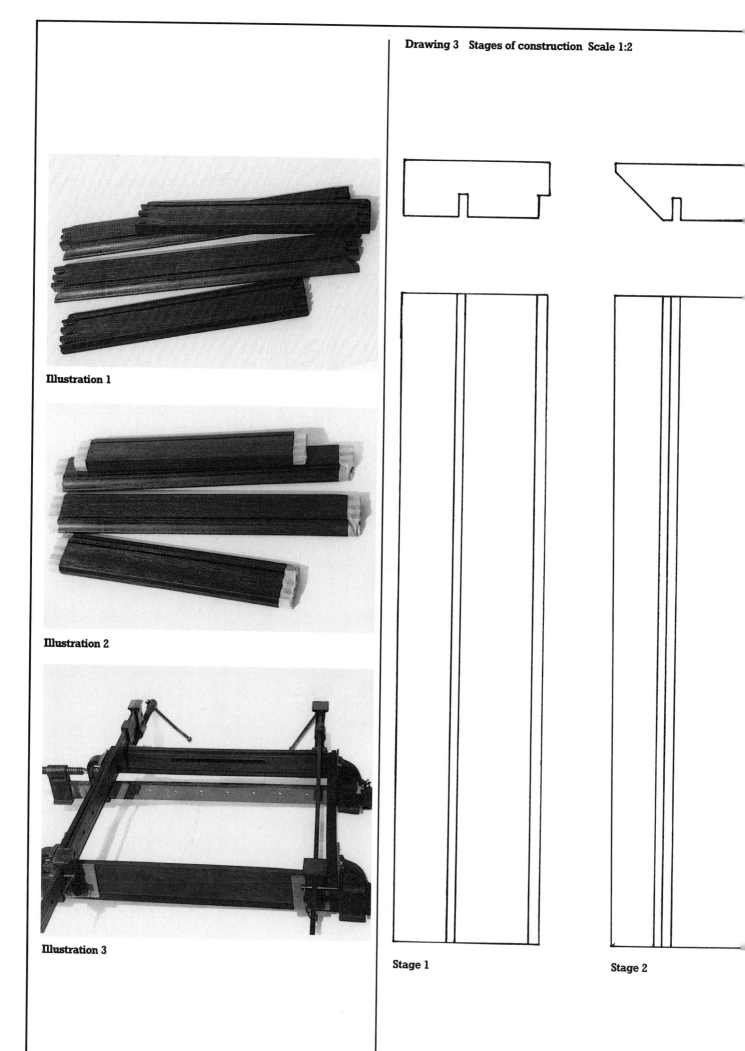

Illustration 1

Illustration 2

Illustration 3

Drawing 3 Stages of construction Scale 1:2

Stage 1

Stage 2

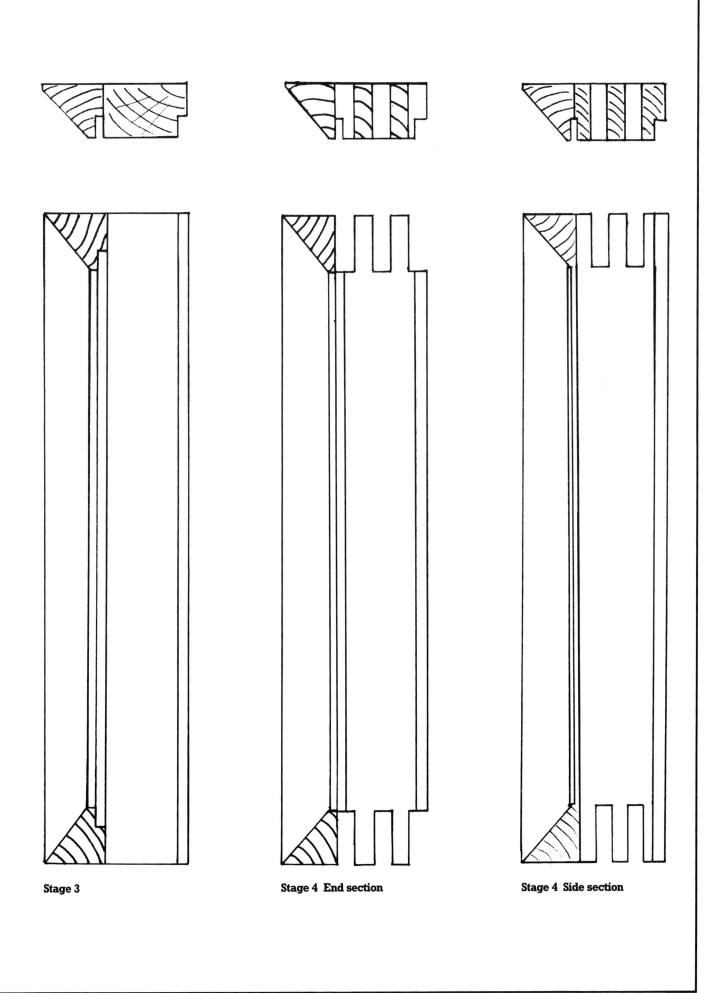

Stage 3

Stage 4 End section

Stage 4 Side section

Illustration 4

contents not to compete with it:- drawing number 3 (stage 2).

With the edge treatment carried out the top corners are then mitred. This can be done on the saw bench using the mitre guide and length-stop to ensure that the opposite sides are exactly the same length. If a mitrebox and dovetail saw are used care must be taken not to cut deeper than the inside of the glass rebate:- drawing number 3 (stage 3).

Corner Joints

The next operation is the cutting of the corner joints. If you have the machining facility, use the combed joint. Fine combing looks discretely decorative in the comparatively short lengths involved:- drawing number 3 (stage 4).

If the dovetailed joint is chosen thought must be given at the setting out stage to the operation which cuts the case in two, by ensuring that the cut passes through a suitable part of the joint. (Preferably through a 'pin' widened at the marking out stage to permit this.)

With the joints cut a 'dry run', with any necessary adjustments, ensures that the case will assemble sweetly at the glueing up stage. At this stage, while the case is assembled unglued, we take the precise dimensions for the glass. Have the glass cut 3mm undersize to the rebate.

Insist that your glass merchant gives you exactly what you require.

Finishing Inside Faces

It is now desirable to finish the inside faces of the case before assembly. Fill the grain with the 'Brummer-Wash' much favoured by pattern makers. This is made by diluting Brummer-Stopping of an appropriate colour to the consistency of single cream with cold tea. It is held that the tannin in the tea hardens the stopper and blends the colours in a subtle way. Whatever the facts behind this we have yet to find a filler to beat it. Having filled, coloured if necessary and rubbed down these inside faces to a fine surface (illustration 1), the final finish is applied. French polish was mainly used but whichever finish is chosen it is necessary to protect the interlaying surfaces of the joints with masking tape (illustration 2).

Assembly

When the finish is satisfactory the case is assembled with the glass and glued up. When glueing up we do not glue the two top mitred joints. The reason? In the unhappy event of the glass ever being broken it is a simple job to cut through the top member into the glass rebate with a scalpel or thin bladed craft knife, lift out the bead formed, replace the glass and replace the bead with two or three veneer pins. Glueing up is a simple operation. Use one of the two part quick setting resin glues, cramping up using four sash cramps (illustration 3).

After the glueing up operation, fit the back 'dry' (unglued) if shelves are to be fitted, glued and screwed if without shelves, and cut the case into two sections on the circular saw using a very fine toothed blade. The two sections are cleaned up with a small block plane set fine. For the less well equipped workman careful work with glass-paper and block will give satisfactory results. Care at this stage will ensure a dustproof case.

Hinges

Now fit the hinges, preferably to the top of the case as a safety measure. If the catches come, or are left, undone, there is little possibility of the front of the case opening with danger to the contents. The hinges being satisfactorily fitted they are removed, the exterior of the case cleaned up, filled, coloured, (if required) and given the final finish. The mating faces of the two sections of the case are also finished at this stage. The hinges are replaced and two small 'throw-over' catches fitted, two mirror plates are fitted to the back and after a final polish over and cleaning of the glass the display case is ready for its contents.

Reference was made during glueing up to assembling the back 'dry' when shelves are fitted. For the method of fitting shelves, to be inconspicuous they need to be housed into the sides of the case. As the shelf cannot be part of the opening front of the case, the housing must only extend through the rear portion. If these housings are cut in the detail stage, before glueing up, they must be stopped housings with the attendent complication of cutting them stopped and making the polishing of the inner faces of the sides that much less straight forward. If the sides are left whole and polished as such, after cutting to form the two sections of the case it is a simple task to remove the back and with a little care and a sharp marking knife the housings can be cut through the back section without damage to the finish. The back can then be finally glued and screwed into place.

Illustration 5

Small fireside stool

This is an unusual departure from the usual flat topped stool. It has a curved top which is carved two ways, bent by the application of handcramps to fit curved rails – that is, an ordinary straight rail with the curve cut out of the top. A bandsaw will do this or it can be easily cut out with a chisel.

Apart from this the joints are straight forward mortice and single cheeked tenons with square shoulders, the ends of the tenons mitred to just clear each other in the mortices which meet in the leg at right angles.

The top rail is haunched sufficiently to enable the curve of the top rail to meet the top of the leg, allowing enough leg above the mortice to enable the continuous curve of the rail to be continued to the outermost corner of the leg when glued up, thus keeping the top rail from twisting.

Wood to Use
Practically any wood with a good straight grain. English oak was my choice as it fits in with my other furniture which is mainly oak. Considering the work which will be put into it, a hardwood would seem to be the order of the day. The field is pretty broad from which to choose. It is surprising what can be done to match any wood with other furniture if an expert is let loose.

Personally, I prefer to stick to one wood in one place. The top having to be bent in two ways, both with and across the grain, will be all the better for having burrs in it as straight grain has a tendency to split when bent across the grain. Burr oak or any burr looks very decorative when cleaned up and polished.

Decoration of Legs
The legs clear of the mortices can be embellished with carving or turning, even just treated with a nice straight chamfer. Mine are carved after being turned to remove the bulk. Of course there is not a deal of bulk to remove but it gives you a guideline where to start and stop carving, providing you don't overdo the turning.

A router or spindle moulder would make clean and precise cuts but in my case I find a good mallet and two sharp chisels – one for taking off the bulk and one for the finishing cuts – more satisfying.

You have decided your wood and selected a suitable way to finish the legs, so now here are the sizes you need.

Cutting List (finished sizes)
Frame
4 legs 1' 3¼" × 1¾" × 1¾"
2 top rails 1' 1" × 3" × ¾"
2 top rails 9" × 3" × ¾"
2 bottom rails 1' 1" × 1¾" × ¾"
2 bottom rails 9" × 1¾" × ¾"
24 pins 2½" × 5/16" × 5/16"
Top
1 Top 1' 4" × 10½" × ½"

Matching the Legs
Having planed all the legs down to equal size and cut to length, put the legs side by side, ends level, and fasten a cramp across all four legs. This having assumed you

have marked the best two adjacent faces and put them in pairs so all the sides to be morticed are in order as they will fit together. It is easy to find yourself with a leg morticed on the wrong side, so double check that the legs are in pairs. (See drawing 4.)

Square lines across the legs as per drawing 3, 1¾" up from the bottom. In case it puzzles you, ¼" is cut off the bottom of the leg after turning to take off the tailstock marks, if you are going to turn the legs, which makes the bottom rail 1½" up from the bottom when finished. (Drawing 3.)

Another line across 1¾" up takes in the bottom rail. Then 8" and mark for the bottom of the top rail, then 3" should mark the top edge of the top rail so leaving the leg to be trimmed off to continue the curve of the rail. (See drawing 1.) The top 5/8" part of the top rail is only morticed ¼" as the rail is launched to fit. (See drawing 1.)

Separate your legs and square the lines round on the adjacent face to be morticed. Having set up a mortice gauge to ½", mark out the mortices. Then you can put into practice your turning on the legs or chamfers or carving, leaving at least a ½" clear of the mortices.

Tenoning the Rails
Clamp your rails together as you did the legs and mark a line across 1½" from each end. Square across another mark 1¼" from each end. This is for the haunching. (See drawing 1.) Carry the 1½" lines round one side and two edges. Mark the thickness of the tenon with the single prick gauge remembering these tenons are only shouldered on one side. (See drawing 2). Do your haunching of the top rails as you fit them. The bottom rails of course do not need haunching.

Making the Pins (or tapered dowels)
Select some straight grained stuff 2½" long or thereabouts and with a sharp axe split it into 5/16

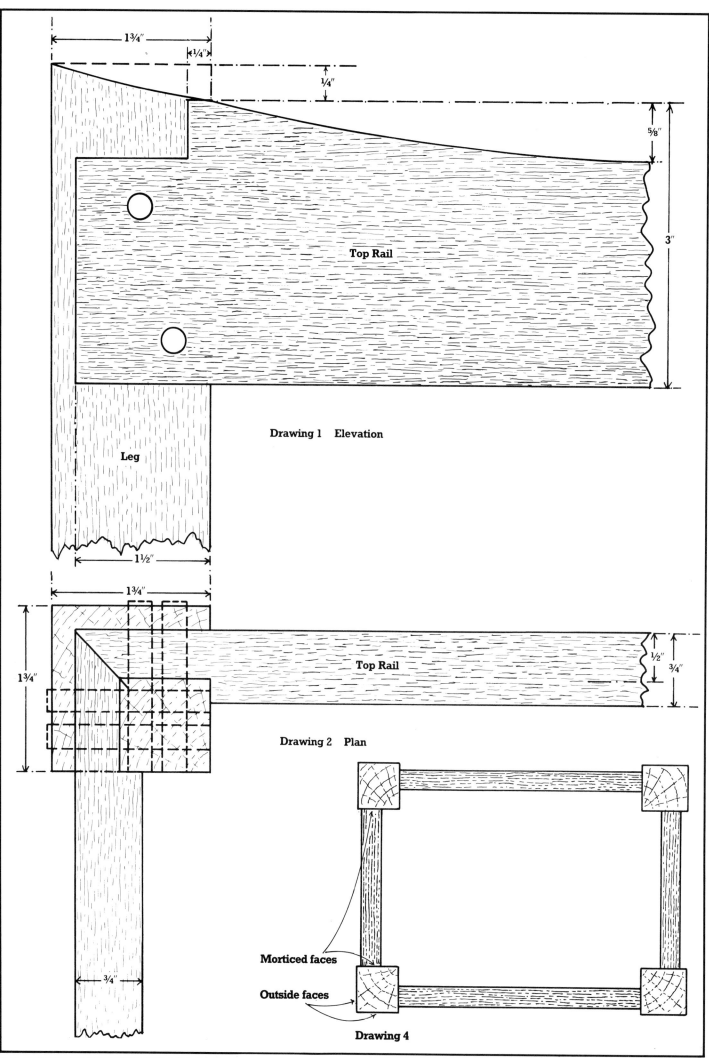

1¾"

¼"

¼"

5/8"

3"

Top Rail

Leg

1½"

Drawing 1   Elevation

1¾"

1¾"

¾"

½"

Top Rail

Drawing 2   Plan

Morticed faces

Outside faces

Drawing 4

thicknesses then 5/16″ till you have at least 24 pieces. Bore a 1/4″ hole in a spare bit of wood preferably the board you are going to use to chisel on. Make your square pin round keeping it as full as possible, turn it end for end and round it off till the end fits in the 1/4″ hole for about 1/8″, thus leaving you with a tapered pin which is used to drive in through a 1/4″ hole in the leg through the tenon and out through the leg again. I became proficient at this in my younger days due to filling several large drawers and buying sticking plaster by the yard to try and protect my thumb and fingers. Make or break tactics!

Glueing up the Frame

Having tied up and fitted all tenons correctly, test for squareness of frame, then mark which rail fits to which leg before taking apart. Take a thin lathe as long as the longest rail and bend it on the top rails to mark a curve about 5/8″ deep. Then draw it on the rail. (See drawing 1) Now glue the two ends up and clean off the pins which are driven in right through the legs, after the legs themselves have been glued of course. (See drawing 1.) The pin holes can be drilled with a 1/4″ drill through the legs before assembling, though you will still have to drill when glueing up to bore through the tenons. Take care here to make sure the pins on one side of leg miss the pins on the other side which is at right angles to it. (Drawing 2.)

Two pins can go in the top rail but only one in the bottom rail as it is narrower. Having pinned up the two ends and cleaned off, join them up with the longer rails making sure the frame is not in twist.

Preparing Frame to Receive Top

Now the bottom of the legs can be trimmed off thus getting rid of any tailstock marks if the legs have been turned. (See marking the legs 4.) Take a good arris off the bottom of the legs and place two winding lathes across each pair to check for twist. Dress the two legs evenly which indicate any twist until all is clear of twist. This ensures the stool sits squarely on the floor if it is level.

Preparing Top and Fitting

Whatever top you have it wants cleaning up especially on the underside. Of course the middle bit is mostly out of sight but the edges can be seen and felt as they oversail the frame.

Take a hand cramp and having positioned the top centrally on the frame, tighten the cramp on the side rail sufficiently to hold it, then try another cramp on the opposite side. The two end rails next, tightening each cramp in turn until the top is drawn to the frame. Move the cramps to where the worst fit is and scribe with a pencil along the rails where the top touches. Mark the top with an X in one corner and the adjacent leg. Take the cramps off and ease the rails where the tight fit was with a compass plane. If you can afford to have two cramps on each long side, so much the better. Make sure you keep the top on the same way every time you fit it, hence the X mark on the top and the adjacent leg. Patience and a slight hollowing of the rails a little bit here and there will ensure a good fit with the top evenly supported on the frame.

This being achieved, 1¼″ panel pins can be driven in dovetail fashion to hold the top securely. You may need them a little closer in one area than another. Remember the top is curved two ways, so any highspots in the middle of the legs or rails will hold it off. As only the edges of the rails and legs are seen it does not matter if

the rest is a little hollow. Also remember the inside of the rails will be seen by people looking at it upside down. A panel pin every 3″ should be enough to hold the top on securely. I adzed my top before I fitted it and as it was burr oak there was scant danger of it cracking. If there is any doubt, remember that more bend can be given on the longer rails, as on the short rails the grain is across for the top. A shallow gouge helps to hollow the rails. On completion, clean up with a fine grade of glasspaper.

Finish

My stool is wax polished. French polish is not so easy unless you have large plain surfaces. That is why a lot of french polished work is completed before it is assembled as near as possible. Messy, as you have to keep it off the joints to be glued. If you wish, you can stain to match anything else you have before polishing. In my case, I fumed the stool before applying the wax.

If by any chance you get marks on the stool, a rub with fine steel wool and a re-rub with the waxed rag brings up the eggshell shine which seems to fit in with the scheme of things on my stool.

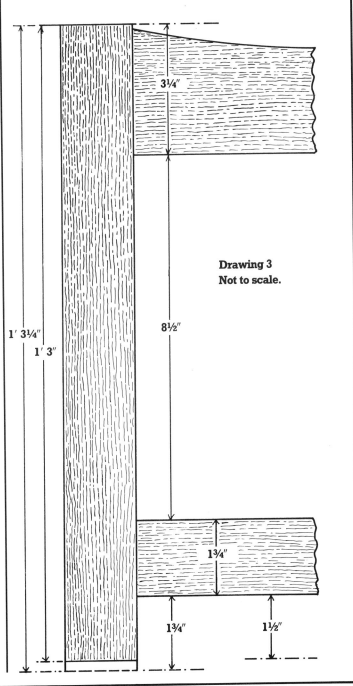

Drawing 3
Not to scale.

3¼″

1′ 3¼″

1′ 3″

8½″

1¾″

1¾″

1½″

Notes

Notes

Notes

Notes

Notes